OUR NECK OF THE WOODS

OUR NECK OF THE WOODS

Exploring Minnesota's Wild Places

Daniel J. Philippon, Editor

Foreword by Kathleen Weflen

University of Minnesota Press
Minneapolis
London

Proceeds from the sale of this book will go to *Minnesota Conservation Volunteer* magazine, published by the Minnesota Department of Natural Resources and funded entirely by reader donations. For more information, visit http://www.mndnr.gov/magazine.

These essays were published in *Minnesota Conservation Volunteer* magazine. For information about other previously published material in this book, see Publication History on pages 265–66.

Published by the University of Minnesota Press
111 Third Avenue South, Suite 290
Minneapolis, MN 55401-2520
http://www.upress.umn.edu

Library of Congress Cataloging-in-Publication Data

    Our neck of the woods : exploring Minnesota's wild places / Daniel J. Philippon, editor ; foreword by Kathleen Weflen.
     p.   cm.
    Includes bibliographical references and index.
    ISBN 978-0-8166-6591-4 (pb : alk. paper)
     1. Wilderness areas—Minnesota.   2. Wildlife management areas— Minnesota.   3. Natural areas—Minnesota.   4. Minnesota—Environmental conditions.   I. Philippon, Daniel J.
    QH76.5.M6O94 2009
                      508.776—dc22

Printed on acid-free paper

The University of Minnesota is an equal-opportunity educator and employer.

For Grace

CONTENTS

Foreword / *Kathleen Weflen*   xiii

Introduction / *Daniel J. Philippon*   xv

Making Camp

TRAPPER'S CABIN / *Sigurd F. Olson*   3
In trappers' cabins, the wilderness always sings.

MY FIRST TRIP UP NORTH / *John S. Sonnen*   7
To camp on Mantrap Lake, the "men" in the family must first
conquer the "machine."

DEER CAMP / *Phil Aarrestad*   12
A deer camp enriches life and inspires growth.

THE PATH BETWEEN / *Holly Atkinson*   16
The author travels the path from girlhood to womanhood
between cabins.

SUGAR BUSH JOURNAL / *Anne M. Dunn*   21
For Ojibwe families, maple sugar camp was a place of intense
work and spiritual renewal.

MOTHER'S DAY IN RATTLESNAKE COUNTRY / *Susan Maas*   26
Weekend camping trips connect a family to their home state.

Paying Attention

DRAWING LIFE FROM NATURE / *Vera Ming Wong*   31
Drawing becomes a way of seeing deeply, a meditation
with open eyes.

LESSONS FROM A YOUNG EXPLORER / *Steve Dibb*   33
A young girl shows her father how to discover the treasures
of the natural world.

BIRDING WITH BEN / *Mary Kroll*   36
A road trip for the birds brings together a mother and her son.

BIRDING IN THE FAST-FOOD LANE / *D. Scott Shultz*   39
The author spots hawks in the Twin Cities.

HEART OF THE HUNT / *Terri Sutton*   44
A vegetarian tries to figure out what hunting means to the hunter.

WHY I'M A BOWHUNTER / *Tom Conroy*   52
Why do thousands of people take bows and arrows and
set out for deer each autumn?

THE APPLE TREE STAND / *Marsha L. Kessler*   55
A bowhunter with a fear of heights inherits an eye-level tree stand.

A PERFECT START / *Dan Brown*   57
His first deer hunt becomes a boy's rite of passage.

Encountering Wildness

THE ROAD TO WILD PLACES / *Don J. Dinndorf*   63
Sometimes the roads don't change, and the magic of wild places abides.

THE BOG / *John Henricksson*   66
This tiny geological wonder is a wilderness by default.

THE WAGON WHEEL / *Joel M. Vance*   70
In the sprawl of the Wagon Wheel, woodcock shooting is at its best.

THE STRIKE TREE / *Peter M. Leschak*   74
A tree delivers fire to its fellows.

ADVENTURE UNDERGROUND / *Cary Griffith*   79
Cave exploring is wet, cold, muddy—and enlightening.

I FLEW WITH EAGLES / *John K. Grobel*   82
High over Lake Pepin, the author encounters unexpected company.

THE LURKER / *Tony Capecchi*   84
A St. Croix fisherman lands a monstrous sturgeon.

Getting Wet

HERON LAKE LEGACY / *Lacey Rose Horkey*   89
A girl inherits her great-grandfather's legacy of
waterfowl hunting.

AROUND THE NEXT BEND / *Tim Holschlag*   92
A river guide never fails to find something new
on the Mississippi.

FISHLESS WATERS / *Jan Zita Grover*   98
An urban fisher learns to see in Minnehaha Creek.

THE RIVER / *Sheila Deyo*   104
The Mississippi weaves its way through one family's history.

GOING WITH THE FLOW / *Jim dale Huot-Vickery*   109
A river bears a canoeist on the currents of his own past.

A SEARCH FOR WHITEWATER / *Hal Crimmel*   115
Desperately seeking rapids to run, a newcomer finds them
in Minnesota's state parks.

RIVER PASSAGE / *Janet Blixt*   120
A woman remembers running the rapids.

KAYAKING THE WILD SHORE / *Greg Breining*   124
A kayaker goes in search of wilderness amid development
on the North Shore.

DOWN AT MILLER CREEK / *Shawn Perich*   132
Progress ignores what a fishing kid understands intuitively.

Embracing Winter

BOUNDARY WATERS WILDERNESS: JANUARY / *Laurie Allmann*   137
Who would live in such a cold, lean region?

BRITTLE BEAUTY / *Rick Naymark*   141
A cold-weather trek puts life in perspective.

LAKE SUPERIOR, WINTER DAWN / *Gustave Axelson*   146
Thanks to a friend, a man encounters a crystalline palace,
at minus twenty degrees.

RIVERING ON THE ONION / *Stephen Regenold*   150
Skiers descend a frozen river toward Lake Superior.

ME AND JOE / *C. B. Bylander*   154
Ice fishing can warm the heart.

FISHING THE ICE / *John Brandon*   158
A father and son learn lessons from a simple pleasure.

A FLASH OF SUMMER / *Jason Abraham*   162
Winter fly-fishing fast-forwards summer.

A THOUSAND CHANDELIERS / *Will Weaver*   165
A northern Minnesotan waits for ice-out on Lake Bemidji.

Doing Science

MEMORIES OF THE LANDSCAPE / *Nancy Sather*   171
Explorations from a boat launch a career as a biologist.

ELUSIVE ORCHIDS / *Erika Rowe*   174
What are the odds of finding Minnesota's tiniest orchid?

A GREAT SMALL UNIVERSE / *David Czarnecki*   178
A lake's green blobs are microcosms worthy of awe.

A RIBBITING ADVENTURE / *Philip C. Whitford*   182
Sometimes you have to take a Breathalyzer test to study frogs.

MY NIGHT LIFE WITH THE BOREAL OWL / *Bill Lane*   188
A biologist's search for the elusive boreal owl often leaves him
in the dark.

COUNT YOUR LOONS / *Eric Hanson*   192
  With more than twelve thousand common loons in Minnesota,
  why try to keep track of them?

SOLO SOJOURN / *Joan Galli*   196
  One rare bird arrives, while another departs.

LAND USE: A BIRD'S-EYE VIEW / *Kim Alan Chapman*   200
  Keeping diverse birds in the Twin Cities region will require
  habitat protection.

Practicing Conservation

ONE SEED AT A TIME / *Sue Leaf*   207
  Is rebuilding a bit of presettlement landscape worth the toil?

GIVING THANKS ON THE PRAIRIE / *Michael Furtman*   213
  A hunter expresses gratitude for the protection of grasslands.

THE DROPPING DUCK / *Tom Chapin*   218
  A conservation officer tells the tale of the ones who didn't get away.

A HUNTER'S JOURNAL / *Dave Schad*   222
  One cabin's old journal tells two connected stories: one of hunters,
  the other of wildlife managers.

THIS OLD FARMLAND / *Blane Klemek*   228
  A farmer witnesses decades of conservation changes wrought
  by his own hands.

Finding Home

THE GRACE OF THE WILD / *Paul Gruchow*   235
  What does it mean to be native to a place?

BATTLE FOR THE COTTONWOOD / *Evelyn Wood Moyle*   239
  Generations of birds convert a dead tree into prime housing.

IRON RED HOME / *Margaret A. Haapoja*   247
  The author recalls growing up on the Mesabi Iron Range.

HOME IS WHERE THE HEARTH IS / *Mary Hoff*   253
  A random act of fire turns a space into a place.

CALL ME ISLAND / *Bill Holm*   256
  A man (whose name in Old Norse means island) recounts
  his island in a sea of grass.

MARKING TIME / *Tom Baumann*   260
  Expectation and hope are jointly fashioned by nature and humans.

              Acknowledgments   263
              Publication History   265
              Geographical Index   267
                Contributors   271

FOREWORD

Kathleen Weflen

Editor in Chief
Minnesota Conservation Volunteer magazine

THE TIME: A WARM DAY, JULY 2008. The place: a metal lawn chair on a balcony overlooking a backyard in St. Paul. A light breeze blows from the east, birds call from the tree canopy, and neighborhood children splash in a swimming pool nearby.

In such a summer time and place, a person could pick up a good book and easily be transported somewhere else entirely. And so I was, over and over again, as I read the manuscript for this book, *Our Neck of the Woods: Exploring Minnesota's Wild Places,* which collects essays that originally appeared in *Minnesota Conservation Volunteer* magazine. As editor of this publication of the Minnesota Department of Natural Resources, I had read each of these essays at least a half-dozen times as I prepared them for publication. Yet, sitting down with this wonderful collection crafted by Daniel J. Philippon, I enjoyed reading all of them in new ways.

Experience teaches that a place can only be understood over time. And so I shouldn't be surprised to discover that these essays, which evoke a sense of place, also deserve return visits.

The idea of publishing personal essays under the banner "A Sense of Place" in *Minnesota Conservation Volunteer* began taking shape after freelance writer Paul Gruchow proposed a series recounting his visits to scientific and natural areas. His first essay, "A World within a World," appeared in November 1994 with the tagline "Close to home, you might find a natural landscape you never expected."

Another personal essay also acted as a catalyst for creating "A Sense of Place." In July 1995 *Minnesota Conservation Volunteer* published "Memories of Laos" by Yer Xiong Stewart. She wrote about her homeland and the hunting and fishing culture that Hmong immigrants carried with them to Minnesota.

Most humans are migratory, moving from one place to another over the course of a year or at least once in a lifetime. Very few people have always lived in the same house or on the same land, like the farmer in Blane Klemek's essay collected here, "This Old Farmland."

Whether travelers or homebodies, humans make themselves at home around a fire, as Mary Hoff eloquently tells in "Home Is Where the Hearth Is." She writes, "In ritual and legend, through all time, fire has meant: You Are Here." Like a well-built fire, each essay in this collection tells the reader: you are here.

INTRODUCTION

Daniel J. Philippon

WHEN I FIRST CAME TO MINNESOTA more than ten years ago, I rented a house from a couple on sabbatical, and I couldn't have asked for a better introduction to the state. Their front yard was filled with purple coneflowers, a stately white pine was growing in the back, and the street on which they lived had a perfect view of the Minneapolis skyline. Wildflowers from the prairie, a tree from the north woods, a city carved out of the big woods—all three Minnesota biomes were represented in that place. Of course, many homes around the state can boast variations on this mix, but this one had something else, something that helped me understand those biomes much more deeply: a wicker basket filled with copies of *Minnesota Conservation Volunteer,* the bimonthly, donor-supported magazine published by the Minnesota Department of Natural Resources.

Whether the owners of that home intended me to learn about their state by reading the *Volunteer* I can't say, but learn about it I did—so much so that I now feel comfortable calling it *my* state (a transition that admittedly took some time). Whenever I had a spare moment, I sat down with a copy of the magazine and discovered something new: an unfamiliar species, a bit of history, an endangered landscape. There was much in each issue to savor, but what captivated me the most were the occasional personal essays that appeared under the heading "A Sense of Place." Here were men and women from around the state, writing about the environments they knew and loved best. Some were professional writers, others were natural resource managers, and still others were ordinary people—biologists and fishing guides, teachers and photographers, remodelers and real estate appraisers—all of whom had something to share with readers: their own experience of the natural world and their sense of what that experience should mean, to them and to us. It is these voices and visions that *Our Neck of the Woods: Exploring Minnesota's Wild Places* seeks to capture.

These sense of place essays officially began to appear in the *Volunteer* in 1996, when editor Kathleen Weflen first created a space where writers could reflect on their personal relationship to the state's natural resources. Such writing had appeared in the magazine before then (though unlabeled as such), and it continues to be found in its pages today (both with and without the series designator). Much of it is nature writing, with its distinctive mix of natural history information, personal responses to nature, and philosophical interpretation of nature. But some of these essays emphasize one of these elements more than the others—such as the natural history essay, in which observation and description predominate, or the nature memoir, in which the focus is on the writer's memories of an experience in nature. Others more closely resemble travel and adventure writing, which detail good places to hunt, fish, and paddle; and some are more akin to science writing, which has the added task of communicating technical information to general readers.

But what matters most is not whether or how such writing is labeled but why it is so vital. In her column introducing the series, Weflen said that these personal essays would "explore places of the heart, from wilderness to, perhaps, a wildly overgrown vacant lot," and she noted that while some writers would look for intimacy in a vast landscape, "others will make themselves at home in smaller corners of the natural world." Which is to say that the first-person singular does more than merely convey information; it also conveys emotion, and with that emotion, a writer's values. Moreover, as Weflen's comment suggests, it's hard to value an abstraction; we love *particular* people, *particular* places, and *particular* things. The personal essay captures these intimate relationships by describing that which is closest to us, those places in which we feel most at home.

Our Neck of the Woods collects fifty-seven essays about these "places of the heart" that have been featured in the *Volunteer* over the past twenty years, since Weflen became editor in 1989. (The magazine itself is much older than this, having celebrated its sixty-fifth anniversary in 2005.) Not every personal essay from this period is included, however, for a number of reasons. Although several authors have appeared in the *Volunteer* repeatedly over the years—including such wonderful writers as Sigurd F. Olson, Peter M. Leschak, and Greg Breining—each is represented here only once. And while this collection does feature a few essays that have appeared elsewhere, it does not include any that have appeared in other magazines or anthologies. Finally, while a few pieces were too brief to include, others had to be omitted because they would have made the book too long. Overall, though, these omissions are few, and the result is a collection that represents the subjects and interests of the magazine's personal essayists fairly well.

The basic concerns of these writers are not likely to surprise regular readers of the *Volunteer,* or anyone with a passing interest in the outdoors, for that matter. What book devoted to exploring Minnesota's wild places would be complete, for instance, without sections on "making camp," "getting wet," and "embracing winter"? Likewise, one would expect a magazine that advocates "conservation and careful use of Minnesota's natural resources" to include writing on such subjects as "paying attention," "doing science," and "practicing conservation." And could you imagine such a publication not also including pieces on "encountering wildness" and "finding home"?

What distinguishes these essays is not the familiar places and activities they describe, therefore, but the specificity and style with which they describe them—and the fact that these descriptions don't always agree! John Henricksson, for example, describes the bogs of the Gunflint region as "miniature natural kingdoms of mist, mystery, and beauty," "mossy grottoes of silence," and "wondrous flower realms, jewel boxes of the far north." Joel M. Vance, in contrast, says that when he goes hunting in a bog, he can "go in one side . . . looking like James Bond and come out the other side resembling Weary Willy," while his dogs emerge "looking as if they'd been mud wrestling with a Vikings middle linebacker." Similarly, Gustave Axelson marvels at the "magnificent diamond sculptures" on

Lake Superior in December, those "giant, jagged boulders" that "collide with a brittle crack each time a new wave adjusts them." But Will Weaver describes the end-of-season ice floes on Lake Bemidji as having "the grace, beauty, and grandeur of exhausted soldiers on a final march." And whereas Phil Aarrestad sees his north woods deer camp as a place where "boys will become men" and "men will become wiser," Holly Atkinson found the pebble-strewn path between her family's cabins on Lake Beltrami to be more like "the path from girlhood to womanhood."

Other themes emerge from these essays as well. Traditional forms of wildlife recreation (such as hunting, fishing, and birding) are of course well represented, but so are many other forms of outdoor recreation, such as skiing, kayaking, and canoeing. Dan Brown and Lacey Rose Horkey each describe their first hunt (Dan for deer, Lacey for ducks), while Tom Conroy and Marsha L. Kessler both explain the thrill of bowhunting, though from different perspectives. The North Shore of Lake Superior turns out to be a popular destination, both for kayaking and for cross-country skiing, as do Minnesota's many lakes for ice fishing (no surprise in either case). The experience of driving is also common to both John S. Sonnen and Don J. Dinndorf—but where one finds it comical, the other finds it heartbreaking. Michael Furtman and Bill Holm both love the prairie; Nancy Sather and Erika Rowe both love rare plants; and Philip C. Whitford and Bill Lane both love the nighttime.

There are also a few unexpected variations on these subjects. Have you ever met a camper who *wants* to encounter rattlesnakes? A vegetarian who hunts? A fly fisher who ties yarn at the end of her tippet? A wildlife biologist accused of public drunkenness just for doing his job? Or one whose study sites keep disappearing beneath new homes? A birder who haunts fast-food restaurants? Or, better yet, one who flies with eagles in an ultralight glider?

Similarly, not all of these essays concern the traditional wilderness landscapes you might expect in such a book. There are plenty of voyages in the Boundary Waters Canoe Area, of course, but there is also an underground expedition in Mystery Cave State Park, a remembrance of growing up on the Mesabi Iron Range, a meditation on the wilderness in a drop of water, a description of piloting a towboat on the Mississippi, a portrait of a northwestern Minnesota wheat farmer, an inquiry into oak-savanna restoration, and an observation of a very avian form of home construction on Lake Minnetonka.

Beyond these common themes and subjects, it's also worth noting two other things about these essays. The first is what isn't here. There's not a lot of history or politics in these pages, although other articles in the *Volunteer* have addressed these subjects in different ways. That's not to say that history and politics are wholly absent, just that these subjects are, as might be expected, filtered through each writer's perspective. In some cases, history becomes memoir, as occurs in Anne M. Dunn's "Sugar Bush Journal," in which Dunn says that she can almost see her Ojibwe elders "walking among the trees, peering into catch-cans, and nodding in satisfaction" as she carries her maple syrup home. Or as Dave Schad tells the story of deer management in the late twentieth century through the entries in his family's old hunting journal. In other cases, history appears as "deep history," the kind of geological past that Jim dale Huot-Vickery considers as he canoes from one end of the Red River of the North to the other. Politics is likewise personalized, whether through the meditations on hunting provided by Terri Sutton and Tom Conroy or the concerns about the pace of "progress" and "development" voiced by so many of the writers featured here, including Susan Maas, Don J. Dinndorf, Tim Holschlag, Kim Alan Chapman, Greg Breining, Shawn Perich, and Michael Furtman.

Another thing worth noting about these essays is the importance that family—and especially parenting—plays in so many of them. Whether it is Steve Dibb learning lessons about perception from his daughter Stephanie, Mary Kroll expressing gratitude for the days she spends birding with her son Ben, or John Brandon cherishing the time he spends ice fishing with his son Joshua, many of these writers connect the value they find in nature to the value they find in family. And while this is not a startling observation, it does say something important about the idea of "sense of place." Just as Tom Baumann finds, in the final essay of this collection, "expectation and hope, jointly fashioned by nature and humans," so too can we observe that "place" is the result of our very human engagement with the nonhuman world; places are likewise "jointly fashioned by nature and humans." And how much more resonant, how much more meaningful, are those wild places we have shared with those we love the most. The more we open our hearts in a place, the more we tend to value it. It really is that simple.

So whether you are a native Minnesotan, a visitor to the state, or, like me, a relatively recent immigrant, I hope you find something in these pages that moves you—emotionally, of course, but also physically, inspiring you to find or develop your own sense of place and to protect that place so that others may share your experience. (Sense of place can drive a sense of loss, remember.) And maybe, just maybe, you might also be moved to share your experience in writing. If so, the *Volunteer* is waiting. As Paul Gruchow writes of Sigurd Olson in "The Grace of the Wild," "Olson was not indigenous to this place either, but he stayed long enough, once he had arrived, to notice, to take account of—to discover—and so at last to learn to sing its poetry."

Wherever you're from, welcome to our neck of the woods.

Making Camp

TRAPPER'S CABIN

Sigurd F. Olson

THE CABIN ON SNOWBANK LAKE was primitive; the unpeeled logs were chinked with moss; there was no floor and only one small window. The cabin faded into the tall black spruces around it as if it had always been there. It smelled of balsam, for in one corner was a bunk full of the resinous tips and on the packed dirt floor needles were the pattern.

The cabin had not been built for summer comfort or view. It had no real-estate value. It had one purpose only: to give shelter at the end of a long day on the traplines, shelter from the gales of winter when the snow was deep and the cold enough to sear a man's lungs.

Even for a trapper's cabin it was small, just big enough for a man and his outfit, a tiny stove, a corner table, and the bunk; there were hand-whittled pegs for clothes and packs, a narrow shelf below the window. But at night when the trees cracked with the frost and the bitter wind whipped the unprotected shore, it was as cozy and warm as a bear's den under a windfall. The roof was low, and the rafters stuck far out from the eaves as though the builder had forgotten to trim them. Those eaves gave the cabin the effect of squatting low beneath the trees, and made it as much a part of the forest floor as a moss-covered boulder or a hummock cushioned with duff. Only a few spruce had been cut for the logs, and with the passing years the little gap had been filled with new growth until there seemed to be no perceptible break between the roof and the low-hanging branches of the trees.

When I entered that cabin I was close to the wild. Here life was primitive and I felt as Thoreau did when he said, "Drive life into a corner and reduce it to its simplest terms." Here, if anywhere, was the simplicity he meant. This was no place for fancy or unnecessary equipment. The cabin meant moccasins, rough wool, and leather—and simple thoughts. The complicated problems of society, politics, war, and peace seemed far removed. The only thoughts that thrived here were of squirrels and birds and snowshoe trails. Here I felt as much a part of the out-of-doors as when sleeping under a ledge.

I liked to lie in the balsam bunk and look up at the pole rafters and study the deer mouse nest in one corner and the lichen and fungi that had taken hold on the rough logs. As the cabin became warm, the mouse thawed out; a slight rustling and suddenly big transparent ears and bright black eyes emerged from the nest. For a long time the little animal would watch me and when convinced that I was harmless, would come down to the table to pick up crumbs.

Sometimes a red squirrel came in through a hole under the eaves. Again the long contemplation and final acceptance. He and I were partners, in a sense—my part to leave something on the table, his to make me feel that I belonged.

This could not happen in a modern mouseproof cabin, and what a pity it is! I have always felt that cabins belong to the animals of the woods as much as they do to us and that the animals should feel as much at home in them as though there were no doors or walls. By shutting them out, we lose their companionship and the feeling of trust that comes only when the barriers of strangeness and fear are overcome.

Sometimes at night I would waken and listen to the tips of the spruce branches rubbing against the walls, caressing them softly. That cabin was still part of the living forest, would eventually be part of the moss and duff again. At such times my thoughts seemed to merge with the trees and the sound of their movement in the wind, their creaking and moaning as they rubbed against one another. It satisfied a longing for closeness to a primitive environment, the hunger to return for a little while to the wilderness. Centuries of caves, of shelters under the trees, of dry spots beneath ledges and windfalls, of listening to the sounds of the night have left their mark. The Snowbank cabin was part of all that.

Another cabin that gave me this feeling was on the Sand River south of my home. It, too, was of logs, but roofed with wide strips of birch bark anchored with stones. The rafters were wide enough in their overlap to shelter a woodpile underneath, an ax, a saw, and other gear, generous enough to heal the break between the walls and the ground. The cabin made a picture squatting there on its little spit of land commanding a view up and down the river. On one side spruces and balsams hedged it closely, but the other side was snuggled close against a great gray rock out of reach of the wind. The trapper who built it may have thought it was just another shelter, but, far more than that, it was a picture in logs and rock that gave pleasure to all who passed. He was probably more of an artist than he knew, unable to resist the view up and down the river, the sunrises and sunsets, and the sound of whistling wings as mallards flew over on their way to the rice beds beyond.

Charley Raney's Stony River cabin was surrounded by high hills, but you could hear the whisper of the river as it flowed across the boulders down below. Here was not only primitiveness, but isolation in a wild and glorious setting. That cabin reminded me of cabins in the Austrian Tyrol, isolated little shelters perched on inaccessible crags reached only by steep mountain trails. There were no sunsets because the dusk settled swiftly between the hills, no vistas, no sense of space—as wild and lonely a place as the bottom of a canyon, and Charley Raney, the mad trapper who built it, found there a mystery and wildness that complemented his own nature. I sometimes wondered how mad he was—whether he was not saner than many who passed judgment upon him. He loved to sit on his stoop and play his violin to the accompaniment of the rapids. He was as much a part of his setting as the Sibelius he loved was part of the forests and lakes of Finland.

There are many trappers' cabins in the north and there are many mansions called cabins. Many of them are comfortable and beautiful in their own way, but when I enter them there is no change for me, merely an extension of civilized living away from the towns. Motorboats, highways, and planes make them as accessible as suburban homes. I find no sense of seclusion or solitude in them, for their conveniences carry with them the associations and responsibilities of urban living. Sometimes they are so comfortable, so removed from all physical effort, that they nullify the real purpose of going to the woods: doing primitive things in primitive ways and recapturing simplicity.

Trappers' cabins are as natural as tents or teepees. They are part of the solitudes and as much a part of the wilderness as the trees and rocks themselves. In those cabins the wilderness always sings. Each time that deer mouse came to feed, I caught a single elfin note. I heard it on the Sand River one stormy night when the drifting snow was full of the sound of wings, and on the Stony when Charley's violin blended with the music of the rapids so closely that I could not tell them apart and I knew he was feeling not only the scene around him but the wilds and hinterlands of Europe's north.

MY FIRST TRIP UP NORTH

John S. Sonnen

IN 1920, WHEN I WAS SEVEN YEARS OLD, I got my first chance to visit the glacial lake country of northern Minnesota.

Dad was planning a five-day camping and muskellunge-fishing trip for himself and my two older brothers, then in their early teens. They were going up to Mantrap Lake near Park Rapids, some two hundred miles northwest of our home in St. Paul.

I remember being somewhat keyed up—not about the trip, but about the family debate over whether I should be taken along. My brothers considered me a tagalong. Dad worried about the tent being too crowded. He had only three army cots. Where would I sleep? Mother suggested he take along our front-porch hammock. He admitted it could be slung between the four-man tent's front and rear center poles—if I was willing to sleep there. I was.

I suspect my two older sisters desired my riddance for a few days, just to have a respite from reading to me or having me read to them. Discordance prevailed for days, but upon my mother's insistence, with added support from my two older sisters, the "men" of the family finally accepted me as the fourth member of their expedition.

On a bright Monday morning in early June, off we went in the family "machine"—a seven-passenger, six-cylinder Premier touring automobile. The Premier was advertised as an "American engineering masterpiece." It boasted an overhead valve engine built almost entirely of aluminum and an electric gear-shifting system. The advertisements said that "a woman could shift gears with little effort." A rear rack held two spare tires with "demountable" rims. Stowed under the rear seat cushion were two sets of "isinglass" side curtains for hurried installation in case of rain.

Two "jump seats" folded down from, and out of, the back of the front seat bench. My brother Charles and I rode on the jump seats because the rear seat was packed with cooking utensils, luggage, fishing gear, and rainwear. On one running board, we lashed down our folded tent, stakes, poles, army cots, hammock, and bundles of rope. I kept thinking about rain, the tucked-away isinglass curtains, and my hammock and the tent on the running board.

As we drove along, it dawned on me that this trip was not going to be the usual Sunday afternoon drive out to the country or a holiday picnic at St. Paul's local lakes. We were long past such personal landmarks of pleasure as Como Park, the State Fairgrounds, Lake Johanna, and the village of New Brighton, when Dad called out: "Over the Rum! On to the Elk! Benchmarks, boys! Benchmarks! Know where you are and what lies ahead. Towns, river crossings, important road junctions. That way, by checking your time, you'll know if you're making progress as planned."

"Is it?" asked one of my brothers.

"Is it what?" Dad countered, as we rolled along the concrete highway toward Elk River.

"Is our progress okay so far?"

"Oh! It sure is! We'll be in Little Falls by lunchtime, as planned."

"But, what if," I interjected, "something happens—a flat tire, a bad road that slows us down?"

"Oh, John, what if, what if!" came Dad's answer. "Don't borrow trouble! The world is full of 'what ifs.' Don't burden your life with them. We have good tires and two good spares. The road is good—you can see that. We're well on our way."

Indeed we were. Highway 3 allowed us to clip along at forty to forty-five miles per hour. A new world, vast and flat, stretched out beyond us. Where are the hills? I wondered. Then I realized we had not seen many trees, much less woods. I thought about asking Dad these questions, but the continuous wind stream made conversation difficult. The noise died only as we slowed down to pass through small settlements—Becker, Clear

Lake, Sauk Rapids, Rice—huddled along the highway. After Royalton, the pavement came to an end, and trouble started.

Forced onto a fifteen-mile ungraded and sandy detour road, which twisted and wiggled its way north toward Little Falls, our Premier engine no longer had a cooling, practically constant airstream flowing through its radiator. Dad shifted into low gear. Soon our engine was gasping and the radiator's water boiling.

Again and again we stopped. Off we boys would go with pail and ladles to fetch what water we could find, while Dad donned his "machine gloves" from under the front seat, threw open both sides of the motor's hood, and unscrewed the radiator's cap and its appendage: a glass disk with a thermometer that displayed mercury soaring up into the danger zone.

At our first emergency stop, Dad told us to look for water in the low spots ahead where the road took some evident dips. At the bottom of the first dip, we found a marsh. My brother Bob filled the pail halfway by dipping it, then Charles and I ladled more water to fill it. Life was everywhere in that place. I was amazed by an incessant buzz and hum, frequent splashing, mysterious movements, continual croaking, and other strange noises. Frogs, blackbirds, turtles appeared in abundance. And now I saw trees. "Jack pines and tamarack," my brothers said. "Now, John, we're getting up north."

Our pail of water cooled the Premier motor, and we made it to Little Falls. But the radiator's thermometer was rising again. A block off Main Street, Dad found a "motor-car garage." We left the car for a radiator "flushing out" treatment while we went to a café for a late lunch. As we sat down Dad said, "Well, boys, we ran into one of John's 'what ifs' this morning, but the machine will be okay the rest of the trip."

It wasn't. We had a hundred miles to conquer before we could pitch our tent on Mantrap's shore. The highway meandered in a northwesterly direction, crisscrossing the Northern Pacific railroad tracks nine times, seemingly undecided about which side of the tracks to travel. The road's condition also wavered. For the first twenty-five miles out of Little Falls, it was graded and had a packed sandy-gravel topping. That was good. Then it turned to an ungraded surface with loose gravel. That was bad. A few short sections had a topping of pine slabs, which rattled and flopped as we drove over them. However, those sections indicated a wetland, which meant water to cool the radiator.

Windmills, which signaled another water source, were few and far between in that sparsely settled territory. Fortunately, more and more lakes began popping up, easing our worries. I remember only two towns before we reached Park Rapids: Staples and Wadena. In each one, we steamed up to the blacksmith-machine shop for assistance.

Finally, in Park Rapids, my father arranged to have the Premier's radiator repaired during our camping days at Mantrap Lake, now only fifteen miles away. The shop mechanic knew the campground location. "Oh, sure! Out there at Dorset," he said. "We'll be out in the morning to get the machine."

Around six in the evening, we rolled into the campground. Dad said, "First things first," which meant raising the tent. My brothers wanted to pitch it close to the lake, but Dad vetoed that idea and chose a site well back from the beach. He explained the sense in placing it under the pines (shaded, sheltered) on pine needle–covered ground (carpeted, dry) slightly higher than abutting spots (good drainage). In twenty minutes we'd pitched and "bridled" the tent.

After we'd set up cots, hammock, and gear, we built a fire and roasted wieners. The "men" drank campfire coffee. It looked terrible, and they coughed a lot. I drank milk, which Dad had purchased in Dorset.

Day slipped into night. After supper, while Dad carried on about the wonderfulness of "up north," sleepiness started to get the best of me. My mind was crammed with thoughts of the day. Yet Dad decided it was time to replace my childhood references to evergreens as "Christmas" trees.

"Fir trees," Dad explained. "They're the ones we use to decorate for Christmas."

Then I learned we chose between spruce, balsam, or "Scotch firs." All belonged to the pine family, he said, along with the red (Norway), white, Scotch, and jack pines.

"The scrubby, useless jack!" one of my brothers exclaimed.

"Oh, no," Dad answered. "No tree is useless. Even jack pines furnish shelter for wildlife. And remember this: the Chippewa Indians used the jack's long, slender roots as threads for sewing their birch-bark canoes."

Despite my anxiousness about getting "up north" that day, I slept soundly in the hammock above the men. I was on the way to becoming one happy camper. My brothers were not destined to be so content.

Each day Dad would take one or the other, in alternating two-hour sessions, out in a rowboat to troll for muskies. That left one brother beached to shepherd me. Thus I enjoyed swimming lessons that advanced me beyond dog-paddling. On trail walks or while beachcombing, a big brother would teach me to identify tracks and skittish animals.

Meanwhile, the fish the men wanted were not biting. Even Dad got skunked—a word that I learned that week. Bob had about thirty minutes of exhilarating success Thursday, our last full day, while fighting and boating a muskie of sizable girth and spirit but two inches short of legal "keeper" length. Dad released it.

"Just think," Bob said to me. "What if that muskie had only two more inches to its tail or snout—well, I'd have it here to show you."

Yes, I thought, what if.

We broke camp the next morning. The mechanic had returned the Premier on Wednesday and advised Dad of a better route home. Homeward bound, Dad asked us if we had enjoyed the north country.

"Yes," I said. "Could we do it again sometime?"

"What if," he replied, "we build a cabin sometime, somewhere up there on a lake?"

Three years later we did.

DEER CAMP

Phil Aarrestad

 THE NIGHT BEFORE DEER SEASON OPENS, a ritual begins across the country. It is a ritual that enriches hunters' lives and inspires them to pass the experience on. Tonight I join in this ritual again, driving remote, icy roads to our deer camp in Minnesota's north woods.

As I drive, I catch an occasional glimpse of lantern lights marking other deer camps tucked in the woods. Finally, I ease my truck to a halt, step out, and draw deep breaths of winter air, laced with the aroma of cedar and wood smoke. At once my nerves settle from the long drive, and a warm voice greets me from the dark. Wayne, one of the oldest men in camp, welcomes me and, as always, makes me feel important. He has done this for as long as I can remember. He is the father of my lifelong friend Joe, who also is a member of camp.

As we talk, the snow crunches under our feet and a chilly wind bends the cedars southward. Wayne and I carry my gear to the shack; the muffled voices inside grow louder as we get closer. Wayne wrestles the door open, and I am met with a wave of heat, cigar smoke, and a flurry of handshakes, smiles, and slaps on the back. An old recording of Hank Williams accompanies the razzing I get for being so late. Before I know it, I am catching up on news and enjoying a beer.

As I am warmed by the lifelong bonds that this ritual has nurtured, I look around the log shack. Measuring roughly sixteen feet by twenty-four feet, it was built in 1918 by a man from Brainerd. He lost it to tax forfeiture in the Depression, and the state put the place up for lease. Our deer-hunting family picked up the lease in the mid-1930s and has passed it down three generations.

History surrounds us here. An old, rusty Swede saw hangs on the wall, and on a table sits a gas cooktop from an old café in Brainerd once frequented by Burlington Northern railroad workers. Balanced precariously on the main beam above me are old hunting regulations, books, playing cards, and tin deer tags from an era long passed. A few times a night, history gets picked up off the floor as these items are knocked from their perch by someone who cracks his head on this low beam.

I also see history in the hunting party that surrounds me. Ranging in age from early teens to seventies, the group represents three branches of one family tree. Wayne, his sons Joe, Gus, and Andy, and Andy's son, Andrew, make up one branch. This is Andrew's first hunt, and as stories and plans unfold, his eyes grow wider. Another branch includes Roy, his son, Rick, and Rick's sons, Ricky and John. The third branch includes three brothers, Ben, Mark, and Nels. I fit in not as a blood relative but as one who has been adopted by friendship.

I bask in this kinship until, at evening's end, we set three alarms and load the barrel stove with wood. The snoring begins, and I reach for tissue to cram in my ears.

My alarm clock wakes me, and I rise in a stupor to start coffee and join the others in the search for clothing, oatmeal, and sandwich fixings. The ritual of attempting to get Nels out of bed begins soon after the coffee starts to boil. After gathering our gear and gulping down coffee, we head out into the cold morning fog and follow the flashlight beam down the logging road. One by one we peel off on our own tree-stand trails. Darkness and trees close in around me as I ease my way down my trail.

I arrive at my stand and with warm hands load my gun. I know that tonight I will unload it with cold hands. I settle in and wait. My senses tune in as the light creeps into the woods.

The season begins with gunfire, which pops like the last stubborn kernels of popcorn in a hot pan. I listen and watch, but no deer move into sight. As the sun rises, patterns of light dance through the red-pine boughs. This opening scene is one of the great rewards of the hunt.

Waiting, I become aware of my heartbeat and the steady exchange of air in my breathing. These rhythms I rarely hear amid the din of daily life. In the silence, I hear again.

The cold starts to work its way deep beneath my layers of clothes. After several hours, I climb down to warm up by doing some still-hunting. I walk into the maze of a cedar swamp and stumble from one root cluster to the next. Great hunters of the past would have been unimpressed by my attempts to be a stealthy still-hunter.

A good set of prints punctuates the deer trail I'm following. When I come across another trail, I sneak into some cover to see if I can spot any deer moving on the trails. As I wait, the sun warms my back. No deer come, so I move on and meet up with some of the crew. We share some warm, gritty coffee and try to figure out who was shooting earlier. We soon realize it was none of us.

While we huddle together amid a swirl of coffee steam, I marvel at Mark's old .30-30. The metal parts are an aged silver color, and the faded stock has an inlaid compass. Once his great-uncle's gun, it has spent more time in the woods than we three hunters combined. As we head back to camp, we plan the afternoon hunt.

That afternoon, I hear a shot close by and figure someone in our group must have been successful. At day's end I arrive at camp without my deer, but my suspicions are confirmed. Hanging from a weathered two-by-four between two red pines is a nice eight-point buck with Joe's name penned on the tag. I hear voices inside the shack rise and fall while I admire the buck. What stories are they telling this season? A story from the past comes to mind about a hunter who was lost. He climbed a big white pine to get his bearings. A buck walked under the tree and snorted. The hunter took the shot from the tough angle and dropped the buck.

Chuckling to myself, I walk to the shack, where the aroma of one of Andy's incredible stews envelopes me. For dessert I kick back in a chair with a cigar and blow smoke rings. As the lazy circles drift toward the lantern, the banter of the crew begins again. Before long, the air is blue with pipe and cigar smoke. A card game unfolds, jokes fly, and guitar music fills the air. The youngsters show us how their guitar-picking skills have improved since last year, and in the corner, Andy is trying to get a debate going with Gus. It seems that Gus isn't interested in rebutting, so Andy is concocting a rebuttal and will debate with himself.

The smoke drives me outside for fresh air. An orange glow from the kerosene lantern on the porch spills onto the snow and the night sky overflows with stars. The Big Dipper and Orion's belt jump out at me, and a satellite slides toward the North Star. I feel trivial in the presence of this vast scene.

Revived, I return to the shack and the sounds of an old Woody Guthrie tune. The night winds down and conversations turn philosophical. After the lanterns are shut off, I settle into my sleeping bag.

Bert—father of Ben, Mark, and Nels—normally would be sleeping on this side of the bed, but last year was his final season in camp. His death, by cancer, has left a void in this camp. He was too young for the final hunt. His sons now must lean on the father within themselves. They hold this legacy of deer camp closer than ever to their souls.

Over the next day and a half, we bring a few more deer into camp, and the season ends for me. As I drive away, I feel a familiar swelling in my throat. I take a few deep breaths and wave. There isn't a deer in the back of my truck, but that doesn't matter. I'm leaving revived and a little more enlightened.

The old timers knew what they were doing up here when they began this ritual. Those who take part in it today know too. Regardless of the hunter's age, the experience of deer camp will enrich his life and inspire growth. Boys will become men. Men will become wiser, and in their wisdom they will continue to make deer camp a ritual of the Minnesota north woods.

THE PATH BETWEEN

Holly Atkinson

 I AM DRAWN TO PATHS: a soft depression in the spring grass, a logging road paved with autumn leaves, footprints in the snow. For me there is a message in an old trail that follows a tumbled-down fence through summer. Paths say, "I found a way through. You don't press on alone."

But there are times in my life when the path eludes me. I teeter on the threshold of an unmarked future, alone and without direction. It is then that I look back. I glance over my shoulder into childhood, to a path on which I once crossed to safety.

The path begins at the thick pine door of my family's rented cabin in the remote north woods of the 1950s. From there it scribbles its way for a half mile through a forest of birch and balsam to another cabin door where my grandmother waits for me in a grove of towering pines.

These cabins were part of Gryce Stine Resort, which lay nestled on the banks of Lake Beltrami twelve miles north of Bemidji. Here I not only traversed a pebble-strewn path between cabins; I traveled the path from girlhood to womanhood on a pilgrimage that spanned more than twenty summers.

My mind journeys back to a bright July morning. My first mission of the day is to run down the path to White Pine to ask my grandmother what time she is having lunch, and if my mother should bring forks. Mother offers to write the message down, but I decline; I am trustworthy. She reminds me not to loiter, but I will. Even the trustworthy dare not squander a Minnesota morning.

Looking back, I am struck with how safe I was walking that path. Few mothers today would allow a five-year-old to walk so far alone. But times were gentler; the world was a kinder place, and home lay at either end.

I close the pine door of Lapping Waters behind me and jump off the stoop without taking the steps. The smell of red pine, spruce, and balsam is strong in my nostrils, and through the trees I can see Lake Beltrami, a bright mirror in the early morning calm. I stop at the woodpile where the logs sit square and neatly stacked. Mr. Locke, the caretaker, has been out early.

He built all the cabins by hand during the late 1920s and early '30s, caring for them as though they were his children. As a little girl, it was hard for me to imagine that Mr. Locke was ever young. He was like the north country, ancient and enduring.

Sometimes I met him on the path, walking resolutely along, his tall, gaunt frame supported by his walking stick. When he saw me, he would touch the brim of his battered hat and nod as he passed by. In young adulthood when I read Tolkien's *Lord of the Rings*, I thought of Mr. Locke and wondered if I had seen Gandalf the Grey walking in the Mirkwood when I was young.

I don't meet Mr. Locke today. I reach into my pockets and haul out a handful of cornbread crumbs, sprinkling them on top of his woodpile for the chipmunks. I never fed them at the cabin. They were wild things, not made for me to corrupt into pets.

The next cabin is not far. Whispering Pine stands in a thick grove of jack pines, around the bend from Lapping Waters. I stop to listen . . . yes, the trees are whispering, telling me to be mindful, to walk softly on these ageless shores.

From Whispering Pine I follow the path up the hill to Birch Crest and Spruce Ledge Lodge. Being up here is like ascending into the treetops. I can see the whole length of the lake, from the rushing springs that first made explorers think Beltrami was the headwaters of the Mississippi, to Mystery River, where the lake empties into Little Fox.

These were the last two cabins Mr. Locke built at the resort, and I always wondered if it made him sad to finish his great work, to lay the last stone in the fireplace, tap the final log into place. But I know now that he was just following the path he had forged for himself, and even in the beginning, he knew his destination.

I take baby steps going downhill, for it is steep and slippery. The damp, round rocks skitter out from under my feet, and tree roots grab at my tennis shoes as I pass by. At the bottom of the hill, the path levels out near a little grove of birches. When I am sure no one is looking, I peel a piece of the smooth bark from one of the trees and stuff it into the pocket of my jeans. Tonight I will write a secret message, and when I return tomorrow I will bury it beneath this very tree. When I am old, I promise myself, I will come back and read my wish for the tree.

Now, recalling that long ago time, I realize that I have yet to keep my promise to the little grove, and I do not remember the message I wrote to the beautiful tree.

Just below the birches I can see Lorelei. This is the oldest cabin left standing on the lake. Mr. Locke built it for Selma and Ed Gryce back in the late '20s when they fell in love with each other and the wild, beautiful lake they claimed for their home. They honeymooned there on a cold winter's night when Beltrami lay locked in ice, and the stars shone pure and white above the newly hewn logs of Lorelei.

Selma Gryce was a true woodswoman. Clad in flannel shirt and men's fishing pants, she walked her own unique path through the male-dominated '50s. She fished, chopped her own wood, carried water from the pump in a wooden pail, and sat in her hammock, writing poems and songs about the lake and her beloved north country. She named all the cabins, the tiny creeks and rivers, and the smallest coves and points along Beltrami. Selma Gryce was my first hero.

As I continue my walk past aging Lorelei, I come to the lodge the Gryces moved into when the resort was finished. It is rugged and beautiful like

Mrs. Gryce, and inside there is a stuffed loon on a baby grand. One time, when I stopped to get the mail, she told me about the day a big wind sucked all the water out of Crystal Cove. "There wasn't a cloud in the sky," she said, "Just a great wind that swept down out of nowhere gathering up the waters."

When the Gryces became too old to run the resort, Mr. Locke built them a new cabin at the most mysterious place on the lake: the site of "The Old Deserted Cabin."

In the early years, my grandmother and I had paddled there in the long summer twilights. Sometimes the setting sun would flash on one of the broken windowpanes, a lamp in the dusk that said someone had come home at last. But Grandmother and I knew that was not so. The only ones who dwelled there were the gray badgers that dug their dens under the crumbling foundation. Only Mrs. Gryce, keeper of the lake's mysteries, knew who had once made a path to the cabin door. Only she remembered who lighted the lamps when the windows were new.

The Gryces lived in their new cabin summer and winter until they passed away when they were well into their eighties. My grandmother passed away soon after, and I never again followed the path of her paddle to "The Old Deserted Cabin." She no longer slept in the Owl's Nest, her bedroom at White Pine, and Selma Gryce no longer spun her stories and songs about Beltrami. Grandmother and Selma had forged a new path.

My path continues along the lake to the sister cabins: Rose Terrace and Balsam Lodge. They are built close together in case two families want to rent side by side. Between them is a plain log bench Mrs. Gryce has set among her wild roses. I stop and sit for a while, looking at the dark trees on the far shore. Mrs. Gryce put the bench there so folks could admire the lake. I do not wish to disappoint her. Now I can see White Pine, the end of my journey. My grandmother is in the yard working in her wildflowers. She stands up when she sees me coming.

"Did you hear the owls last night?" she asks, straightening her back. She is tall and thin, like a reed beside the lake.

"No," I say. "But I heard the loons."

"Yes," she says. "I heard them too. It was one of those nights."

We go into the cool darkness of the cabin. Grandmother pours me a glass of milk from the wax milk carton that looks like a megaphone. I tell her that my dad says it is moose milk, and that is why it is in the funny carton.

"How does it taste?" she asks.

"Fine," I say.

"Well then," she says.

I ask her when we're having lunch and if Mother should bring forks.

"Fish will be ready around noon," she says. "When the menfolks come in. We have forks, but we need extra spoons for the cobbler."

She takes a small beaver stick from her apron pocket and places it in my hand. "Take this back home with you," she says. "The beaver have marked it; it will make your bones strong."

I put the little stick in my pocket and hug her neck. The wind has kicked up, and Beltrami is running with whitecaps.

"Hurry on now," she says. "Your mother will be watching for you." This time I take the path at a run.

When I come in sight of Lapping Waters, Mother is standing on the stoop, her hand above her eyes shading them from the sun.

"Grandmother needs spoons," I call out.

SUGAR BUSH JOURNAL

Anne M. Dunn

 THE CRUSTY SNOW CRUNCHES under our feet as we break trail into the sugar bush. The cooking scaffold looks like a lonely skeleton with its arms flung out in welcome. Soon it will be the hub of our busy camp.

Like a grid, the scaffold's shadow marks the place where we will build the campfire. As we dig down through the snow and matted leaves to the rich, black earth, the children gather bundles of dry sticks and bark. Then they wigwam the sticks over bits of paper and bark, strike the match at the windward side, and start a little fire, which they feed with larger sticks. Soon a brisk blaze is leaping toward the sky.

We have no storage buildings here. Each spring we stack our inverted catch-cans and cooking pails near the scaffold and cover them with tar paper, held in place with heavy poles. Now we dig them out, fill the pails with snow, and hang them from the scaffold with strong wire. As the eager fire licks at the black pails, we add more snow until we have enough water to wash and rinse three hundred catch-cans.

The men have begun to replenish the wood supply, and they fell a large dead maple. To our dismay we discover it has been home to several flying squirrels. We count seven as they glide down among the trees to seek new hiding places. It's unusual to see them during the day, and seven are more than many people will see in a lifetime.

As the men cut and split the wood, the women and children haul it to the camp on a long toboggan. There they stack it around the scaffold, as if building the walls of a log cabin. The gaps between the crisscrossed wood allow the air to pass through and dry the wood quickly in case of rain or snow. The log stack also serves as a shelter from the cold wind.

It takes several days to get the wood ready. There will be no time to gather wood when the sap begins to run. When we have stacked enough wood, we go home to wait. I watch the box elder trees near our home because we know that when the box elder begins to weep, the sap is rising in the trees to begin another growing season, and it's time to tap the maples. The process is triggered by the fluctuating temperatures of freezing nights followed by thawing days. How anxious we become as the days go by. At last, we see the bright tears glistening in the branches of the box elders. The sap is running!

We return to the camp armed with a small hatchet, a bit, a brace, and a box of clean taps. The children scurry from tree to tree, distributing catch-cans. The older children know which trees will be tapped and how many catch-cans each tree will need. Small trees are tapped once on the sunrise side, so they will begin to flow early in the day. Larger ones will produce more sap and may be tapped more than once. One great tree holds five cans well spaced around its huge trunk. We call this tree Grandfather.

It takes three days to set three hundred taps. Setting the tap requires drilling about two inches into the tree, about three feet from the base. As the bit is turned, a long curl of moist wood is drawn out. The wood suddenly darkens when the bit is deep enough.

When the bit is removed, a spout is placed in the hole, and a can is quickly hung in place. We watch a drop of sap appear, glitter in the sunlight, fall from the spout, and, with a musical *ting*, splash into the bottom of the can. Another harvest has begun!

The two thirty-gallon storage barrels are scrubbed clean. We will use one for a larder until the sap is running fast enough to fill both barrels. Eventually, the sap will run so fast and hard that we will not be able to boil it all down in one day. Then we must not allow the sap to remain in storage too long because it will sour. Sour sap must be discarded. To avoid such waste, we rotate the stored sap carefully, cooking the older sap first.

The first sap of the season runs crystal clear and produces a mild syrup. As the season progresses, the sap turns amber, producing dark, strong-flavored syrup.

Because the sweet-tasting sap contains only about 3 percent sugar, we must collect and boil more than thirty gallons of sap to make one gallon of syrup. As the sap boils, the water evaporates. The sap tastes like sugar water until it has boiled long enough to concentrate into a dark, sweet fluid that releases the maple flavor. (Box elders and birch trees also produce a sweet sap that can be boiled down into a pleasant-tasting syrup.)

We watch the sap closely, for we have worked too hard to let it boil over and be lost in the fire. To slow the rolling boil, we remove the pails from the heat with long, slender poles cut from green aspen. The poles are fashioned from a sapling with a good crotch; one end is cut to form a four-inch hook with a flat bottom. With this pole, a person can tend both sides of the fire, using the crotch to pull pails from one side and the flat end of the hook to push pails out the other. Touching the rolling sap with a green balsam branch will also slow the boil.

Although the sugar bush is a place of intense work, it is also a place of spiritual renewal and great personal enrichment. It's hard for me to imagine a better place to be in March.

When I get to camp early in the day, I find the sap still frozen in the spouts. I lay wood for a large fire—about ten feet long and four feet wide—and brew a pot of coffee made with sap instead of water. Then while the fire spreads, I fill the cooking pails with sap from the storage barrels and hang them over the fire.

As the sun climbs, the grove begins to warm, and I walk away from the snapping fire to listen for the sap-song. I hear it begin far away. *Ting.* The sap is thawed. *Ting.* It falls into empty catch-cans. *Ting, ting.* Soon I am surrounded by the happy rhythm. As the cans fill, the song subsides.

In some of the trees we have found the sumac taps left by other families that used the groves before us. They look like withered nipples almost covered by dark folds of gray, furrowed maple bark.

Other trees bear scars from long ago when the trees were slashed near the base and a carved cedar trough was pressed into the wound. The trough directed the sap into seamless birch bark bowls set on the ground. Some of these slashings are now four feet off the ground.

Although the sugar bush is rich in quiet memories, it would not be complete without the laughter of children. So, like generations of families before us, we have brought the children, and the grove rings with their excited voices.

The children spend many hours swinging in the arms of an ancient maple, broken by storms and age. The giant seems unwilling to resign itself to the earth. Propped up on huge crumbling limbs, it invites the children to many adventures.

The children also learn to be comfortable with wild things. Near the camp two ospreys make their summer home. Their ragged-looking nest clings to the top of a dead aspen. We welcome their return from the south as they circle our camp like great winged sentinels.

The staccato of a hungry woodpecker punctuates the quiet. Squirrels and chipmunks visit us for handouts and flick their tails in salute of our generosity. The well-dressed chickadee and nuthatch entertain us with their acrobatics.

A less welcome visitor is the masked bandit who has discovered our larder. We must be very clever to devise ways to keep the raccoon out of our food.

Two playful weasels have come to live in our wood stack. They make us laugh as they chase each other through the wood stack and suddenly pop up between the sticks. Then almost before we see them leave, they are blinking at us from somewhere else. They go so fast it seems we are watching six white weasels running around in the wood.

But the children also have work to do. As the season progresses, the sap flow increases, and we must work until long after dark. We have seen the snowy trails turn muddy, and now we must empty the cans at least twice a day. Using small pails, the children collect sap from cans near the camp.

In the evening we sit in the glow of the fire in private worlds of thought, but as the darkness gathers round us we draw closer to each other. Families are knit and friendships sealed around the fire.

Kookookoo-oo an owl cries in the night. Looking up, I find the stars of our late-winter sky entangled in the bare branches above us.

Each night we carry our precious burden of steaming syrup home. Walking down the trail, I feel close to the people who came to this grove long ago. I can almost see them walking among the trees, peering into catch-cans, and nodding in satisfaction. I can almost hear the mud sucking softly at their feet as they go to warm themselves at our abandoned fire, still glowing with hot coals.

To make the coveted maple sugar cakes, we must boil the syrup again. When the syrup reaches the pollywog stage (250–260 degrees), we remove it from the heat and beat it with a wooden paddle until it loses its glossy look. Then we pour it into molds.

Sugar is made by heating the syrup in the same way. But it must be beaten for a very long time. It seems that the syrup will never change, but suddenly it becomes granules of maple sugar—an excellent reward for such hard work.

When the tree buds begin to expand to the size of squirrel ears, we remove the spouts and allow the trees to heal so the sap will flow uninterrupted up into the trees for another season of growth.

Now it's time to celebrate our thanksgiving for the maple harvest. We invite our friends to the annual potluck feast. It's an open house without a house. People come and go all day. Everyone enjoys sap-coffee and sap-tea. For the children we make hot chocolate with sap and milk. Of course, we have plenty of Indian fry-bread ready to dip into the fresh maple syrup.

On closing day we get ready to move out of camp. We linger over small tasks, but at last we can find no further reason for delay. One by one we pick up our packs and leave. Single file, we move down the muddy trail.

One by one we pause at the fork in the trail to look back. Silently we promise to return next year, when the box elder begins to weep.

MOTHER'S DAY IN
RATTLESNAKE COUNTRY

Susan Maas

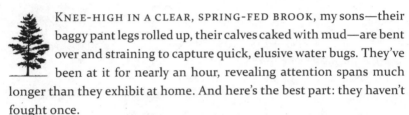 KNEE-HIGH IN A CLEAR, SPRING-FED BROOK, my sons—their baggy pant legs rolled up, their calves caked with mud—are bent over and straining to capture quick, elusive water bugs. They've been at it for nearly an hour, revealing attention spans much longer than they exhibit at home. And here's the best part: they haven't fought once.

They haven't caught a single water bug, nor will they for the rest of the weekend. But the futility of their pursuit never seems to diminish their zest.

The pleasure of watching them from my camp chair a few yards away—where neither of them has made a single demand on me—is a superb Mother's Day gift.

My husband, six-year-old son, three-year-old son, and I are camping at Whitewater State Park in early May. The forest floor is a riot of white, yellow, and purple wildflowers. Before even pitching our tent, we've seen beavers, turtles, sandpipers, bald eagles, and flycatchers. Timber rattlesnakes live here in southeastern Minnesota among the limestone cliffs; before the weekend is over, we'll have seen at least one—in a program at the park interpretive center—though we're hoping for more.

Crotalus horridus probably won't make its way onto a Hallmark greeting card anytime soon, but Mother's Day is as good a time as any to learn about this fascinating species. Recent research has revealed that the long-persecuted and feared timber rattlesnake has never been exactly the surly, aggressive villain humans have perceived it to be. The female timber rattler has a somewhat convivial family side. She can recognize her siblings, even after years in captivity, and seeks their company.

Female timber rattlesnakes show other traits of sociability, including group defense and maternal care of the young, which they bear live (in litters of seven or so) every three or four years. In the face of predators, disease, habitat loss, human persecution, and tough competition for food, timber rattlesnake families seem to stick together and make sacrifices for one another.

My parents saved each year to give us a two-week lakeside vacation with plenty of fishing expeditions and walks in the woods. "Roughing it" meant a housekeeping cabin with no dishwasher. My husband and I aren't exactly wilderness backpackers: we rarely camp for more than three days at a time, and almost always within fifteen miles of a breakfast diner. But, for us, the campfire and sleeping outside—the hot dogs, marshmallows, ghost stories, and night sounds—are key. What a child might miss in a snug cabin bed, solidly separated from wild animals and potential storms, is the faint but thrilling hint of risk. Little girls and boys love a whiff of danger—the far-off howl of wolves, a glimpse of a bear . . . or the telltale shake of a rattlesnake's tail.

For his Saturday morning interpretive program about the long-abused timber rattlesnake, park naturalist Dave Palmquist brought a live specimen: a snake he acquired a decade ago from a woman who'd moved into a blufftop housing development and discovered the reptile in her backyard. Palmquist told us that fearful humans often illegally capture or kill these essentially timid creatures, which are protected by state law.

"Unfortunately, we often kill what we don't understand," he said. The timber rattlesnake, he added, "is a symbol of what's left of the bluffland wilderness."

My beloved paternal grandmother was from bluff country, born and raised in Winona. In 1919, when she was a girl, Whitewater State Park was established as part of a burgeoning local effort to protect the region's natural resources. I imagine my grandmother might have picnicked here in the meadows with her family, perhaps strolled on hilltop trails with a high school suitor.

"Can we camp at this same park next time?" our six-year-old asks as we approach the end of a two-and-a-half-mile hike. We are all uncharacteristically quiet: For minutes at a time, I can hear only birds chirping, small tennis shoes padding on the dried-leaf-strewn trail, and our younger boy tapping the ground with his walking stick each time he takes a step. We're watching eagerly for rattlesnakes.

Habitat loss poses a grave threat to the timber rattlesnake. The snake is inextricably tied to its bluffland habitat. Attempts to save displaced snakes by relocating them are usually unsuccessful. Even when placed with existing rattlesnake populations, relocated adults eat poorly and often leave the new site, perhaps in an effort to return to their original home. Humans are, of course, more adaptable in this regard.

I'm from Michigan, but most of my childhood vacations (including the lakeside cabin getaways) were spent catching up with family and friends in other states. Now that my husband and I have children, we spend a lot of precious vacation time driving or flying out of Minnesota to relatives elsewhere. Our weekend camping trips in Minnesota are important for our sons to feel connected with the soil, trees, and water of their home state. Wherever they go, I want them to really be *from* somewhere: they're Minnesotans.

I like to think that my bluff country grandmother, a lover of wildflowers and beauty, admired the false rue anemone sprinkled here on the forest floor like thousands of tiny fallen stars. Maybe she, like her great-grandsons, also speculated whether the funny mayapple plants, with their rubbery stems and enormous leaves, could be umbrellas for woodland gnomes. And I wonder if she ever saw a rattlesnake in the wild—there certainly were many more of them around then—or if, on a future camping trip, we might be so lucky.

Paying Attention

DRAWING LIFE FROM NATURE

Vera Ming Wong

As a child in Chicago, I found refuge on the shores of Lake Michigan. Imprinting on this landscape, I unconsciously developed a sense of air-land-water equity: an expanse of land must be balanced by an equal vastness of water, all of which is balanced by a more-than-double volume of sky. Intellectually, I know now that my equations are way off, that water on this planet far outweighs the emerged land, and the sky has infinity on its side; but my gut sense of air-land-water balance persists.

The Boundary Waters Canoe Area Wilderness reaffirms my sense of equity between land and water. Are we on land, surrounded by water, or on water, surrounded by land? Here one eventually feels amphibious, moving on land, water, or ice with equal ease and care.

In the BWCAW, we meander through constantly changing layers of landscapes and innumerable glorious compositions of sky, plants, land, water, rocks. Chinese and Japanese gardens aspire to reproduce these landscapes. Every gesturing boulder, every intriguing bog, every downed tree tangle, and the endless arc of every reflected bulrush catch my eye and my breath. How can I paint it all, in the sliver of time between paddling (or skiing) and sundown? And how can I avoid being intimidated by the perfection that surrounds me?

I remind myself that small pieces can catch the essence of a big place. Trying to catch everything at once usually produces nothing at all. So I seek a slice that can reveal the temper of this place: not a generic scene, but a particular constellation of plants, among rocks, sharing water, dancing with shadow and light.

Within each painting is inquiry and revelation. What forces cause this place or organism to be? What dynamic interactions—geology, climate, biota—keep it alive? And which forces must it resist to persist?

In a system left to its own devices, as in the BWCAW, such interactions are for the most part undisguised. Ancient glaciers, past logging, former roads, and years of drought or high water are all inscribed on the land and biota. More recent winds, storms, ice, and fire add new layers. When I paint or draw, I practice time travel, reading clues that tell the history of place—lines on the rocks, species of plants, growth forms of trees.

Since ancient times, drawing (and painting, which is drawing with color) has documented images for history, science, posterity, religion, nostalgia, memory. Beyond the usefulness of the end product, however, is the value of the process. Drawing from life requires extended focus on a small part of one's environment. The deeper I look, the more questions I find. And wrestling to balance details within the big picture (can I draw the forest for the trees? or the trees for the forest?) opens paradoxes: shall I narrow the focus to gain a wider view, or widen the focus to gain a deeper view? Drawing becomes a way of seeing deeply, a meditation with open eyes, a working reflection of a relationship growing between artist and subject.

Why not simply take a quick photograph? Sometimes I do, but can the camera catch what strikes me? If I only take a photo, will I really see, the way one sees when one looks piercingly, analytically, empathetically for as long as light holds? It's the looking and trying that make the connection, that create the spark, that travel from snow, sky, and tree, to eye, to mind, to hand, to paper; that let me, briefly, become part of what I draw. Painting and drawing, for me, are a learning process, through which I merge with parts of nature and pay my respects. So even if I only have time for three lines and a scribble, I still try.

LESSONS FROM A
YOUNG EXPLORER

Steve Dibb

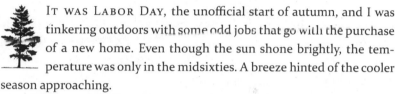

IT WAS LABOR DAY, the unofficial start of autumn, and I was tinkering outdoors with some odd jobs that go with the purchase of a new home. Even though the sun shone brightly, the temperature was only in the midsixties. A breeze hinted of the cooler season approaching.

As a stream of blackbirds flowed overhead, I realized that with the exception of a few fishing trips and a couple of family picnics, I had hardly set foot in the country all summer.

Casting aside my hammer, I laced up my boots, pulled out my hunting jacket and hat, grabbed my six-year-old daughter, Stephanie, and left for what I thought would be a routine walk through the woods.

We drove to Moonan Marsh Wildlife Management Area, where a series of dikes trapped water brought by ditches from the surrounding farmland. This system created a large area of marsh and flooded woodlands. Although it's a popular spot during the waterfowl and deer seasons, it gets few visitors the rest of the year.

We had parked in a small lot and started across a narrow footbridge over the first drainage ditch when four wood ducks flushed about fifteen yards to our left with an uproar of wing beats and peeping. Though startled by their exit, I was promptly brought to earth by a small voice behind me that asked, "What kind were they, Daddy?" Collecting my fatherly thoughts, I croaked "Woodies," amazed that my daughter, no doubt equally surprised, had found time to wonder what kind of ducks they were, why they were sitting there, where they were going now, and so on.

We started down the edge of the woods, following a trail made by deer and widened by years of treading by human feet. I walked slowly, relishing the warmth of the late afternoon sun, not searching for anything in particular.

I glanced back from time to time to see Stephanie picking up things that caught her eye. When we were ready to turn into the trees, I asked her what she had found. She held out her small hands, which held an assortment of feathers, bones, flowers, pretty rocks, and weeds. It struck me as funny that her young, perceptive mind had found such a wealth of treasures, where I had found none.

As we marched through a backwater dry from that year's rainless summer, I looked with interest at the bottom of a familiar swamp. Old snail and clam shells lay in the mud. Sticks that had pulled at my waders last fall were now in plain sight.

Even some of the ditches in the swamp were dry. As we walked down one of them, my own awareness started to sharpen as Stephanie continued to stop and investigate each clue to the ecological puzzle. A beaver's feed pile was now high and dry, prompting a question about how beavers survive in dry years. In the mud we read a book of natural stories. Tracks of deer, raccoon, and mink betrayed favorite crossing or feeding spots. Stephanie was in her glory, picking up this, kicking at that, stopping to muse over a hole in a hollow log.

As I stood watching her, I realized how much adults have to learn from children: to slow down and observe the world around them, to stop and smell the wildflowers once in a while. We go rushing through life, meeting deadlines and quotas, dragging our children with us as we go. But given the chance, they find their freedom to ponder and discover what this natural world holds for them. My six-year-old teacher was giving me quite a lesson.

The sun was starting to set, so I turned back in the direction of our truck and blazed a trail through the hip-deep swamp grass. I saw that

Stephanie was struggling, so I swept her up and planted her atop my shoulders to continue our journey through the cool grass.

Eventually, we reached a mature stand of maples, oaks, and basswoods. I gave my young explorer the lead and directed her down a narrow trail. When we stopped for a short breather, I pointed out some old deer droppings, explaining that the trail we were on was quite likely created and used by deer.

Not knowing what response this would bring, I was surprised but delighted to see her bend down for a closer look. Finally, she straightened her legs and peering down the trail, she murmured, "Neat, Dad."

Ultimately our trail led us back to the ditch where we started (much to the amazement of my young companion), and while we were walking back to our truck, a red-tailed hawk, circling in the late afternoon thermals far overhead, screeched as it swung southward.

Watching the hawk's departure, I felt a small hand slip into mine and a young voice asked, "What day is it today?" "Well, sweetheart, it's a special Monday called Labor Day," I replied. Squeezing my hand, she added, "Well then, this has been the best Monday I've ever had!" I looked down into her bright blue eyes and answered, "Me too, sweetie. Me too."

BIRDING WITH BEN

Mary Kroll

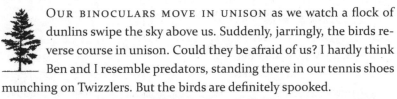 OUR BINOCULARS MOVE IN UNISON as we watch a flock of dunlins swipe the sky above us. Suddenly, jarringly, the birds reverse course in unison. Could they be afraid of us? I hardly think Ben and I resemble predators, standing there in our tennis shoes munching on Twizzlers. But the birds are definitely spooked.

Then we see it. Soaring casually near the flock is a peregrine falcon, looking for lunch. The flock frantically switches direction, corralled like skittish calves by the peregrine. Then, the falcon is gone. Perhaps it isn't hungry, or it has spied other prey. The manic shorebirds skitter to a relieved, exhausted stop on a nearby sewage pond.

Yes, we are standing next to a sewage pond. By choice.

For many people, birding may seem like a leisurely activity with walks through colorful, trilling woods that lead to views of birds (which hold long poses while you thumb your Sibley's field guide). Actually, birding is partly a procession of small-town sewage ponds. Shorebirds—the birds we were looking for that spring day—find food and refuge at these less-than-aesthetic places. To bird there, you must lift binoculars and hold your nose at the same time.

And I'm addicted to it.

It's all Ben's fault. Ben is my twenty-year-old son, a fine man in the making and already an accomplished birder. As a kindergartner, Ben boarded a cavernous yellow school bus, unbalanced by his oversized backpack, clinging to a Peterson's bird field guide. He couldn't read, but he would try to match the birds he spied from the bus with the pictures. By age ten he was rattling off the warblers he saw in our backyard—magnolia, Blackburnian, Nashville. Frankly, I thought he was making the names up. But like a dutiful mom, I peered through his outstretched binoculars and assured him, yes, I could see the white eye ring. Sure.

As Ben got older, it occurred to me that he knew what he was talking about. I watched as he fell in with a group of seasoned birders in Grand Marais, high-fiving each other like division champions when they found a black-legged kittiwake (a small gull) in the harbor. Ben held his own on field trips, and other accomplished birders would fully accept his identifications when announcing their "roll call" of birds at the end of the day. Clearly, he wasn't making anything up.

We're into the second day of a three-day birdathon, and the sky is overcast. It seems as though Ben is navigating our car under a giant swash of rain. To the north, south, and west I see clearing, but Ben has a destination in mind and keeps us pinned under clouds, as if he were consulting a divining rod, not an atlas, for directions.

Finally, we arrive at a sprawling wetland in Kandiyohi County. It looks like any other spongy grassland. "Let's call some rails," Ben suggests, as he pulls out a CD player and slips in a bird-sound disc. The faux Virginia rail crackles loudly. Right away, a bird returns the sound. Ben and I share smiles; and then, suddenly, the rail is at Ben's feet. Quickly realizing its mistake, the bird turns on its nonexistent heels and skitters off through the grass.

"Let's consider that our mascot for the trip," I suggest. "We could name it Roger. Roger the Rail." Ben smiles and shrugs. I think he sometimes wonders why he's birding with such an amateur.

Later in the day, his quick "Oh, wait, pull in here" has me making a fast right into the flooded parking lot of a cement manufacturer. Not exactly my idea of habitat, but I strain to see what Ben has sensed. Then I notice the sand and silt, washed in from a nearby flooded stream, forming small

islands among the standing water. Shorebird habitat? Ben spies a beautiful, brownish shorebird with a black chest and face mask. It is busily
turning over stones with its bill. Aptly named, the ruddy turnstone is
looking for insects and grubs. I sometimes think Ben has bird ESP.

We meander through southern Minnesota. The area is spackled
with small towns and their grain elevators rising next to railroad tracks.
We stop at each crossing to listen for the distinctive *coo-cooo-coo* of the
Eurasian collared-dove, an exotic bird from India that was introduced
into the Bahamas in the 1970s and migrated to Florida. Its range now
spreads north into Minnesota. In these small towns, Ben and I find con-
venience stores with microwaveable hot dogs and lilac bushes the size of
urban condominiums, but no calling doves.

Doves or not, I love the march through these small towns, with their
modest homes and gardens lined by neat rows of rhubarb. We leisurely
drive from bird feeder to bird feeder, checking chickadees and nuthatches
off our list, moving on before we alarm homeowners who might wonder
why we are staring at their yards with binoculars. We stand on street corners and listen for the distinctive twittering of chimney swifts overhead,
as locals crane their necks to see what we find so interesting.

Our final stop is a cemetery, where we look for warblers and other flitting things. I can identify many of these small birds, but sometimes I'm
not sure. Some warblers are yellow with olive streaks, or yellow with blue
gray wings, or gray with yellow heads, or gray with yellow rumps. They are
a maddening puzzle. I pretend I know them anyway. Ben is happy when I
locate a new warbler flitting among the branches of a Norway spruce, and
he identifies it before I make a bad guess.

Sewage ponds. Parking lots. Cemeteries. These days are so sweet, with
my son. They last from sunrise (warblers move in the morning) to late at
night (owls). They are long days, full of moments and scents of raw sewage. But none of this matters as long as I'm birding with Ben.

BIRDING IN THE FAST-FOOD LANE

D. Scott Shultz

HIGH ABOVE ME IN THE OVERCAST SKY, spinning tighter and tighter circles, a female peregrine falcon closes the gap on a terrified common grackle. The falcon throws out her talon-tipped foot once, twice. The third time convinces the hapless grackle that gravity is his friend. Folding his wings, he tips over and plummets, still dodging attacks from the peregrine. They drop to earth in seconds and vanish behind the Target store at Interstate 494 and Penn Avenue.

The Target store?

Perhaps the lunchtime shoppers were amused by (or wary of) the sight of a bearded bear of a birdwatcher, binoculars glued to his eyes, turning circles in the parking lot. But while they worried about the price of paper towels (or the parking lot lunatic), I witnessed the savage drama of nature played out above an asphalt stage.

Yanking the binoculars from my eyes, I jumped into my truck, almost on top of my forgotten Burger King Value Meal, and raced to the scene. I searched for evidence of the outcome of the sky chase. Finding none, I returned to the edge of the parking lot to finish my lunch. As I chewed the last bite, I glanced out the side window and saw the falcon winging my way. I eased out of the truck and stood stone still as she crossed directly in front of me, ten feet above the lot. She headed for the distant Norwest Bank tower and disappeared.

. . .

In March my wife and I took our dog for a walk early one morning. The rhythmic drip of melting snow and the crisp scent of evergreens transported us to the north woods. Ten minutes into our trek, we spied a male Cooper's hawk zinging his way through still-naked maple and elm trees. He landed in a tall spruce and disappeared among the dense needles. Around the next bend, I spotted a silhouette near the top of a pine. As the bird turned to study us, I saw the hooked beak and larger-than-crow size of a female Cooper's. Meanwhile, the male had returned to the air, flying courtship circles above the tree canopy, *kakking* in full voice.

"I bet they're going to nest near here!" I told my wife.

"Near here" was, in fact, a residential neighborhood with a smattering of deciduous and coniferous trees in each yard, located just south of the University of St. Thomas in St. Paul. Not what the field guides would call typical nesting territory for a shy woodland hawk. Perhaps it is time to revise the field guides.

One summer evening a freshening breeze drew my wife and me out for a leisurely walk around our neighborhood near the College of St. Catherine in St. Paul. As we neared two teenagers tossing a Frisbee, a juvenile male Cooper's hawk rocketed past them at knee level and directly in front of us. He headed down the side street, crossed two front lawns, then shot up near the top of a cottonwood. We jogged to the tree and studied the hawk while he ignored us.

Dusk was gathering, and this bird was seriously hunting: his head swiveled and jerked left, right, center, then right again. Starlings had flocked to a few cedar trees to our right. All their quarreling and jockeying for the best perch had revealed their hiding spot. Then, as the hawk launched from his perch, the cedars fell silent as a green tomb.

Like a brown-and-white fletched arrow, the hawk shot through the curtain of cedar branches. Starlings bailed out in all directions. They fled in twos and threes, flying hard and emitting terrified squeals.

We could hear movement in the dense foliage, wings slapping branches, talons scraping bark. Suddenly a starling shot out with a chocolate-brown streak hot on its tail. Predator and prey disappeared behind the houses, and we could only guess the outcome.

Seeing a hawk in action—that is, in hot pursuit of its dinner—is the true reward for an urban raptor watcher. The secret recipe to doing this successfully, I have found, is this: first, do not expect to see it; and second, keep your eyes on the prey species.

The actions of a lone gull first alerted me to the Target store peregrine. Perched on a light pole, calmly surveying the sea of asphalt and automobiles, the gull abruptly snapped to attention. Pulling its feathers in tight, it swiveled its head to gaze skyward. I looked skyward too, and spotted the peregrine descending on the grackle.

Another surprise sighting occurred at a park in south Minneapolis. While snacking on a Wendy's Big Classic before my evening class, I was watching the antics of a gray squirrel as it scavenged from a trash barrel. In an instant the squirrel froze, then dashed to a nearby tree. Within seconds, a red-tailed hawk made a pass at the base of the tree, apparently trying to flush the squirrel. The wise squirrel scrambled to the lee side and hugged the bark. The redtail swept up to the top of a tree thirty feet away. She sat with her back to the rodent but watched over her shoulder for any sly escape attempts. Eventually a passing bicyclist spooked the hawk, and the squirrel was free to scavenge again.

Perhaps a third "ingredient" to successful urban hawk watching is this: eat fast food. Three summers ago I kept track of a pair of red-tailed hawks nesting on a utility tower near a bustling Burger King off Interstate 35W at County Road C. I watched them build a partial nest, then rebuild it on the tower's next higher cross arm. I checked their progress daily as I hurried to work. On weekends I watched them feed a single, rapidly growing chick, while I gorged on a Whopper with cheese.

One morning as I was wolfing down an Egg McMuffin in a parking lot near downtown St. Paul, I watched a flock of starlings feeding on the ground. A group of robins perched in ornamental trees nearby. Suddenly both species took to the wind, and I knew a cruising raptor was near. A mere three seconds later, a female sharp-shinned hawk—a smaller version of the Cooper's hawk—came cruising over the spot where the starlings had been feeding. She rose and fell over the contours of the land, probably hoping to flush any stragglers, but the starlings were long gone.

Other noteworthy city bird sightings: a red-tailed hawk atop a field light at Midway Stadium watching most of the fifth inning of a St. Paul Saints baseball game; an adult bald eagle flying at treetop level over the College of St. Catherine campus escorted by a few hostile crows; an adult peregrine grabbing one of a trio of pigeons as they flew parallel to the Lafayette Bridge; and on two occasions, a grackle—a nonraptor—chasing and catching a house sparrow.

My favorite urban raptor viewing began in March 1995 in Fridley. The weather was unseasonably tolerable, and I had taken to eating my lunch in the library parking lot. Munching Taco Bell tacos in the delightful ambience of my truck, I heard the enraged squawking of several crows—a fairly reliable "raptor-sighting alert." Stepping out of the truck, I watched their careening flight. Then, there she was: a female Cooper's hawk, cruising the edge of a woodlot, casually fending off the crows' half-hearted attacks. She was soon out of sight, and I returned to my lunch.

Before I had finished my second taco, she returned and landed on a decrepit squirrel nest. She began rearranging a few sticks atop the nest, and I realized she would be nesting there. Because I worked only three miles away, I made plans to eat lunch in the lot on a regular basis.

According to most literature, the Cooper's is an uncommon and secretive bird-catching hawk, at home in mixed deciduous and coniferous forests. What was this bird doing in a tiny woodlot three hundred yards from a big shopping mall and fifteen yards from a busy library parking lot?

Two weeks later I deduced that the pair was in full incubation mode, and I expanded my research time to include the hour before work. The female, often only visible by her long striped tail protruding over the nest edge, would leave the nest only when the male arrived. As soon as she left—leaping and free-falling for a split second before turning on her rapid-fire wings—the male settled down for his turn at incubation.

One morning I spied a gray squirrel working its way up the nest tree. When it had climbed to a spot directly below the nest, the female stood up. The squirrel shot up an adjacent branch, barely a foot from the nest, and the female rushed at it. The squirrel scampered back to its hideout below. A moment passed, and it went back up. Foolishness or bravado overtook the squirrel this time: it crested the edge of the nest and leaped in! Of course, it instantly leaped back out, followed by the female. This time she flew after the squirrel at breakneck speed, footing at it and just barely missing. Twenty feet down, she slammed to a stop on a branch and watched the squirrel descend, then returned to her nest and settled in.

The squirrel was actually climbing up again when the male hawk arrived. This time the rodent scrambled all the way down and disappeared. The stress of the squirrel's visit must have flustered the female, for she refused to relinquish the nest to her mate.

I changed employers before the chicks left the nest and had to wish the Cooper's family the best of luck. My research grounds moved to the east side of St. Paul—the Wendy's on Maryland Avenue, the Hardee's on Rice Street, and, of course, the McDonald's on University. I did see a pair of ospreys once, over McCarrons Lake on Rice Street—by the Taco Bell and Burger King.

HEART OF THE HUNT

Terri Sutton

AL SCHROETER AND I are bumping down the Echo Trail out of Ely in his battered pickup, catching the day's first gold on the hilltops, falling into shadow on the swampy bottoms. My hands gingerly cradle a scalding tin cup of coffee. I've sworn off caffeine, but I'm sipping this thick stuff because I'm cold, and because I've already stepped so far out of the comfortable shell of opinion and habit known as "me" that all rules are off. I'm wearing a blaze orange acrylic stocking cap. I'm going hunting. My kick-started brain spins. I feel lost. Good, I decide. I think that's why I'm here.

A week before, on the phone, Al's guffaws bounced on the wires between Ely and Minneapolis. He's a rangy, beetle-browed giant, with a voice to match. "Sure, I'll take you hunting," he enthused. "But, Terri, *why*?" Al has known me as a dedicated non-meat eater for the decade-plus since his shaggy punk-rock band first slept on my floor in San Francisco. I've known him as a loony outdoorsman since I heard that he—three days into a Lake Calhoun ice-fishing marathon—resolutely ignored a fed-up girlfriend screaming from shore. Al moved north a few years ago, with a vegetarian wife who mostly doesn't mind sharing him with two bird dogs and the woods.

For a moment, I couldn't think how to answer him. Because I don't get it, I finally said. Because I've never understood what hunting means to the hunter, and maybe it's time I should.

The October sun is brightening the high yellow aspen leaves when we park in a rutted clearing amidst the Superior National Forest. In the quick calm we hear the dogs—Maybelle and her daughter Dixie—whining and scratching back in their kennels. Before Al lets Maybelle out, he slides his shotgun out of its Naugahyde casing and shows me the short barrel—chosen for its easy handling amid dense forest growth, Al says. He passes me the unloaded pump-action shotgun. I bobble it, my hand slipping with the pump. "Eek!" I exhale and almost throw it back at him.

Al buckles a bell collar on Maybelle. "Hunt 'em up!" he says sternly. She races off into the brush and we saunter after her, Dixie weeping hopelessly behind us. For a short bit we walk trail as a huffing Maybelle streaks through the scrub. So this is hunting, I think: the dog does everything. Then we're over our heads in saplings, and it's all I can do to keep upright. My confounded eyes offer up screwy snapshots: branches at two inches; mossy log underfoot; Al's gun to the left and ahead; branches at zero inches. It's as if we're hiking through a moving kaleidoscope, which might feel divertingly trippy except that one of us is packing.

Tutored with stories of stealthy Hiawathas, I'd envisioned the hunt as a hushed, contemplative endeavor. Instead we're crashing through crunchy leaves and brittle saplings, Maybelle off to the side a-ringing her bell. And Al's talking: directing the dog, directing me, and simply jawing, because he does that. "Yeah, you don't tell people about your favorite covers—the locals'd use 'em like walleye holes. May-*belle*! Come! We're gonna head round this way. See this leaf? That's woodcock splash. It looks fresh." Surrounding all our noise I hear the forest, which on this windless morning sounds like merciless patience.

Then the bell stops. Al stops me. Silence. "She's locked up." Al locates the dog, her body poised in midstride, head angling off to her right. "That bird's just staying put," notes Al. "Sure it's invisible." We step closer behind Maybelle, quiet. "There it is, about four feet off her nose." I look, and I see brown leaves. The moment extends liquidly around us, filling our lungs.

Later Al will tell me: "When Maybelle goes on point, I know I have time to think about the bird's probable course, what my best shots are; I have time to adjust my hat." For me, watching, it seems like we all become something other than conscious—more like functions, levers, within an old and efficient machine. The bird appears to fly up at the same time the gun goes off; it is falling, light to dark, even as it rises.

"Down bird!" Al commands, and Maybelle leaves her point to snuffle for the woodcock. "Was that loud?" he asks me, grinning. "Not really," I say, although the shot still echoes. The whole moment was loud, not just the gun.

Maybelle brings Al the bird, and he brings it to me. Patterned in deep brown and black, the woodcock fits exactly in Al's wide palm, its neck draped over his wrist. "How do you know it's dead?" I wonder anxiously. Al wiggles the loose little head, with its thin stilt of a beak. I can't see where it's shot, but Al has blood on his hand. I hold out my two, and he tips the bird onto them.

The body is hot. I didn't expect that. The eye is black and glassy yet, the white ring around it emphasizing the gleam. Drawing out the wide wing, I can feel its tensile strength. The needle bill, with which the woodcock probes dirt and wet leaves for earthworms, opens to reveal a slim tongue. These details escaped me the last time I stalked woodcock, a spring evening years ago when some friends and I drove to Elm Creek Park Reserve near Osseo to witness the male's whistling courtship flight.

Crouched low, uncertain in the deep dark, we heard above us the trill of the wind through the male's wing feathers and his chirping song, inscrutable music to an invisible dance. This bird, leaking warmth into my hand, cannot hide itself. But its weight, the tactile substance of its soft feathers and bony bill, strikes me as a mystery equally bottomless and off-balancing.

As Al drops two more woodcocks and a pair of grouse, missing a single cunning grouse that refused to fly, the thunking reality of all these interrupted ascensions chips away at the wonder of a bird in the hand. Whatever your respectful intentions, a shot bird still flops cruelly to the ground. My eye tries to keep the downed bird flying into the what-if dimension, into the web-work of ghostly flight paths envisioned by writer Robert F. Jones. Jones would have it that spirit birds, forever "winging on out as if they'd never been hit," eventually weave the hunter's "rough winding sheets." I'm not sure nature writes its stories with such satisfyingly karmic ends.

The hunting creed assumes that the lives of prey can and should be sacrificed for the sustenance, physical or emotional, of the hunter. Most people who eat meat pay someone else to kill food for them. Hunters pay to kill. Their refusal to distance themselves from killing intrigues me: I don't know whether they deserve my disgust or my respect. It's the latter that has shot up lately.

Nearly two decades into vegetarianism, I've lost a bit of the self-righteous edge: I keep running into contradictions. Plant eaters tend to trumpet the animal cruelty and environmental destruction caused by meat eating—a valid, constructive criticism, and disingenuous too. At the mouth of the Mississippi in the Gulf of Mexico, researchers have been watching runoff pesticides and fertilizers from heartland farms liquidate the ocean life over an area the size of New Jersey. Part of the dead zone bears my name. Whatever you eat, because you eat, something else doesn't. The hunter doesn't try to elude responsibility for human appetite and its consequences.

A year earlier at Thanksgiving, Al presented our gathering with his fall harvest: woodcock pan-fried, baked, and served with a reduced red-wine sauce. I did not refuse a sample—because of the worm diet, it tasted rich and steaky—partly because I knew that these birds had enjoyed a wild, unfettered existence, and partly because I wanted to acknowledge the labor that had brought this food to the table. I'm a gardener; I plan and plant and weed and water, coaxing life and dealing death. Al scouts and trains his dogs and talks woodcock for months, preparing for the hunting season. Perhaps the hunt and the garden should be considered together, the hobbified versions of ancient, essential pursuits. Perhaps when you shoot, as when you dig, you remind yourself that food is not just bought, but earned.

At our final stop on the Echo Trail, Al strolls up to an aspen stand and pronounces: "Last time there was a grouse here." As if summoned, a grouse rattles up, brushing our teeth for us. I think I am uneasy around these deaths because *I* have not earned them.

Brad Gatzlaff has been up since 3:30 a.m. hunting. First he and a friend drove to Weaver and huddled in their duck boat, grousing as mallards and teals landed in the middle of the water, out of reach. Then he walked out to his deer stand, which he has used for more than twenty years, and did some housekeeping. Now, ten hours since his first cup of coffee, he's heading to public lands south of Kenyon and West Concord, aiming for pheasant.

"We need something for the game bag!" Brad cries. His wife, Mary Madison, who doesn't hunt, laughs from the backseat. Their blond Labrador pup, Blue, who is learning to hunt, eagerly leaps into the front and is shoved affectionately back.

Two years ago my longtime friend Mary wed this sandy-haired, straight-spined guy from south-central Minnesota—the co-owner of a forest management business—and moved south. Whenever I make the trip for dinner, the three of us end up in long, tangled conversations in which we high-five over the essential stuff (love, family, nature) and argue stubbornly about anything slightly less abstract. The fact that the urban liberal consciously made her bed with the small-town conservative, and he with her, keeps us semicareful. Hunting, of course, is one locus of disagreement. "I can't come around on the deer thing," Mary admitted before I came down. "This year it's even worse—maybe because of Blue."

Now we near the long decline of land, with its thicketed creek, and Brad wails. "Aaak! Look at all the trucks." I count five, and pick out nine orange figures spread across the furred draw and grassy rises. It's odd to see so far, after the close focus of the northern woods. Brad passes the trucks, parks a couple hundred yards up the road. "We'll try these fields, see if they left anything for us."

The day is fairly balmy, the low sun scuttling behind quilted clouds, but the north wind is blowing fit to buck any lingering duck all the way to Louisiana. I wade into the left side of a thick scrub stand with Mary. Brad and Blue take the right. Nose to the ground, Blue chugs through the mounded prairie grass like a low-slung vacuum cleaner. I shuffle and wait, shuffle and wait, hoping to raise up a showy red-faced rooster, the bird Al disdainfully typed "a balloon with feathers." Instead I find tawny big bluestem, the labial seedpods of the milkweed, and a foot-chilling grassy swamp. Fleeing the water, Mary and I forge through a thicket and lose Brad; this open prairie sweep is deceptive.

When we catch up with him, my nose is dripping and my hands are numb. But we've discovered palm-sized bird nests cradled in the crooks of sapling branches. We drop down with the slope to a wind-ragged creek. "If I shoot into the water here, you can see the shot pattern," offers Brad. I nod, and he fires. The water dimples in a two-foot-wide oval swath. It's the first shot we've heard in an hour—the first I've heard, close by, since Al downed our last grouse. The sound hits me like a slap: *Hey, lady. This ain't a nature walk.* "You wanna try it?" Brad asks. I slough off my gloves. The gun weighs heavy and cold in my arms. Brad shows me how to jam the gun butt into my shoulder.

I aim, realize the gun has fallen away from my shoulder, readjust, aim again. Press the safety. Squeeze the trigger. Simultaneously, I feel the kick, see the water spray, and squeal. "Wow!" Brad and Mary are laughing. Mary steps up, takes her first-ever shot: the barrel rears upward, as I'd felt it leap in my arms. "Where did it go?" she squeaks breathlessly. "I think you hit the trees," says Brad.

I'm jealous—I want the gun back. Brad passes it over from Mary. I try again, fumble less, spray the water just where I want to. I'm thrilled all out of proportion. I feel electrified and huge, like my bones are lit up in neon. I realize I could stay here all day, shooting that gun.

Returning to the truck, I fall back, trying to warm my aching hands, diligently shuffling the straw. Mary's gathering a bouquet of dogwood stem, sunflower pod, and bird's nest. Blue swims the grass between Brad and scent, milkweed seed fluffs rising behind her like bubbles. A hundred feet from the truck Brad and Blue stop, the dog pushing hard in the straw. Mary calls out to me, and I turn to answer; when I look back at Brad, the hen has flown. The day's only bird, and I've missed it.

In the Suburban, with the heater booming, Brad gripes about his day. "I would've liked to have at least seen more birds." Blue is sacked out in the backseat. The warmth loosens up muscles stiff from leaning into the wind. Brad talks about some wild turkeys that fooled him into thinking a deer was approaching his stand last week. "You just about puke out your heart, you get so excited. 'Can't be a squirrel, no—Oh, it's a gol-darned turkey.'

"What else gets your heart racing like that? Besides running, and—that's not really it. If it *is* a deer, you *really* lose it. And if it's a buck, well, you're going to be there the next year, that's for sure."

I think: That's the clearest explanation I'm going to get.

The next morning, I watch Blue fasten in on a scent. She thrusts her nose into a hillock of grass. A long-tailed rooster bursts from the straw, whirring upward, iridescent yellow and brown and red. The bird pauses once, the gun's barrel resting with it, then they both rise and shudder, together, in the air. The bird drops.

I wake up with the shot still in my ears. My first kill, I think, groggily. In the dream, I was the hunter, wearing Brad's clothes. And I was also the fallen bird. Something has died inside me. And something else is winging out now, "as if it had never been hit," into the real world.

I'm sitting in the woods near Ely in the dark, no gun, hunting deer. I'm wearing a blaze orange vest and hat, though I can't see them. Also: long underwear, flannel jeans, socks, mukluks, shirt, sweater, scarf, and down jacket. Temp's around thirty. Time's a little after 6 a.m.

I close my eyes for a bit and drift, coming to as I'm falling backward. Straighten up. Breathe. The moon lights up a snow crystal at my feet. When I next open my eyes the black pines have defined themselves against graying air. The forest is so still I can hear the absence of sound. It's a struggle to get a full breath, I'm listening so intensely.

A rifle booms, far away. A crow flies first. Then a jay and my beloved chickadee, leaping above, it seems, from tree to tree. A plane buzzes over. More rifle shots, still miles away. A small red squirrel hurries by, not three feet from my boots. Behind me, a tree creaks.

I hold my breath. And the sound comes again, but from farther to my left. And again: a dry leaf, heavily crunched. I'm straining to sit still; my pulse is slamming in my ears. What *is* this stealing up on me: reverence or terror? The silence eventually extends. I gulp air. My heart slows. The day brightens. At 8 I walk out, teeth chattering.

During dinner in Ely the night before, we'd bumped into a hunter still adorned in piecemeal blaze orange. "How'd it go?" my companion had asked. "Well, I got a little buck," the man admitted, with noticeable distaste. "I let him pass by, but my buddies bugged me until I went back after him." His mouth pursed.

"I wasn't ready. It's not the killing I'm into so much as the hunt." The answer struck me then as pat, though his discomfort didn't. This morning, I think I understand. This morning, I finally feel I have earned, if such a thing can be done, the deaths of those first birds with Al.

I realize that I have to keep earning them: if hunting demands anything, it is a constancy of attention, a kind of faithful listening to prey and gun that only begins in the ear. I don't know when—or whether—my aim will stop a bird's rising flight. I do know this: my mother-in-law has offered me her father's old 12-gauge, and I haven't said no.

WHY I'M A BOWHUNTER

Tom Conroy

FOR ALMOST TWENTY YEARS we gun-hunted deer together, in one area near the Minnesota River in southern Minnesota. While other hunters came and went, our annual hunting party always included the three of us—Dad, one of my brothers, and me.

Our November hunt grew to become as much a family tradition as any holiday or birthday. It was a special reason for the family to gather, even if only the three of us actually hunted.

That tradition was severely weakened, however, on the cold December evening in 1985 when I found Dad slumped behind the wheel of his car, dead of a heart attack. (I still wonder if it was more than coincidence that he died at an old family picnic site, a grassy clearing along a wooded creek, just downhill from where we'd hunted in later years.)

Circumstances chipped away at our hunting tradition. Two years later my brother, who was now living in Wisconsin, decided to save the cost of a nonresident deer hunting license, about a hundred dollars, and stay home with his wife and new baby. I could understand his decision; nevertheless, I was disappointed. We'd collected a lot of memories during those twenty years, and it bothered me to think it might all be coming to an end.

In fact, much of what had been so appealing about our annual deer hunt had changed. We no longer met at the folks' house for an early breakfast on opening day. Nor did the family gather there again that night. Now, just my friend and I hunted, and we had considerably less room to roam.

For most of twenty years, my dad, my brother, and I were lucky to have much of those woods and sloughs to ourselves. A longtime family friend owned the land and gave us free rein. That began to change, however, as the farmer's sons and their friends grew old enough to hunt. Now, encounters with other hunters were becoming too frequent. The November woods began to seem frantic as orange-clad figures scurried about with a sense of urgency—such a short time to get a deer. My head told me it was time to let the tradition die, but my gut argued otherwise. Clearly, it was time for a change.

Bowhunting, I hoped, might give me back the unhurried solace of the woods. It might also renew the excitement of hunting, providing a greater challenge, with the odds clearly in the deer's favor. However, on the day I drove home from the sporting goods store, new bow and arrows on the backseat, I had mixed feelings—excited about the future but reluctant to let go of the past.

Several years later, I'm still betwixt and between—a gun hunter sometimes, a bowhunter at others. Nevertheless, I've come to understand the compelling nature and growing popularity of bowhunting.

We bowhunters are a contradictory bunch. On the one hand, the high-tech compound bow—the marriage of a traditional bow to a block-and-tackle pulley system—makes shooting easier and deadlier than ever and has contributed tremendously to the popularity of bowhunting. On the other hand, the philosophers among us realize that if our equipment becomes too modern, we lose our sport forever.

Some fifty years ago, conservationist Aldo Leopold warned against the advent of the "gadgeteer, [who] has draped the American outdoorsman with an infinity of contraptions, all offered as aids to self-reliance, hardihood, woodcraft, or marksmanship, but too often serving as substitutes for them. . . . The American sportsman . . . doesn't understand what is happening to him. . . . It has not dawned on him that outdoor recreations are essentially primitive, atavistic; that their value is a contrast-value; that excessive mechanization destroys contrasts by moving the factory to the woods or to the marsh."

It's the "primitive, atavistic" nature of their sport that avid bowhunters treasure most. Ironically, that primitive nature is also what antihunters target in their campaign against bowhunting. Because the bow and arrow is so primitive, it is ineffective, they say, the cause of lingering death and too many wounded deer.

In the hands of the unskilled or undisciplined hunter, the bow and arrow (like any weapon) can indeed be ineffective and wound deer. When used with restraint, the weapon is highly efficient. And it's the restraint implicit in bowhunting that makes it perhaps the most humane of all methods of hunting.

"'Humanity' is a curious invention," writes Dennis Olson. "The constraint of positive emotions, love and care, is placed upon human potential for carnage. The remainder of nature is simply indifferent. Plants and other animals don't need moral control because they don't have our omnipotence. We feel we should be humane to other animals.

"Fairness is humane. The bow and arrow I hold are more fair than cannons. A wolf would use every means it has to make the kill and, if it could, would think me too generous."

In some situations, however, fairness has little to do with bowhunting. Expediency is all. When deer gorge themselves on gardens and million-dollar apple orchards, when they are killed by cars on suburban streets and by airplanes on runways, bowhunting is sometimes the only feasible, effective means of controlling deer populations. Shotgun slugs whistling through Bloomington or Flandrau State Park at New Ulm meet no one's idea of good sense or public safety.

Bowhunting is quiet, unobtrusive, and relatively safe. The record number of bowhunting fatalities for one year in the United States was three, in 1989; by contrast, forty people died from bee stings and eighty-six from lightning strikes in this country in 1991.

Firearms hunter numbers have declined in some areas. At the same time, however, bowhunter numbers have increased. I find that interesting, something to think about.

While the appeal of bowhunting is multifaceted, the solitary nature of the sport is of particular importance to me and many others. In today's hurried world, it seems, we don't allow ourselves much time to just sit and think. Plenty of time for that when you're bowhunting, though. Plenty of time to sit and think, watch and wonder. Might even get a deer. Maybe. Maybe not.

THE APPLE TREE STAND

Marsha L. Kessler

MY FAVORITE DEER STAND isn't anything fancy. In fact, it couldn't be simpler—a board nailed across a couple of tree limbs, camouflaged because it has aged gray, a near match for the gnarled trunk of the tree. The stand sits five feet above the ground on the edge of a pasture, just off the crest of a gentle slope. It faces a sparse windbreak at the top of the rise. And most important, the stand faces the deer trail, which passes just below the height of land and connects one coulee to another.

I wish I could claim that I am the creator of this stand, but that would be a lie. I like to think that the real designer had a moment of inspiration as he checked on his livestock late one spring afternoon. The apple blossoms on the field's edge caught his eye; and while standing under the tree, he noted the main branches that spread from the tree's crotch, creating a palmlike seat. Tempted, he climbed up and realized what a great hideaway he had found among the limbs of the apple tree that surrounded him on all sides. Trees on the slope below furnished a thick backdrop. By pruning a few branches, he created a window onto the game trail above him.

Decades have passed, and I am now the benefactor of this inspired farmer. I am a bowhunter with a fear of heights, so I was intrigued when I discovered this eye-level stand. Most likely, I had found it in the same manner as the original builder—drawn to the apple blossoms on the pasture's edge.

It took several minutes for me to realize there was a deer stand in the tree's center. Although the board was aged, I judged it firm enough to hold me, so I climbed up. With one branch acting as a backrest, I stretched my legs out along the board's length and leaned back—as though sitting on a recliner. In short, I had stumbled onto something really special, a deer stand that was perfectly sited, safe, and comfortable.

Since my discovery, I have hunted from this stand exclusively and with great success. Every year I have been presented with plenty of shooting opportunities demanding very little effort on my part.

I hunt primarily to put meat on the table, so up until last season I had been happy to take does and let the young bucks pass. Then, one crisp fall morning, I was sitting back against the tree, contentedly listening to the blue jays wake up the world. Out of the corner of my eye, I caught movement, brief glimpses of antlers moving along the far side of the trees toward the stand.

I held my breath, sure the buck could sense me and would bolt. But to my surprise, he cut through the windbreak and popped out thirty yards directly in front of me. He stood motionless for a few minutes and then calmly lowered his head to graze some tasty tidbit. He seemed relaxed, oblivious to my presence.

This was the first time I had ever seen a buck hang around, and I admired him for several minutes without a thought of taking a shot. As the buck continued grazing and showed no sign of moving on, I debated shooting. On the one hand, I was after meat only; on the other, he was a good-sized deer. I was reluctant to shoot any buck, but he continued to present me with the perfect opportunity. I struggled to make up my mind.

Finally, I gave in and took aim. A solid *thunk* told me my shot was true. The buck ran off. As I sat back to wait for him to drop, I started shaking with adrenaline. I waited until I could no longer hear the buck's movement, then climbed down and followed his trail about seventy-five yards to where he had dropped. I had a clean shot and my first buck—a healthy ten-pointer. He has provided meat for my family all year. Every time we grill a steak, we raise a toast: "Here's to the deer, and here's to the old apple tree stand."

A PERFECT START

Dan Brown

THE ALARM CLOCK CLANGED AT 4 A.M., awakening my senses to the sizzle and smell of frying bacon, the rattle of dishes, and the aromas of gun oil and coffee.

Despite a fitful night's sleep, I felt energized and excited on this morning of my first deer hunt. After years of hearing my dad and uncles tell and retell their hunting and deer camp stories, I was now taking part in this rite of passage, this fall tradition.

Hearing floorboards creaking overhead and a quiet bustling throughout the cabin reminded me that I didn't want to be last to the breakfast table, so I dressed quickly and went upstairs from the basement.

I ate breakfast with my uncles Tom and Joe, while Dad and my uncle Dewain studied an aerial map of the Chippewa National Forest and explained our options for the morning's hunt.

I had grown accustomed to the incessant, deprecating humor my uncles directed at me, so I was surprised when Dewain asked me which stand I'd like to use, based on the rub lines and scrapes I'd found while scouting the area the previous weekend. It occurred to me that since my arrival the night before, I hadn't been the source of any jokes. My uncles had welcomed me to deer camp, and I began to feel like a respected member of the group, instead of just a fifteen-year-old nephew.

We left the cabin at 5 a.m., taking two vehicles up the highway to the north end of Little Sand Lake. Along the way, we dropped off Joe and Tom at trailheads to trudge through the dark, snow-covered woods to their stands. Dad, Dewain, and I walked a trail together until it forked.

As we parted ways, I received some last-minute encouragement, and we exchanged good lucks. With a blanket of snow on the ground, I found it fairly easy to follow the faint logging trail by starlight. I arrived at my stand thirty minutes before shooting time.

Sitting with my rifle resting across my legs, I had time to relax and listen in the predawn woods. I heard the cadence of distant hunters as they walked through the woods, their boots crunching the snow and leaves and snapping twigs and branches. I noted the sharp, high-pitched squeaking of nails in cold wood as hunters climbed ladders and settled into their stands; the mice scurrying through leaves and over the bark of fallen trees; and the distinct, low hoot of owls.

As the sun neared the horizon, I picked up the distant sound of something heavy moving through the woods, a sound unlike the rhythmic strides of a hunter. I checked my watch and was surprised to discover that only a few minutes remained until shooting time.

Through the trees, I could see Dewain sitting very still, looking down at the trail that eventually wound its way to my stand. A few minutes later, he waved his red cap high over his head, and I could only assume that a deer was heading in my direction.

In the half-light of dawn, I saw a large deer fifty yards down the trail, heading my way and closing ground quickly. Quietly, slowly, I shouldered my rifle, eased the safety off, and watched the mature buck through the gun's open sights as he neared my stand. I forced myself to breathe, certain the deer could hear my heart beating as I waited for him to quarter away. The gun roared; the report echoed through the woods until the air fell silent again.

A number of years later, Uncle Dewain admitted to me that, yes, that deer, my first deer, passed directly in front of him only minutes before my historic shot. When I asked him why he let the buck pass, he smiled and replied, "Danny, we all knew how excited you were that day. And I guessed that buck would stay on the trail until he reached your stand. I watched you through my field glasses; and I gotta say, it took nerve and patience to wait as long as you did for that shot. That was a great first deer."

It has been twenty-three years now since that memorable weekend. It took some time and reflection to understand why my uncles treated me with courtesy and something approaching reverence. For those three days, they recalled old emotions and saw again their first deer hunt through my eyes: they wanted my first deer-hunting experience to be perfect.

Encountering Wildness

THE ROAD TO WILD PLACES

Don J. Dinndorf

WHEN I WAS MUCH YOUNGER, in those thrilling early years of duck hunting, my father and I would leave home the morning of opening day and drive the half hour or so to the marsh he and his buddies had leased for the season. Up Highway 238 north of Albany, my hometown, through St. Francis, then into Upsala and left at the gas station. Then past the house with the A's on the shutters, turn right and continue for a few more miles, as gravel rang in the wheel wells.

Then, there it would be, sparkling in the autumn sun, that wondrous chain of marshes, and under the sweeping branches of a great white oak, the waiting cars of my dad's friends and their sons.

Thinking of the road makes me smile even now, almost thirty years later. Traveling the road was part of the whole adventure, especially looking for the house with the A's on the shutters for the first time each fall— usually when we were going to the marshes to build blinds and drop off boats, two weeks before the season opened. The weather was warmer then, and I would find puffballs in the pasture, big acorns by the oak tree, snails and frogs, and maybe even an empty painted turtle's shell near the water.

Perhaps it was then that I began to treasure "getting there" as a part of the experience, and not just see it as a trial to pass through on the way to a goal. Today I know adventure begins the moment I sit down inside the car to drive to wild places.

But the road to the marshes is one I don't drive anymore. Change is the reason I stop far short of the house with the A's on the shutters.

One Saturday in early September, I took my fourteen-year-old brother to see the marshes our father and I had hunted years before. The hunting party lost its lease when my brother was still far too young to come with us. The original landowner passed away, the land was sold, and our connection to the land was broken. None of us had been back since.

I found the road all right, and my excitement was building, just as it had before. Nostalgia circled as thick as wood smoke. I began rehearsing a pitch to the current landowner for a new lease. Then suddenly, I slammed on the brakes. There, by the curve in the road, stood the oak tree where we used to meet. But I hadn't seen the marshes. I turned around in the same approach we used so long ago, and drove back along the road, a sick feeling growing in my stomach.

On the hill, the thick woods had been turned into a smoldering pile of bulldozed and burned logs and brush. A new ditch ran through the shallow marsh nearest the road, the place I stalked teal during slow times. The deep waters of the big marsh farther back were being bled away in a deep channel through its heart.

My throat tightened. I couldn't answer my brother when he asked, "Is *this* it? Is this where it *was*?"

Minnesota has other roads like that—a road once bounded by woods where houses now squat, a highway where I can recall a vanished wetland for every mile of pavement.

There are roads I try not to travel for a different reason. One is a road I can see from my office window.

For the past twenty years, springtime has meant wild turkey hunting for me. That part of my hunting life began in the southeastern Minnesota blufflands, and that's the place I think of as the snow shrinks away and cardinals begin their spring song. For me, the gateway to turkey hunting is where Interstate 494 drops into the Mississippi River valley just before joining Highway 61. At that point, it is as if the bluffs begin and the familiar low hills and forests of home are left behind.

When turkey hunting was new to me, the hunting and scouting trips were the only times I took that road and, likewise, the only times I heard cardinals. But today cardinals have expanded their range to include my backyard feeder; and while I'm not complaining about their presence there, familiarity means the loss of their song's power to transport me to Aprils long ago.

Now that I work in South St. Paul I could take that road to my office, but I take a different route, at least partly, to preserve the magic of that gateway.

The road to Baudette is another route I came to know as a boy, when my family would travel north to Lake of the Woods. The big water was close to paradise for a young fisherman.

For me, the route to Lake of the Woods has remained the purest— not only because I rarely travel it unless I am going to the big lake for walleyes, smallmouth bass, and northern pike, but also because it has changed the least.

Forests still border most of the route. Just off Highway 64, I watch for the "trees in a row" at the state nursery at Badoura, just as I did after my dad first pointed them out thirty years ago. I still see deer and beavers and watch for bear. The last time I passed through Walker, the A&W drive-in was still selling root beer. And near the bogs around Red Lake, I can still gaze in awe at the state's largest wetlands.

When, at last, Baudette comes into view, I am eager to get out on the water again. I've already been there for hours, remembering each outing before.

They say you can't go home again, and the same could be said of the roads that take you there. Home and the roads that lead there change, sometimes sadly, sometimes because they just look different to older eyes. But sometimes the roads don't change, and the magic of the wild places abides.

There might be things people can do to preserve the magic—concerted action to protect the land and water—or perhaps a person can hold on to magic by simply taking a different route to the office. Other times, travelers might just get lucky and find that familiar landmarks endure, old forests still stand, and the fish still bite, as surely as we remember them.

THE BOG

John Henricksson

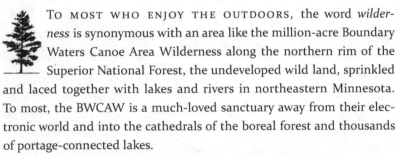To most who enjoy the outdoors, the word *wilderness* is synonymous with an area like the million-acre Boundary Waters Canoe Area Wilderness along the northern rim of the Superior National Forest, the undeveloped wild land, sprinkled and laced together with lakes and rivers in northeastern Minnesota. To most, the BWCAW is a much-loved sanctuary away from their electronic world and into the cathedrals of the boreal forest and thousands of portage-connected lakes.

But *wilderness* is a word we use very carelessly. The bogs of the Gunflint region forest are the only true wilderness in this area: undisturbed, obscure, and a little otherworldly. Not the riverine or embayment bogs, or the vast peatland bogs, but the enclosed bog, usually less than ten acres of coffee-colored water, the sedgemat- and stunted-spruce-surrounded Camelots of wilderness. Miniature natural kingdoms of mist, mystery, and beauty.

There is nothing in the bog anyone wants—nothing to cut, mine, sell, or develop—so it is a wilderness by default because no one covets its contents. Bogs grow and disappear at glacial speed, tremble with mats of decomposing vegetation and sphagnum, sometimes thirty feet deep, and are usually freckled with miniature forests of bog willow, tamarack, black ash, sedges, and stunted black spruce several hundred years old. Bogs are mossy grottoes of silence.

Over centuries the decaying vegetable material turns into peat, which records and preserves everything imbedded in it—seeds and pollens, insects, sometimes even human corpses. The word *bogeyman* comes, of course, from *bog*. Manuscripts of Nature, J. E. Potzger calls them in *Bogs of the Quetico-Superior Country Tell Its Forest History.*

Some of the plants growing there are often also found in either the Arctic or the tropics. Tiny anomalies. In *Bogs of the Northeast,* Charles Johnson describes the bogs' ambience well: "We find them intriguing, yet we shun them as somewhat peculiar. They remain mysterious—neither solid land nor water but a realm in between. . . . An aura of spirits still emanates from them to stir our imaginations. . . . While the scientist in us seeks to understand them, the poet in us wants to keep them away from complete discovery, safe in some shadow of mystery."

In the summer they are wondrous flower realms, jewel boxes of the far north, revealing bottle gentians, rosemary, bog laurel, sundews, cotton grass, the leathery brown blossoms of the pitcher plant, moccasin flowers, the uncommon rose pogonia, dragon's mouth, and bog orchids.

Because of the acidic water and lack of food there, wild creatures usually only pass through on their way to someplace else. Red-necked grebes, Lincoln's sparrows, great gray owls, common yellowthroats, sedge wrens, and Connecticut warblers are the birds most often seen in bog environments. Damselflies and whirligig beetles disturb the water's surface, and a copper butterfly is found most often in the bog habitat. Frogs seem to like the bog; there is usually an abundance of chorus frogs, gray treefrogs, northern leopard frogs, and wood frogs.

Occasionally a moose will amble along the shoreline if aquatic vegetables, such as water lilies, grow there. The moose stands near the water's edge and puts its head under water, groping with huge leathery lips to wrap around a stem of the plant near the bottom, and then, with an explosion of water, jerks it out by the roots and stands for minutes leisurely chewing on the water lily tuber, which American Indians used for years as a potato. The name *moose* comes from the Indian *moozo,* meaning *twig eater,* and browse is the dietary staple; but the root is the favorite snack of most Gunflint moose.

There are no manmade trails to these bogs because they aren't fishing spots; the water is too acidic from the rotting vegetation for fish. This is not game animal habitat and the open water is too small to canoe, so these bogs are virtually unknown. They are mapped but not named or labeled. Forest ecologist Chel Ànderson showed me how to find them on topographic maps by searching out small free-form or circular, tightly packed, depressed concentric lines with no creek running in or out. The spot might be just a sharp dip or a dry glacial scour. Then again, it might be a ten-thousand-year-old ecological relict full of wonders. The only way to find out for sure is to bushwhack in or talk to timber cruisers, trappers, loggers, or conservation officers—someone whose job takes them into the trackless parts of the forest.

Some bogs in this area are home to the *ellefolk,* strange little people who emigrated here from Norway at about the same time the people of that country made new homes along the North Shore of Lake Superior and in the wooded uplands of the Gunflint region. Ellefolk lived originally in the bogs of Denmark, but they are solitude-loving creatures and the almost constant ringing of the Danish church bells upset them so they finally moved to wilder, quieter places in Norway. After residing in the Norwegian bogs for years, the ellefolk found that country too became noisy and crowded.

Norwegian immigrants who came here to fish the waters of Lake Superior wrote home about the natural beauties and remoteness of the Gunflint region of Minnesota, and it wasn't long before a colony of the ellefolk decided to follow. Just how they got here is still a puzzle, but the ways of little people have always been shrouded in mystery. They can travel with great ease through air, fire, wood, water, and stone. The females can even travel on moonbeams. Ellefolk are light elves, associated with flowers and natural beauty, not the dark elves who will lead you astray.

The ellefolk men wear broad-brimmed black hats and red sashes and are about the size of children because they only grow during moonlight hours. When they first came, many lived in the forest, but after so much of that was cut down they moved to the more secluded bogs. They usually live under the crests of small hills at the edge of the bog, and they grow fabulous gardens, which are hidden in the moss. They aren't seen by many people because they come out only during the hours of dawn and dusk, and the males spend a lot of time sitting on the edge of the bog telling stories or playing their odd, little flutelike instruments made from bog reeds and willow bark.

Some people who have poked around the bogs have found strange, flattened sedge rings and were puzzled by them. Actually, those are the rings where the ellefolk dance, and if you step into a ring you can usually feel the musical vibrations of the dance. That can be dangerous because it is said you may die if you stay in the ring too long. Many strange deaths have occurred in the bog, but it is more likely that the Norwegian legend has been mistranslated and transformation is more likely what is meant. What the ellefolk legend says is that "you will never be the same."

Most dismiss the whole concept as folklore, or worse, but I have met ellefolk at bogside several times, and was once told by Petra Woodencloak, one of the prominent little people, that in order to see them one has to believe in them. For me, that is enough, but I have often found it hard to explain to others. Fortunately, the Troll Lady was available to help me out. In real life the Troll Lady is Norwegian-born Lise Lunge-Larsen, storyteller, actress, authority on the little people of Scandinavia, and author of *The Troll with No Heart in His Body*.

Discussing the little people in her book, she muses, "I think they have withdrawn into an elusive world, parallel but not easily accessible to ours. In our civilized world, most people have lost touch with nature and aren't capable of seeing the beings that live there. In Norway our lives were informed by stark and dramatically beautiful surroundings, so I knew where the trolls lived and I knew where the wood elves would play their music."

For those who never want to lose touch with nature, it might be well to discover and adopt one of the Gunflint region's bogs. Because of its isolation and uselessness to the economy, it will always be there for you— wild, mysterious, and magical.

THE WAGON WHEEL

Joel M. Vance

 GREAT SPORTING ART does not feature a ruffed grouse hunter with one foot buried to the knee in a bog hole, the other painfully trapped by an alder fork, trying futilely to move a gun barrel six inches in any direction through a sprout thicket.

That, in my experience, describes Minnesota grouse hunting. Lyrical writers would rather deal with more scenic coverts. George Bird Evans writes about the splendid King Ruff, pointed by an immaculate Belton setter, in the rhododendron thickets of West Virginia. Burton Spiller took us to the golden aspens and old apple orchards of New England. Bob Abbett turns those magic words into paintings that make the hunter's heart beat faster.

Though it's relatively flat terrain, the Wagon Wheel makes my heart beat faster too—with extreme exertion, the way a climber's heart is thumping at about twenty feet from the summit of K2.

Where is GBE, Spiller, or Abbett when I stumble through the Wagon Wheel, like someone trying to negotiate an obstacle course blindfolded at midnight? The only painting that could sum up the Wagon Wheel would be Edvard Munch's *The Scream,* or maybe some of the more lurid Gustave Doré illustrations for Dante's *Inferno.*

The Wagon Wheel is 130 acres of typical Minnesota swamp, somewhere north of Minneapolis, south of Duluth. Because it is my discovery and my love, you could not drag its precise location out of me with thumbscrews (although I am open to generous bribes).

It is public land, in common with thousands of acres of tax-forfeited land on the plat map of any north woods county. You can find your Wagon Wheel, too, if you look long enough.

The Wagon Wheel is at once an exercise in endurance and an always-productive hunting covert. I don't know of another spot that is so reliable. If I don't move grouse, there will be woodcock. Usually there are both.

The Wagon Wheel is shaped like your hand: a large area of upland from which fingers extend into an alder swamp. Woodcock filter onto the fingers that rise just above the water table. Grouse lurk on the back of the hand.

This covert is light years from those golden coverts of sporting art. The whole place is a sprawl of blowdowns, laced with tangles of alder, thickets of poplar, and blackberry briars. You can go in one side of the Wagon Wheel looking like James Bond and come out the other side resembling Weary Willy.

My dogs exit the Wagon Wheel looking as if they'd been mud wrestling with a Vikings middle linebacker. And they have a frazzled expression, as if they'd just attacked what they thought was the neighbor's cat, only to find it was Simba, king of the veldt.

My hunting buddies and I named the place the Wagon Wheel because the adjacent landowner mounted his mailbox atop a wagon wheel, with a half-axle as the post. The landowner moved out several years ago, leaving a ramshackle house, which had been under construction for a dozen years but always seemed to be slipping back toward ruin. Apparently he took the wagon wheel with him when he left, which is understandable—it probably was worth more than anything he owned.

It takes about an hour to hunt the Wagon Wheel, more if you stop to catch your breath at the log by the Pine Ridge. Often there is a grouse near that log, so it almost surely is a drumming log. There is an open area in front of the log, typical of a drumming site.

Once I shot the probable drummer over a point by McGuffin du Calembour, my best friend. Guff brought the drummer to me, and we split an apple and he took a nap while I smoothed the bird's feathers and felt the regret I always feel with a warm, limp partridge in my hand.

For several years I wandered blindly in the Wagon Wheel, knowing that sooner or later I'd happen on an edge and figure out where I was. But the maze of fingers and the ever-present swamp tricked me more than once. I'd find myself stranded on high ground—three inches above standing water—not knowing how I got there or how to get back with dry feet.

There are no landmarks in a Minnesota bog; it all looks the same. A truck on the distant highway is as good as a landmark in the Wagon Wheel. As long as traffic goes by, I know where north is, even if I can't get there except by wading.

Dozens of motorists pass the Wagon Wheel every day, and I doubt any know it is public land or that it holds grouse and woodcock. In sixteen years I've never seen another hunter there. How could anything so public be so private?

I've flushed a low of one and a high of five grouse—not a super covert, but one worth working. As consistent as the grouse hunting is, it is the reliable presence of woodcock that brings my hunting buddies and me back year after year.

Some years they are resident birds, especially if the weather has been warm and they haven't been given a subarctic reason to move south. Other times, when the ground is hard from early frost, they'll be the vanguard of migrating woodcock.

Woodcock migrate singly, but often drop into a covert in bunches, a "fall" of woodcock. Then we'll find them on every little finger of the Wagon Wheel, every bog edge. Other times they'll be concentrated in only a spot or two. But always we find woodcock.

They're a wonderful bird for a dog, especially a wide-eyed youngster on his or her first trip into the brush. They hold tight, squatted to the ground immobile, relying on their mottled forest-duff coloring to hide them. Woodcock depend more on their camouflage than on flight. In fact, a woodcock is supposed to be the slowest bird of all in the air.

But they must be among the quickest to spring into action. I've spied a woodcock on the ground, then the next instant it was eye level and climbing, gone off the ground so fast my eye couldn't register it.

In the sprawl of the Wagon Wheel, woodcock shooting is at its best. None of the open-woods shooting of a Bob Abbett painting. Here, the birds dart among the alders like bats in an insect swarm.

Once as I tried to follow such a jinker with my gun barrel, the barrel tangled in the alder whips and the stock cracked me so hard alongside the head that I saw stars. Wagon Wheel hunting can be more injurious to hunter than hunted.

I hunt far more scenic grouse coverts, but each year I look forward to the first hunt in the Wagon Wheel. It also is the first hunt of the season after many months of not hunting. The Wagon Wheel will be hot and tangled with clinging fern. I will take my shots, if any, through a screen of alder and aspen leaves. I'll forget a water bottle and will be tempted to crouch by the dog and lap from the same bog hole when thirst grows incessant.

Then I'll stop by that drumming log on the far side where it is quiet and I am at peace with my dog and the day. No one will chance by to disturb me. I can think or not think, my choice. Usually I don't think—other than to sense that this is a moment all too fleeting, all too soon gone.

THE STRIKE TREE

Peter M. Leschak

IN EARLY AFTERNOON OF JUNE 6, while transferring tomato plants from a cold frame into our backwoods garden in northern Minnesota, I noticed a thunderhead in the south. A single storm cell, dark and burgeoning in an otherwise clear sky, was churning in my direction. I hustled the last three plants into the soil, fixed for whatever moisture might fall. As the cell roiled overhead and the sun disappeared, a few plump raindrops splattered in the dust. I heard a lone crack of thunder; but in a few minutes, sunlight returned. I hand-watered the tomatoes.

Several hours later, at dusk, the Department of Natural Resources' fire duty officer phoned to say a fire had been spotted in the woods near Beatrice Lake, about three miles north of our cabin. I was on call for the Side Lake station, so I threw on fire-resistant Nomex shirt and pants, slipped on my lug-soled boots, and harnessed a radio to my chest.

As I drove to the DNR Forestry garage to pick up a fire engine, I switched on the radio and monitored voice traffic from a local volunteer fire department that had also been paged. I heard access to the fire was difficult, and no one had reached it yet. Once in the fire engine, I radioed the duty officer to request a couple of additional DNR firefighters.

About ten minutes later, as I drew near the scene and wound down a gravel road hemmed in by dense conifers, one of the volunteers radioed in from the fire. He said the fire might be five acres—hard to tell in the dark—burning in a Norway pine plantation. "It's a circle," he said. "A ring of fire."

I immediately thought of the thunderclap I'd heard seven hours earlier. Had a lightning bolt ignited this fire? It tallied. For a blaze to grow that large in calm weather beneath the humid forest canopy, it must have been burning for hours. Because it was remote, it probably wasn't set by humans. Would there be a strike tree out there, evidence of lightning surging through a trunk to the ground? My mandatory report would demand a cause.

Around the next curve, the woods flashed red with the light of a fire engine's rotating beacons. I parked behind the truck and approached the fire chief for a briefing.

The blaze, he told me, had been spotted by a teenager on a four-wheeler. He'd sped home to dial 911. I raised an eyebrow, but the chief said he didn't suspect the kid started it. The boy had guided a department squad into the fire, more than one hundred yards off the trail. I agreed it didn't fit the profile of an arson set.

I locked in the front hubs of my fire engine, shifted into four-wheel drive, and followed the kid on the four-wheeler to the fire. The old logging road quickly narrowed to a trail. The ground was firm, but branches and stems brush-whipped the body of the truck, rattling the mirrors and twanging the antennas. A half mile in, my guide stopped and pointed to the right. I got out and peered into the darkness, sniffing the sweet aroma of singed pine bark and burning needles, but not seeing any flickers of flame.

"Just go that way," the boy said. "You'll find it."

I affixed a headlamp to my helmet and slung a five-gallon pump can onto my back. Before leaving the engine, I turned on the emergency flashers to serve as a beacon. Fighting fire at night can be disorienting, and it's embarrassing to lose your truck. I steered toward voices in the dark.

In a few minutes my headlamp beam was diffused by thick smoke, and I heard the crackle of combustion. I stepped onto blackened ground and saw an arc of fire ahead. The flames were about two feet high and backing leisurely through a stand of twenty-year-old trees. Four volunteer firefighters with pump cans had knocked down most of the blaze. I joined in to finish it off, vigorously working the can's "trombone."

In ten minutes the two DNR firefighters I'd requested arrived; in less than half an hour, only scattered embers remained, glowing in the dark like distant stars. I released the volunteers, and my partners and I patrolled the perimeter of the burn to ensure the edge was cold before we left it for the night.

Next morning we returned to hunt for hot spots and for the cause of the fire. A couple of punky stumps were openly smoking. Other remnants of fire we ferreted out with our noses and by using bare hands to probe for latent heat in suspicious places, such as a swath of white ash (denoting hotter burning) along the bole of a deadfall.

We crisscrossed the burn, about two and a half acres. Sniffing, poking, and scratching, we exposed a half dozen hot spots that we dug out or chopped up with pulaskis and sprayed with pump cans.

As we pursued elusive heat, I kept an eye out for evidence of ignition. Since the initial report mentioned "ring of fire" and there'd been little wind to shove flames in one direction or another, it made sense to focus on the center of the burn as point of origin. But a search there turned up nothing.

The terrain was essentially flat, so slope would have exerted little influence on fire spread. (Fire runs faster, therefore farther, uphill.) A lofty snag towering above the canopy might have been a likely suspect for a strike tree, but the pines were more or less of uniform height and there was nothing like that.

After more than an hour hunting, I revisited a hot spot we'd worked first thing that morning. There, on the north flank of the fire, closer to the perimeter than to the center, I ran my fingers through the ash to ensure it was cold, then pulled the strip of pink flagging we'd tied to a branch to mark it. As I turned to move on, I saw the strike tree.

I've seen mature trees that were literally blown apart and shredded by a lightning bolt, with limbs and chunks strewn like shrapnel for yards in every direction. By comparison, this strike appeared almost gentle, a christening rather than a kill shot. The fresh scar looked as if the roller nose of a chain saw had been frisked down the trunk, barely cutting through the cambium.

It appeared likely the young pine would survive this lash and continue to grow. I found that pleasing. This tree had taken the hit, served as conduit for the lightning that started the fire that helped to nurture neighboring trees. It had delivered fire to its fellows.

Actually, it was a lovely burn. The fire had been low intensity, burning evenly through the plantation. It lightly singed the tree trunks at the base, cooked encroaching brush, and released the nutrients in the duff. Hundreds of pines were encompassed by the black, but not a single one had been killed or even seriously damaged. If we'd purposely ignited the fire for timber-stand management, it would've been termed a success; and we joked that it was unfortunate the teenager spotted the flames before they'd had the opportunity to beneficially scorch ten, twelve, or twenty acres. A look at our maps and plat book showed the fire was on private land (owned by a timber company), so when it was reported we had little choice but suppression. If it had been a state plantation, and assuming we had sufficient resources to maintain control, we might have let it run for a while, especially since it was a lightning start.

I was reminded of an American Indian folktale set in the prehuman era when animals and trees could talk. It seems the pines were the sole possessors of the secret of fire—a significant ecological element of boreal forest and nearly every other ecosystem on the planet, working chiefly as a quick decomposer and recycler. The pines selfishly refused to share fire with other inhabitants of the earth, but during one especially cold winter, Beaver—ever busy—pilfered an ember from the pines and spread fire to the willows, birches, and other trees, who passed it along to the rest of the creatures; and thus the world as we know it arose, shaped by fire.

The earth is struck by lightning about a hundred times per second, and the myths of many cultures associate thunderbolts—the celestial fire—with cosmic creative force. Our strike tree was an agent of the process, linked to the earth and sky by electricity, a pine that shared the flame. Geologic mechanisms that provide chemicals (nutrients) are too gradual for the needs of the biosphere. Fire historian Stephen Pyne wrote,

"The necessity for decomposition on a grand scale is such that if fire did not exist, nature would have to invent it."

I called my firefighters over to inspect the evidence of ignition. There was nothing to indicate why that particular tree had been struck, or why the burn had progressed asymmetrically from it. Perhaps the storm cell had spewed robust downdrafts with a distinct directional component. Or maybe fuel had been more plentiful south of the strike, drawing flames that way. We didn't know. But how fine it was to witness the source, to touch the tree that was drummed by lightning.

ADVENTURE UNDERGROUND

Cary Griffith

 My headlamp illuminates a crawl space big enough for a house cat to squeeze through. The hole flattens out beneath a five-ton slab of limestone. Beyond, everything is pitch black. But I can hear the animated voices of the nine group members who have already pulled themselves through the hole.

This isn't a nightmare, just the first dicey section of a three-hour wild-cave tour. Two guides are leading us through a latticework of crawlways, dark holes, dramatic cave formations, running water, pools, and slippery clay. We have already seen bats, stalactites, stalagmites, crystal-flecked walls, and some geologic oddities so wondrous they defy imagination. And until now it has been worth every remarkable, easy walking step. But after an hour, we've come to a point that requires much more than a simple crouch and scuttle.

"You OK?" one of the guides calls back through the hole.

"Sure," I answer, lying.

On this side of the limestone slab, I get down on hands and knees and watch the boot bottoms of a fifty-eight-year-old fellow caver disappear. When I first saw this hole, I felt certain it was impassable. But in the past couple of minutes, I have seen two men almost twice my size wriggle through it. Finally, it's my turn.

Flattening myself against the cave floor, I see a rocky protuberance jutting up in front of me, making the space appear even tighter. I crawl into the gap, no more than eighteen inches high, and ease my body forward with fingers and toes.

My helmet strikes the limestone slab overhead. I turn my head side-ways to get over the jutting rock. Once over it, I find myself hugging the clay floor of the coffin-sized space. Until this moment I'd never consid-ered myself claustrophobic. But in this tight spot, with tons of earth and rock between me and the surface—cave ahead and cave behind—a small wave of anxiety begins to crest into full-fledged panic. My breath comes in shallow bursts, and all I can think is, *I have to get the hell out of here.*

This cave complex is part of Forestville/Mystery Cave State Park in south-eastern Minnesota, and one of the largest cave complexes in North America. Of the more than thirteen miles of passageways, about one mile is open for public tours that require nothing more strenuous than an oc-casional crouch.

Exploration of the other twelve miles of wild cave requires a knowl-edgeable guide. One of our guides is Allen Lewerer, president of the Minnesota Speleological Survey. (*Speleology* is the technical term for the science or study of caves.)

Unlike public tours, this excursion requires much more equipment than a lantern and jacket. We wear kneepads, elbow pads, helmets with two lights (one a backup), gloves, coveralls or other warm clothes, and boots with ankle support and gripping bottoms.

Discovered in 1937, Mystery Cave has been largely surveyed and named. Some sections are named for peculiar geologic formations. Some straight, wide, and clear stretches have street names.

During the first hour of caving, our route took us down Fifth Avenue—a long, straight stretch as wide as a subway tunnel in places. From there we crossed 17 Layer Rock, climbed over fallen slabs into the Dome Room (where water drips from the ceiling into a glistening pool), then proceeded to Diamond Caverns (where tiny crystals sparkle in lime-stone) and Blue Lake (where six-foot pillars hulk beneath the blue water). We traveled across the Hills of Rome, down Fourth Avenue, and finally into the Smoking Chamber, where we entered this coffin-sized hole.

. . .

In my tight spot, all I can think about is getting out from under. I take a deep breath and try to get ahold of myself. I'm low enough to see lamplight flickering ahead, on what appears to be the walls of a spacious cavern. Thankful for the beacons, I belly crawl forward.

I find enough room to rise onto my hands and knees, and Allen reaches down to offer a helping hand.

"You sure you're OK?" he asks.

"Sure," I say, my pulse still jiggering.

"Good," Allen says, smiling. And I smile back, because I am beginning to feel what cavers describe as the thrill of the crawl.

After a ten-minute rest, we scrabble through more amazing passages. One passage requires us to step sideways through a canyon that's only a foot wide. Another requires creeping over a mud-caked floor. These passages are more thrilling than scary. We see fossils, flowstone, ribbons, draperies, and other remarkable formations. Allen explains how each was formed.

Finally, after two hours underground, we reach the edge of Enigma Pit. Two jagged rock walls drop thirty feet down into a narrow canyon. Water drips from the walls and vanishes into this dark pit. We could reach several hundred more cave feet through an opening in the wall on the other side of the chasm. Allen edges across to three natural footholds, and climbs to the top and back down unassisted. It is a feat for anyone, but Allen is old enough to be a grandfather, and he's a big man. I'm impressed, but the rest of us decide to skip it.

We retrace the remarkable passages we crossed to reach Enigma Pit, and I'm only slightly unnerved by the prospect of having to wriggle back through that narrow hole. There's only one way back. After almost three hours of caving, I follow another pair of boots into the opening. This time, buoyed by our adventure in this remarkable geology, I am more exhilarated than anxious.

Before long we reach the surface. My clothes look like they've been swabbed with clay-colored paint, and my boots are caked. I'm happy to be out in the open again, with new appreciation for sunlight, fresh air, trees—and the haunting beauty that lies below.

I FLEW WITH EAGLES

John K. Grobel

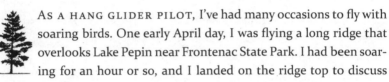As a hang glider pilot, I've had many occasions to fly with soaring birds. One early April day, I was flying a long ridge that overlooks Lake Pepin near Frontenac State Park. I had been soaring for an hour or so, and I landed on the ridge top to discuss weather conditions with fellow pilots. As I looked east, I noticed several birds soaring over the park. I mentioned that the turkey vultures must have returned from their migration and I thought I'd join them in flight. I'd always enjoyed flying with vultures because they're never aggressive and will allow a hang glider to fly within a few feet.

I launched my biplane, tweaked in a little right rudder, and ran along the ridge, gaining altitude until I was seven hundred feet above land. I watched the soaring birds as I made my way east. Soon I realized they were bald eagles—thirteen of them. Suddenly, two mature eagles, the highest of the group, broke off and headed my way.

As the birds approached, I slowed my flight. One eagle flew within a few feet of my right upper wing. The other stayed twenty to thirty feet above. Both eyed me intently. I was excited and had no idea what to do next, so I started talking to them clearly and calmly to reassure them of my good intentions. After what seemed like endless scrutiny, they simultaneously rolled right and slowly tracked the ridge east toward the others. I did the same while trying to detect any sign that might mean I had gone too far. As I drew closer to the two, I was astonished that they let me fly with them. Within minutes I had entered the air space of the other eagles.

Seven of the eagles were mature; six were immature. I kept a hundred feet from any bird and never tried to approach the young eagles. I did, however, witness the show of a lifetime as the eagles soared, played, and practiced their techniques. On a couple of occasions, an eagle would fly over the top of my upper wing and stay where I could almost touch it. At least two mature eagles stayed within one hundred feet of me at all times. I'm convinced they were watching me with concern for their young. In fact, the adults seemed to be training the young eagles. From two to four mature birds would single out an immature bird and escort it down below the ridge top and then allow the young bird to soar.

The apparent lesson was soaring, because if the young bird flapped, the adults would immediately corral it and ride it below the ridge top. Sometimes they would land on top of its back or bump it. At other times an adult would fly under the young bird, lock talons, ball up, and pull it down. All the young birds seemed reluctant to go below the ridge top, which was where most of the coercion occurred.

Finally, twenty-nine minutes and some odd seconds after I had joined the eagles, the activity ceased. Within thirty seconds the birds climbed to a thousand feet, broke away from the ridge, and headed toward Lake City. I was unable to follow, and I'm still not sure why they left.

I've never been able to describe the exhilaration I felt. For the next twenty minutes, I simply reflected on what had transpired. Then I headed west to share the experience with my fellow pilots.

THE LURKER

Tony Capecchi

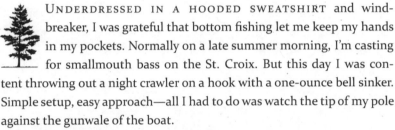 UNDERDRESSED IN A HOODED SWEATSHIRT and wind-breaker, I was grateful that bottom fishing let me keep my hands in my pockets. Normally on a late summer morning, I'm casting for smallmouth bass on the St. Croix. But this day I was content throwing out a night crawler on a hook with a one-ounce bell sinker. Simple setup, easy approach—all I had to do was watch the tip of my pole against the gunwale of the boat.

Other than the cold that made my breath visible, the morning had been unremarkable. That changed around seven thirty—an hour and three walleyes into my day—with a slight twitch of my pole. I fed it some line and waited, counting to *five-Mississippi*, like my grandfather taught me, before setting the hook. The instant I yanked my pole, I realized I'd hooked a monster.

It ran upriver, then shot out of the water in an explosion that changed my definition of huge. I had heard such sturgeon swam St. Croix's deep waters, but I had also read stories about the Loch Ness monster. When you only hear tales about a creature, it lives in an abstract world. Now reality was bending my pole to its limits.

A zinging sound filled my ears; the sound of my reel stripping line. The sturgeon leaped, adding to the chaos. I gasped at the sight: the dark brown beast with its suction-cup mouth shook its head and danced on its sharklike tail.

Two more jumps and forty minutes later, the big fish finally tired. I gradually worked it up to the boat, which led to an interesting conundrum—how to land it with my woefully undersized net. I scooped its head into the net with my left hand. Then, moving quicker than I ever had, I dropped my pole and grabbed its tail with my right hand. Adrenaline took care of the rest, and the creature landed in my boat.

I measured its length at 54.5 inches, and I guessed it weighed about forty-five pounds. Sandpaper skin stretched tightly around its dense body. Its stomach bulged like a stuffed sausage, exceeding the grip of my extended hand. To support the fish properly, I slid my hand closer to its head and was startled to feel its dangling whiskers. My breath had not yet resumed its normal pace, but the sturgeon seemed unfazed. Its black, beady eyes stared ahead. Those eyes had probably seen a lot over the decades. A sturgeon's lifespan can run one hundred years.

I asked the fisherman in a nearby boat to take a picture of this once-in-a-lifetime moment. The vision that's stuck in my head, though, came during the release: the monstrous sturgeon, which looks the same today as it did in the days of the dinosaurs, returning to the murky depths of the St. Croix.

Getting Wet

HERON LAKE LEGACY

Lacey Rose Horkey

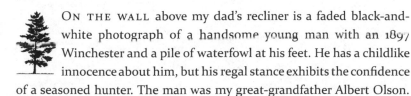

ON THE WALL above my dad's recliner is a faded black-and-white photograph of a handsome young man with an 1897 Winchester and a pile of waterfowl at his feet. He has a childlike innocence about him, but his regal stance exhibits the confidence of a seasoned hunter. The man was my great-grandfather Albert Olson.

Albert enchanted his eight children with tales of tromping about Heron Lake in the early 1900s as a hunter and guide. His stories instilled a passion for hunting in his six boys. When Albert's youngest son, Louis, grew up, he shared the family lore with his nephew, my dad. Armed with well-oiled shotguns and coffee, the two found a home in the reeds of the lake.

On a frosty fall morning when I was thirteen, Albert's legacy was passed from the men in my family to me.

It is the morning of my first hunt. My dad's creaky footsteps on the wooden stairs break the silence and my slumber. His whisper announces the arrival of dawn, and I awkwardly rise from a warm mattress. I'm drowsy, yet aware I must endure the cold for this opportunity to have my dad to myself. While I tightly cinch his thirty-six-inch-waist camouflage fleece pants around my waist and slide into his monstrous boots, he zips my 20-gauge Benelli and his 12-gauge Winchester into their carrying cases.

Mesmerized by the oversized footprints I am leaving in the frost on our driveway, I slowly march toward the truck. The chilly October air bites my cheeks as I watch my dad load the truck with hunting gear. With his scruffy cheeks and burly mustache framing his overlapping front teeth, he is the handsome and rugged hunter one sees when thumbing through the pages of *Outdoor Life*.

Once the packing is finished, we slam truck doors and depart for Heron Lake. A makeshift path links the two-lane highway with the wilds of the lake. On our left, an unharvested plot of field corn bounces past the window. On our right, a line of maples hides the lake beyond. As we drive over hardened clumps of grass and mud, Dad's keys jostle against the steering column.

My great-grandfather made his trek to the lake in hunting boots. He never sat behind the wheel of a car, though Henry Ford's Model T was introduced in 1908.

My dad and I ride without speaking until the crunch of water-worn rocks beneath the tires signals our arrival at the lake. The moon still lights the rugged landscape as my dad transfers the truck's contents into my outstretched arms and I place them in the canoe at water's edge.

Waves lap at the canoe as my dad paddles us to the cattail-covered duck blind he designed and built. Halfway there, I take over the paddling. As his daughter and a descendant of hunters, I want to prove I'm a worthy hunting companion. I want to claim our family's hunting stories as my own.

When we reach the hunting blind, my dad wedges the canoe into the bulrushes. The sky lightens as we toss decoys of mallards and teal into the icy waters. Then, we wait.

Crouching on plastic pails padded with seat cushions, we whisper about the wind and water and weather. I giggle as my dad admits to past adventures plagued with tipped canoes and leaky waders. The hunting stories span four generations of foggy fall sunrises.

"Lace, look!" The words fly out of my dad's mouth as his finger points out a distant flock of targets in flight.

In the next few moments, my eyes dart from the flock to my dad and back again. He grasps the wooden mallard call suspended from his neck and begins an atonal conversation, negotiating where the birds should land. The rhythmic flapping draws closer to our hideaway, and we lift our guns to our shoulders. In my head I hear my dad's shooting lessons, and I am aware that his words echo guidance given by my great-grandfather to Louis, and Louis to him.

I stare down my gun's barrel toward the mallards suspended in flight. As they catch themselves midflap and expose their thickly feathered chests to our sights, we pull triggers. Powerful bursts erupt from our gun barrels.

At once, I am linked to my dad, my great-uncle, and my great-grandfather.

My dad and I retrieve our harvest among the painted decoys, then paddle back to the sunlit shore we'd left in the darkness of early morning. Behind us, the swirling trail of our canoe vanishes into the water. Nevertheless, we've left our imprint on Heron Lake, and my great-grandfather's legacy has been carried forward for another generation.

AROUND THE NEXT BEND

Tim Holschlag

HE HAD NO IDEA it would be like this. Childlike excitement revealing itself like a rocky riffle in low water, James attempts a detached tone. "Do you get many that size here?"

I'll play the game. Deadpan, I reply, "That nineteen-incher you just caught was about the ninetieth smallie over seventeen inches I've taken on top this summer." I pretend not to notice the tremble in his hand as he lays the fly-rod popper on the water again.

James, my guiding client, has just discovered the upper Mississippi River. A world-traveling angler from St. Paul, he had never fished the Miss' because he'd envisioned the commercial river, the one girded by cities, locks and dams, and industrial plants. This river, just forty miles north of the IDS Tower, is new to him. Lured here by the smallmouth bass fishing, James says the Mississippi's fishery rivals that of congested western trout rivers.

"But it's so quiet here," he observes. Indeed. Floating this five-mile section, we see little development along the wooded shore, and few other anglers. Here, the Father of Waters is like an undiscovered wild waterway. Eagles soar and ospreys dive. This is Montana's Yellowstone River sans hominids.

Of course, this all seems perfectly normal to me. I work on the Mississippi every day. And I grew up on moving waters, wading and floating rivers since the summer days when Ricky Schmidt and I would walk a mile and a half to fish Plum Creek for chubs. We were six then. Now I'm nearing nine times that age, and still following the river around the next bend.

And that's exactly why I love rivers so much. The next bend always has new fishing potential, new water, new adventure. And each river is a world all its own. Large or small, fast flow or slow, wild or civilized, opaque or crystalline, every river I know has a unique character.

The Mississippi actually has multiple personalities, even within Minnesota, from its remote Itasca headwaters to the barge-bearing metro river, to its vast Lake Pepin reaches. I guide on a fifty-mile stretch just north of Minneapolis, where the channel is maybe six hundred feet across and rocky throughout—handsome water in a semiwild setting. Here, the mighty and often murky Miss' is certainly no easy book to read, but after years of plying its waters I sometimes think I've seen all its moods. Then it thoroughly surprises me.

During the floods of '93, when the river flowed full for months, I found fish in places I hadn't seen them before and haven't seen them since. And just last year I discovered a new Mississippi right where the old one flows. Tom, a die-hard angler and regular client, and I were floating an island-studded section of river near Monticello. A late start, good fishing, and the waning days of September left us still on the water as evening approached. Earlier in the day, my heretofore faithful eight-horse had died, so I knew it would be oars all the way and a late landing. This was just fine with Tom. After casing the rods, I laid into the oars.

As the harvest moon rose, we quietly approached the islands. Although I thought I knew the area as well as I know my own boat, now it was a mysterious world of shadows and nighttime splashes. Snaking through dark channels and past unseen river critters, I had about the best float of my life on a brand-new river.

I've been guiding on the upper Miss' for more than a decade, but I still get a kick out of rediscovering it and bringing newbies into my river world. Surprising them with the natural beauty and fecundity of their backyard river makes me smile.

Naturally, people's reactions to the river depend on their expectations. James, Tom, and dozens of others who come with few expectations and little knowledge of the river often find it delightful. The uncrowded quietness and superb fishing make them instant river fans. One client, a California fly fisher, had been avidly pursuing smallmouth for twenty-two years. Heavy rains had roiled the river, and the current was fierce; but during his first morning on the Mississippi, nearly five pounds of smallmouth fell for his fly—his biggest bass ever. Now he makes the long trek to our Minnesota rivers every year.

A few aren't so easily impressed. With heads too big for their hats, they regard themselves as whiz-bang anglers and expect the Mississippi to deliver instant gratification. But this river has a way of humbling this type of guy.

A classic case was the CEO of a Fortune 500 company. Armed with the priciest tackle and a smidgen of lake-fishing experience, Mr. Fortune expected the river to be a pushover. An above-normal flow that day meant stiff currents and big bellies—that is, slack loops in the fly line. But rather than heeding my hook-setting advice, he ignored the current and insisted on using his wimpy lake technique. Many fish rose to his fly, but after a frustrating seven hours he had landed just two of them. Despite his status, the river was his boss. His fishing partner, however—more modestly equipped, but more open to my advice—caught eleven fine fish that day, including the biggest smallmouth of his life.

The occasional unruly client notwithstanding, most folks are great, eager to learn and willing to accept that I'm the captain of our little ship. Many of them ask what it's like to work on the river for a living. Well, it's not all fun and game fish. There's a generous measure of tedium to the job—get up, pack lunches, load boat, drive, meet client, shuttle, launch, rig up, row, instruct, maneuver boat, unhook fish, row, take photos, row, unhook fish, row, tie on flies, row, take out, drive, clean boat, dinner, bed, get up, pack lunches. Except farmers, no one complains about the weather as much as a river guide does. There may be as many adverse conditions as days in the fishing season. My mission is to catch fish in everything from drought to flood, from cold rain to blazing sun to howling gale—no matter how inexperienced the client in the boat.

But I can't complain. I enjoy the challenge, and the occasional odd client adds spice. (I still have the portrait of me drawn by a fellow who wanted to catch just one bass on his delicate bamboo fly rod, and then spent the rest of the day talking about becoming a sketch artist in Boulder.) The best part of the job is just being out there. Five, sometimes six or seven days a week, I'm on moving water.

Certainly other jobs, including some I've had, pay more and offer better security, but for me nothing measures up to the one I have now. This despite (actually, because of) the job being so physical. My craft is propelled mostly by current and oars, with nary a battery on board. High-tech, doze-in-the-boat fishin' it ain't. There's no machinery, no electronics, no intercessor between me and the river and its fish. That's also why I love fly-fishing so much. Modern fly rods may be fancy graphite, but they catch fish only with practiced effort. Even the flies are strictly hands-on. Personally tied by myself and friends, they fool many bass (plus the occasional walleye, catfish, and pike). But the angler must constantly work the fly—casting it, twitching it, drifting it.

Nonpiscine nature also figures prominently in my life on the river. The *kik-ik-ik* of the eagle is a regular and reassuring sound, as is the *cheep, cheep* of the osprey. Watching these acrobatic fish hawks plunge into Snuffy's Rapids, sometimes emerging with a tasty sucker, is almost as enjoyable as a big bass on the line. And when you spend your days in a slow and quiet craft, low to the water and near to the banks, even closer animal encounters are bound to occur.

Once a client almost caught a deer—on his fly. He was an older gent who loved placing his popper inches from the shoreline, and one wind-blown cast went slightly awry. When it landed in waist-high grass a few feet onto shore, Ed gave a mighty pull to dislodge the fly. The grass quivered from the tug, then exploded, as a bedded whitetail burst forth. Ed's fly flew free and the deer bounded into the woods. It was difficult to say which of us was more startled. Doubtless that deer had a good story for his friends, but so did my client. For several more years, he excitedly re-counted the "near deer" tale every time we fished together.

An otter encounter was even odder. That summer an adult otter with three exuberant pups was a regular sight along a secluded stretch. A good mother, she gave a warning chitter when the boat drifted too close and always managed to get the pups to hide in the grass until we passed. Then for a week, no otter show. Until one day just a single otter, about the size of one of the pups, bounded along the rocky bank. Instead of running or swimming away, this fellow matched our speed as we floated down the river.

Amazingly, after scampering along the shore for fifty yards, he dove into the river and started swimming right for us! We were a short cast from the bank, with John's floating fly and floating line directly in the otter's path. He tried to get it out of the way, but too late. Swimming into the line, the pup was temporarily tangled, then continued toward the boat. As he neared, I gave him a little splash with the oar. But even this didn't immediately deter him. He swam around the boat for several more seconds then turned and headed back to the bank, where he perched on a boulder. Was he looking for Mama and his siblings? Did our moving boat seem like an island to explore? Did he just want to visit? I dunno.

Fish, of course, are the river wildlife I remember most vividly. Floating along, I see a familiar boulder and remember the eighteen-incher with only one eye that we caught four times one summer from exactly the same spot. Or the small eddy below the NSP rapids, where a humongous smallie once struck at a floating lure with such enthusiasm it leaped completely out of the water and over the lure. And a "secret" little island channel, where my Kansas clients once hooked and landed two four-pounders simultaneously. Fond memories are around every bend.

Fortunately, some folks have given thought not just to memories of the past, but also to conservation for the future. A few years ago the Department of Natural Resources, at the urging of The Smallmouth Alliance conservation group, placed catch-and-release smallmouth regulations on forty-seven miles of the Mississippi. This wise move has made the upper Miss' a world-class fishing destination. And it should serve as a positive example for many other Minnesota waters.

But danger also lurks around the bend. Developers and homebuyers have discovered the waterway in recent years. More sprawling houses now overlook the river. Clearing the wooded shorelines for their picture windows, folks are actually degrading the river they've come to view. The clearing increases bank erosion and reduces water quality.

Instead of sterile, chemical-laden lawns creeping to the water's edge, the Miss' and its splendid smallies would do much better with at least a twenty-foot buffer of natural vegetation. Protecting such a strip of river-bank wouldn't encroach on anyone's livelihood or domicile; it would simply be a sensible way to protect a priceless public resource.

Limiting development depends on understanding that the real beauty of the river is its wooded wildness and unpredictability. That fishing and floating the river in the company of eagles and otters is far better than simply being able to see it from the living room.

If this viewpoint competes with those who would manage and mani-cure nature for their private purposes, naturally, I'm rooting for an un-tamed future for this river and her fish. And I'm hoping everyone else who loves the Mississippi will stand up for her too. I intend to keep fol-lowing that winding water all my life, but what lies around the next bend is up to all of us.

FISHLESS WATERS

Jan Zita Grover

 MY HOME STREAM FOR FOUR YEARS was a Zen fishing paradise: a mazy, meandering tailwater that ran twenty-eight miles
from dam to mouth, most of it beneath a pleached archway of
elms, ashes, cottonwoods, and poplars. Kingfishers, green-backed
herons, great blue herons, white-breasted nuthatches, tree and barn
swallows, swifts, hooded mergansers, goldeneyes, and Canada geese rode
its waters and dived from its streamside trees. A few warm days in winter opened up channels broad enough for casting, and in summer the
water was usually high enough to provide two to three feet midstream,
and often more along the grass-lined outer bank.

But a *Zen* stream? Well, yes. This creek offered fishing, but no fish—a
daily ritual of casting, feeling the water eddy round my legs, noting the
changes in water level and temperature, the progress of seasons marked
by vegetation, insects, and birds. But as for fish, those were few and far
between—according to the Department of Natural Resources' metro
manager, a few sunfish, the vagrant bass or pike that washed over the
dam far upstream.

In any case, the creek's few finned beings were wholly safe from me.
I not only didn't seek them, I didn't even cast a fly. But I was nonetheless gratified when I ran into fish—or rather, when one of them ran into
me. One late spring morning, for example, I was standing midstream,
casting against the current, when something with the resilience of an
inflated inner tube bumped hard into my left calf and briefly wrapped

itself around my leg. A dark shape glimpsed, then gone beneath the hard-running water. My first and only thought was a pike—several years ago, a child angler had caught a respectable eighteen-inch snake, as small pike are sometimes called locally, in a pool just upstream of where I now stood. But before I could further puzzle out the fish's identity, rain began dimpling the water, and the crowns of the creekside trees fanned open beneath a heavy northwest wind. A late May storm was coming on, thunder predicted, so I reluctantly reeled in and left the water for the morning. Five minutes later, when the storm broke, I was already at home in southwest Minneapolis.

My home water was Minnehaha Creek, which is fed by Lake Minnetonka and regulated at Gray's Bay Dam by the Minnehaha Creek Watershed District (MCWD). The creek may have been fishless for all intents and purposes by the time it reached Fifty-second Street and Xerxes, where I faithfully haunted its waters each day, but it was in every other way an interesting stream.

Before it was dammed for lumber, furniture, and gristmills in the 1850s to 1870s, Minnehaha Creek swam with pike, bass, sunfish, and suckers. In 1852, Colonel John Owens, publisher of the weekly *Minnesotan* (St. Paul), wrote about an expedition he and his party had made to Lake Minnetonka, during which they "caught fish enough to feed all twelve hungry men" from Minnehaha Creek. "Fishing for about twenty minutes more, they brought in more than a total of about forty pounds." Even the first generation of dams on the creek apparently didn't destroy its fish populations; Coates P. Bull, whose family farmed alongside one of the creek's tributaries around 1900, recalled pickerel, bass, sunfish, and other fish in great numbers: "Suckers and Redhorse each spring swam from Lake Harriet through the outlet into Minnehaha. . . . They 'paid toll' aplenty; for settlers, even from Eden Prairie and miles to the west, brought their spears to harvest bushels of these fish to eat and to feed pigs."

But as the wetlands adjoining Lake Minnetonka and the creek were drained for farms, roads, and homes, the creek's water level began to drop and to fluctuate dramatically. There were years when the creek almost dried up. By 1928, when Otto Schussler published his *Riverside Reveries*, Minnehaha Creek had "almost ceased, for a great part of each year at any rate, to be a stream." Finally, in 1963, the MCWD was formed to regulate water levels and water quality in the creek's 169-square-mile watershed. At the Gray's Bay Dam on Lake Minnetonka, waters above a set minimum level are released into the creek. Creek levels are also increased during peak canoeing/tubing season (July to August) unless there's a drought. In 1979 the Creekside chapter of the Izaak Walton League cleaned up the creek from Gray's Bay down to Minneapolis; the garbage they collected filled two dump trucks.

Living about twenty-one miles downstream from Gray's Bay Dam, I witnessed the creek's almost daily and seemingly fickle fluctuations. In early May, despite snowmelt and ice going out on Lake Minnetonka, the creek was usually starved for water throughout its Minneapolis course. Even the old millpond below East Minnehaha Parkway at Thirty-fourth Avenue receded from its usually brimming banks. Farther upstream, every storm drain leading into the creek hung suspended three or four feet above the usual water level. Ducks waiting for open water crowded into discontinuous puddles like so many commuters pressing onto rush-hour trains.

And then, just as inexplicably, sometime during the night near the end of the month, the water would begin spilling over the dam again. The next morning, the creek was a good three feet higher, its muddy flats vanished. Buffleheads and mallards floated contentedly on winter-cold pools beneath the naked trees.

Most of the Minneapolis miles of Minnehaha Creek provided great opportunities for everything that makes fly-fishing gratifying, *except* the likelihood of hooking fish. The creek's width varied roughly between ten and twenty-five feet when the water was running 150 cubic feet per second or more. Its structure was classic: runs, riffles, pocket waters, pools filled with many of the same aquatic invertebrates I had learned to expect to find in trout waters: Stonefly, mayfly, and caddisfly nymphs colonized the rocks that dotted its sand bottom; blackfly larvae clung there too, swaying by silk threads in the current. Winter and summer, fine blooms of midges lifted suddenly into the air at twilight, followed in summer by great cartwheeling hoards of swallows and swifts, which picked them off as quickly as they arose from the water. In late June and July, iridescent blue damselflies courted and mated in midair, on the surface of the water, on the yellow flag and cattails at the water's edge.

By forgoing the opportunity to cast for fish, I was able to sample other pleasures in a focused, relaxed way. No two-and-a-half-hour drive, no burning of hydrocarbons to get my conservation-minded self farther and farther out of town; no night driving. In exchange for the absence of fish, I got everything else that made small-stream fishing worthwhile. Need I add that the creek was uncrowded? The only time I found anyone else casting there, it was because I had told Sam and Kim about it. But I did not see them on the creek again.

Plenty of people stopped their cars alongside my stretch to ask if there were really fish in Minnehaha Creek or to comment on my casting. After I told them that the creek was practically fishless and pulled my line from the water to show them the yarn at the end of my tippet, most of them just stared at me, bemused or disgusted, shook their heads, and climbed back into their cars. I, in turn, was bemused by sidewalk anglers whose view of fishing was so instrumental that they were flummoxed by my admission that I wasn't even rigged to catch anything. But I savored the company of others who stopped to reminisce about their favorite streams, try a few casts with my rod, or comment that midcity, midstream casting looked like a great way to unwind after a day's work.

After two years of faithful attendance on the mostly fishless waters of Minnehaha Creek, I woke one day and decided I wanted to fish not so much *for* fish as *in the presence of* them. I wanted to stand in waters that the DNR had designated as trout waters. This had less to do with my growing appetite for blood or hookups than with my curiosity about how fishy waters differed from what I knew about Minnehaha Creek. My curiosity had grown, as had my confidence: I thought I knew now what to look for when exploring new waters for fish. So I began driving to the nearest certified trout streams: Eagle Creek, Hay Creek, the Kinnickinnic and Rush rivers, the Brule. And I found that what I had learned on Minnehaha

Creek served me well: sometimes I found fish where I expected to, and occasionally I even caught them.

But those streams, beautiful and "productive" (as fisheries biologists call them) though they were, lacked the heart-tugging familiarity of Minnehaha Creek. I missed knowing what occurred on those distant streams during the many days when I couldn't visit them; I missed the dailiness of time spent on a nearby stream. What those fine waters offered in terms of fish per mile couldn't compensate me for what they couldn't give: the knowledge earned through daily intimacy. Was the creek up or down today? How close to hatching were the caddisflies in the riffle downstream of the big cottonwood? Had the chubs and shiners built their nests yet?

Today I am lucky enough to live close to not only two neighborhood streams but to ones with resident trout and lake-run fish. Like Minnehaha Creek, stretches of them are cool, leafy, seemingly untouched. In spring I can lie on warm streamside boulders and stare down into their transparent miniature pools at shiners and nervous little brook trout, just as I used to watch chubs on Minnehaha. These are streams I not only savor but work to protect; I have come to see the need to fight for such precious urban waters. I doubt that I shall ever be more fond of them, though, than I was—still am—of Minnehaha Creek.

It is the place I first fell under the spell of moving waters and came to see them as animate, storied, and plastic enough to accommodate and challenge me, no matter how little or much I knew. It is the place where I first kept faith with a part of myself I hadn't known before: the creature capable of a great, unexpected patience, a faith that I could crack the code of waters, the skills of casting and fishing. It is the place that taught me that faithful attendance on a single place—in this case, a stretch of stream no more than five hundred yards long—could yield unimagined complexity, a microcosm so rich that I am still its beginner, its postulant.

Minnehaha Creek taught me a way of seeing that enriches my life and my writing. Just now, on a visit to Minneapolis, as I sat alongside the creek's edge once again, admiring it from my truck on a mid-June morning, a great blue heron drifted weightlessly across the opaque white sky. A leaf green inchworm bobbed from his silk line beneath a drooping elm branch, and I saw both of them. Because my eyes had been opened in and by this place, I knew how succulent a surface-feeding fish would find the inchworm, and how such fish would gather eagerly beneath the branch, waiting for him to drop.

The rains had finally come after an exceptionally hot, dry spring, and now the creek flowed wide and shallow. Water grasses that wouldn't have been there most years until mid-July streamed in the current, and the heavy thickets of grasses anchoring the north bank crowded out over the water, their pale heads already seeding up.

This was a place that humans nearly destroyed and then helped to rebuild. That handsome curve on the inside of the creek just below me covered with mosses and grasses wasn't even there three years ago when I moved north to Duluth. It was a human-made structure concocted of sandbags, mesh, and soil designed to narrow the creek where it was throwing up sand and cutting back into the bank.

I felt enormous satisfaction in these evidences that people could partially heal what we have damaged, that a place like Minnehaha Creek has restorative powers of its own. I learned these lessons on an urban stream, and I believe they made me a different and a better person. The prospect of revisiting the creek whenever I travel to Minneapolis remains exquisitely exciting. Each time, I strain forward over the steering wheel, peering eagerly through the windshield, waiting for my first sight of it.

"Jeez, *Mom*," my daughter protests. "It's not like you ever caught anything there."

But I did. Fishing in that nearly fishless place taught me what I most wanted to learn: the patience, attentiveness, and submission needed to love a place well.

THE RIVER

Sheila Deyo

 "THE RIVER." I wonder how many times in my life I've heard or spoken those words: countless times, I'm sure, and always with the same implied meaning, the downtown St. Paul harbor of the Mississippi River.

The spring before last, I had a chance to join the Great Mississippi River Cleanup, a volunteer project to clear trash on stretches from Harriet Island in St. Paul to Fort Snelling in Minneapolis. I thought volunteer work, especially on the river, would be a good experience for my three daughters. Though they don't remember it well, the river was once a big part of their lives. Their father and I had met there, worked there, and spent most of our time with river people. Our two oldest daughters even had towboats named after them: motor vessels *Katie Rose* and *Jillian Rae*. My own nostalgic reasons for wanting us to help take care of the river went even further back.

I grew up on St. Paul's West Side. The river was a backdrop for our neighborhood. For my friends and me, the highlight of walking downtown on Saturday afternoon was the trip across the river. Time was unimportant as we stood on the Wabasha Bridge, watching our saliva plummet into the wind. I can still feel the knot in my stomach as we jumped across broken planks in the old sidewalk, trying not to notice just how far below the water flowed. And the tremors at the north end of the bridge, as traffic built at the stoplight, felt like an earthquake to me.

Some Saturdays we didn't cross the bridge. We'd skip going downtown altogether and instead climb down the bluffs. We'd stop to explore the mushroom caves and eventually make our way to the riverbank. It was all territory our parents had forbidden us to visit. "Bums live down there," they'd say.

The caves were scary—pitch-black, cold, and damp. When we entered, we could hear the screaming echoes of kids already deep inside. Once, as we ran through the blackness, our friend Donna suddenly somersaulted down an incline and into a limestone wall. She stumbled out of the cave, dazed and with blood dripping from her ear. With some difficulty we escorted her back up the steep, wooded bluff, all the way discussing our predicament. Inappropriate as it seems now, our main concern was what to tell her parents.

During the long walk home Donna kept asking, "What time is it?" We would tell her, and in a few minutes she would ask again. She did not reply to our repeated question: "What's your name?" This unsatisfactory dialogue left our club of twelve-year-old girls with no recourse but to tell her mother the truth, and hope she wouldn't tell our mothers.

Donna was fine, diagnosed with a slight concussion, and most of our parents never found out about our excursions. But that trip down the bluffs was our last. Maybe we realized that our parents might be right, that it was a dangerous place, or maybe we just grew older and lost interest—I can't remember.

I had to do a little convincing—arm twisting, really—to get my daughters to donate a summer day to the river cleanup. In exchange for our labor, we would get a ride on a paddle-wheel boat, free food, and entertainment. I thought it sounded like fun. To three girls, ages eight to fourteen, it sounded boring.

In the morning, we roamed Pike Island, picking up bits of trash, mostly cigarette butts and Styrofoam peanuts. I was surprised at how little trash there was. On the first Earth Day in 1970, my St. Matthew's grade school classmates and I picked up hundreds of times more trash near the riverbank.

As the girls and I glided back downriver that beautiful June morning with our task complete, I felt sentimental about days gone by. Watching the Omaha Railroad bridge swing open for our passage reminded me of a friend named Jan who spent hours in that little house opening and closing the bridge. I have waited for that bridge to open countless times.

During my summers in college, I worked for the excursion boat company that sponsored our cleanup. During the day I did clerical work and sold tickets; at night I served food and drink to passengers. But the real fun began when the trips were over. In the wee hours, the crew would swap stories while swabbing the decks. The camaraderie grew as we joked about the eccentricities of our passengers and the antics of our employer. It was a great job, cruising up and down the river, watching the city lights reflecting off the night water.

That's where I met Mike, a towboat pilot who occasionally ran the excursion boats. Soon after we married, Mike started a barge-switching business. Large towboats from down south would come up river with fifteen or more barges in a "tow." Our small towboats dispersed the barges to various points along the Mississippi and Minnesota rivers, where they were emptied of their cargo, cleaned, and filled again, with anything from coal to grain.

The river consumed our life back then, workwise and socially. Most of our friends made their living on the water. At every gathering, sooner or later, "she," the river, became the topic of conversation. Once it began, the river lore, lies, and storytelling went on for hours. Many of the women in the group were convinced that their mates had more passion for the river than they had for them. Some of them were right.

Our small business employed thirty to forty workers from late March to November. The boats worked twenty-four hours a day, seven days a week. Work shifts ran twelve hours on and twelve hours off. The work was physically exhausting, especially for the deckhands who assembled and disassembled the tows with heavy steel cable.

The phone rang day and night. Somebody didn't show up for work, or the loading docks weren't on schedule, or the boat was still waiting to go through the lock. One call over the marine radio I'll never forget. The *Katie Rose* had gone downriver to Lock and Dam No. 2 near Hastings to help one of our other boats, which was having trouble with a tow of twelve empty barges in a strong wind. In an effort to assist, the *Katie Rose* had run up against an underwater sand ridge and flipped onto its side from the weight of the barges. The pilot and deckhands jumped overboard as the boat rapidly took on water and sank. The crew was quickly rescued. Luckily, no one was injured. The boat was a wreck, destroyed by sludge.

In the 1980s, most small barge companies were forced out of business or bought out by large international corporations. The company whose contracts we ran closed its operation, except for the barge switching, which it began to do itself. We were left with large payments and boats that had no work. We were out of business, with a third baby due in months.

Sometime later, Mike left for New Orleans to pilot towboats—live-on boats they're called—six weeks on and two weeks off. After a while, I didn't care too much for the river life.

A few years later, I found myself living a completely different life— no longer married or in contact with river people. I felt like she, the river, had won the poker hand. But, little by little, the river has crept back into my life.

My brother moved onto a year-round houseboat. And my father developed a passion for boats that propelled him into the excursion business with a 118-passenger paddle-wheel boat. It's funny to think that some of the river people who are now a part of his life and my brother's were once a part of mine.

Not long ago, it seemed that the Mississippi River was noticed only by those who worked or lived there. Now hardly a day goes by when the river isn't mentioned in the local media, as though it has just been discovered, as though it were gold and everyone wanted to stake a claim.

The federal government has designated a seventy-two-mile stretch of the river, from Dayton to Hastings, as the Mississippi National River and Recreation Area administered by the National Park Service. The city of St. Paul is betting that riverfront development will fuel downtown renewal.

Meanwhile, commerce and industry continue to use the river to transport bulk goods. Excursion businesses compete to carry tourists, wedding parties, and school groups. Recreationists enjoy boating, hiking, fishing, bicycling, and jet skiing. The river gives people open space, scenic views, and a vital water supply.

Environmentalists work to protect the river's wild assets. The riverbanks are home to herons, egrets, marsh wrens, beaver, woodchucks, deer, turtles, and other wildlife. Its waters teem with aquatic life.

Stepping back to look at these interests and assets, I've come full circle in my regard for the river, and for that I am glad. I can see that the river is, and always has been, a nucleus for existence here.

At the end of the cleanup, my youngest daughter, Madeline, who had spent most of the day crabbing about the work, heat, and bugs, leaned over to me and said with an apologetic grin, "I'm sorry I complained so much. I really did have a good time."

I knew Madeline was more pleased about winning the contest for finding the most unusual piece of trash—a small metal object resembling a spaceship with legs—than about making a contribution to the environment. But that was all right; all I had really wanted to do was to share some memories with my girls and bring them a little closer to the river.

GOING WITH THE FLOW

Jim dale Huot-Vickery

SOMEWHERE ALONG THE RED RIVER OF THE NORTH, on the
Minnesota–North Dakota border, perhaps just shy of Manitoba,
I realized I had to keep going north with the flow. I had to keep
canoeing the river's 550 miles, keep freighting mayoral mail and
a U.S. flag, and keep my eyes open to the beauty of a little-known river.
I was, after all, on a mission.

It had become my challenge and honor, in May–June 2000, to canoe
from one end of the Red River of the North to the other, from Breckenridge,
Minnesota (and adjacent Wahpeton, North Dakota) to Selkirk, Manitoba,
north of Winnipeg. The trip had been organized by Bob Backman and
Christine Holland of River Keepers in Fargo-Moorhead, and although
there would be almost a hundred paddlers participating in the thirty-
four-day Red River Millennium Tour, people coming and going, I was the
only one committed to paddling all the way. Hence my personal pack
held the folded and packaged U.S. flag given to me by the Veterans of
Foreign Wars to bring to Mayor R. S. "Bud" Oliver in Selkirk. Ditto for
the "mail"—a batch of Red River of the North proclamations plus various letters and history books—given to me by mayors along the river. In
other words, I had unusual cargo on an unusual canoe journey, and I was
determined to do all I could to stay the course.

The media, meanwhile, were watching.

There was TV coverage of the tour, press coverage (particularly Brad
Dokken's series in the *Grand Forks Herald*), and, because I was the

long-distance guy, a lot of attention came my way. There were questions about the tour's purpose (to emphasize the Red's historical, environmental, and recreational values) and, inevitably, questions about my particular presence on the river.

What came out of my mouth matched my heart.

I've always had an abiding love for rivers. They are the living blood of all landscapes, the veins and arteries, the flowages and corridors of the vibrant earth. All life seeks their shelter, their quenching nourishment, their beauty. By getting to know a river, one gets to know its wildlife, seasons, rhythms, and human history. This became clear to me at an early age, for I was born along northwestern Minnesota's Red Lake River, the largest U.S. tributary of the Red River of the North. As one boyhood year led to the next, I couldn't look at a river without wondering about its flow, its connections.

This wonder was true of the Little Black River, which flowed through my grandfather's farm en route to the Red Lake River near the village of Huot. This was true for the Clearwater River, which flowed into the Red Lake River in Red Lake Falls, my boyhood home. And where did the Red Lake River flow? To the Red River of the North, of course, the *Rivière Rouge du Nord* of the early French Canadian explorers. And so, as I aged, moved away, and became a roamer of rivers, I knew I must someday return and canoe the great Red River, certainly its northern half with its countless bends through the Red River Valley, the prairie, the old bison country, until my mind and senses were saturated with the river's cottonwoods and mourning doves, its far sky, the mud and bones and murky waters, the snappers and catfish and starlit reflections, the kingfishers and blackbirds and morning dew, whatever I'd find: all flowing, funneled, into one single waterway, draining, essentially, my native home.

Here, in the Red's watershed, my great-great-grandfather, Joachim Huot, is buried. So too my great-grandfather, and grandfather, grandmothers, and mother, and uncounted cousins. The blood, the water, the connections are interwoven like branches of elm, oak, and swaying willow on the dawning riverbank of my days.

More than this, however, resonated for me when the millennium tour departed on its grand journey down the serpentine Red. There was the geological lure of the place. Always, whether paddling north, east, west, or, sometimes, even south, I was conscious of moving through a vast, flat land created—like much of Minnesota—by glacial ice and water. Yet, in the Red River Valley, the geology, hydrology, and exposed land are relatively recent. The last stage of glaciation ended about eleven thousand years ago. As the ice retreated northward, it created a large lake behind it: Glacial Lake Agassiz.

But Lake Agassiz wasn't a lake as we think of a lake in the fishing skiff—or, for that matter, canoe—sense of the word. Agassiz was big. Geologists, such as George Schwartz and George Thiel in *Minnesota's Rocks and Waters*, claim Agassiz once stretched more than 700 miles south to north, reached a depth of 700 feet, and covered about 110,000 square miles (larger than the combined area of today's Great Lakes). Like an amoeba, the lake changed shape and size, covering northwestern Minnesota, northeastern North Dakota, western Ontario, much of Manitoba, and part of Saskatchewan, making Lake Agassiz, according to Thomas Waters in *The Streams and Rivers of Minnesota*, "the most extensive body of fresh water ever to have existed on the North American continent."

That's big.

My point, however, is that when Lake Agassiz drained—at first southeast via Glacial River Warren and then northward via Lake Winnipeg and the Nelson River to Hudson Bay—it left behind a vast, fertile landscape, the Red River Valley, not really a valley at all, but essentially the bed of a lake, rich in sedimentary silts and lacustrine clay, and flat, flat, flat. Flat as a calm, dirt sea.

Through the heart of this country, twisting this way and that, still draining the rain and melting snow of seasons, flows the Red. It is a young river, perhaps only 8,500 to 9,000 years old; and on its surface a paddler, a voyageur, glides through a ghostly memory of big water and glacial ice.

Red River water is a sight to behold. As the Red meanders through the old, muddy bottom of Lake Agassiz, the river becomes increasingly turbid as the water gathers fine particles of silt and clay into minute, mottled swirls that blend together. Time and again, I glanced at my paddle blade as it sliced into the water to see if I could visually measure clarity. Five inches of visibility? *Three* inches? The farther north we paddled, the murkier the river became. Runoff from torrential storms near Larimore and Fargo increased siltation until there seemed to be no visibility at all.

River color?

Greenish brown in the Red's upper reaches. Grayish brown lower down, or, as tour section leader Tom Tolman put it, "the color of wet cement." At times I noticed plain gray or the blue of reflected sky, but never—in 550 miles of travel—did I see the Red River red.

Perhaps the river's name, as some historians suggest, is rooted in the reflected red sunsets over Upper and Lower Red lakes at the head of the Red Lake River; or, possibly, the name comes from the blood spilled by warring Dakota and Cree clashing in contested territory.

I found the river, notorious for its floods, more beautiful than expected. For most of the Red's length, up past Fargo–Moorhead, Grand Forks–East Grand Forks, Oslo, Drayton, Pembina, and on into Manitoba, the banks are dense with woods: oak, elm, cottonwood, and willow. Brush, in June, is lush. Grass: waist high. Patches of nettle mingle with pink blossoms of wild roses.

Stray scents of moist dirt and plants, sometimes minty, eddied in the air as we glided by. Always the river felt like a liquid ribbon unfurling in forest, an undulating corridor through walls of woods rich with the dark green of ripe spring.

Yet at our country camps, or when stopping for a break, we sometimes walked up through the narrow belt of woods to view the open farmland, once prairie. Fields of black dirt, with small *islettes de bois* (islands of woods), stretched as far as we could see. No hills. No lakes. A few swales. Tiny cars and trucks on distant highways, along with scattered farmhouses and, occasionally, a town's water tower, reminded us we were not far from civilization, that we were, in fact, voyaging down the natural heart—so sequestered and ripe with fecund life—of a settled, populated land.

Flocks of geese, honking, took off from shoals to curve against big sky and circle around. White-tailed deer browsed along the banks, bounded away, or stood their ground and watched us pass. Bald eagles perched on dead trees or took to the air, soaring. Orioles. Swallows. Scarlet tanagers. Magpies. Mourning doves. Great blue herons. Small brown owls, name unknown, flew off downstream or back into the woods. Snapping turtles, sensing a canoe's strange motion, scuttled from shoreline sun into swallowing waters at river's edge. Fish—carp, sucker, catfish, walleye, bass, perhaps sturgeon—startled us when they whipped into motion with a sudden splash, or leapt into the air, next to our canoes.

Adding to this mosaic of life, and carrying us to Selkirk right on schedule, was the swelling river itself. We had passed Red River tributaries almost every day.

There was the Wild Rice River south of Fargo, and the Red Lake (which enters at Grand Forks, hence the city's name), Buffalo, Sheyenne, and Goose rivers. There was the Park River, the Turtle, Pembina, and, in Manitoba, the Roseau, Morris, Seine, La Salle, and the great Assiniboine River, among others, all gathering their waters, their blood of the land, into the main stem of the Red. This quickened the current, and although the Red's gradient is low, averaging a half foot per mile, we sometimes rode current speeds of three to five miles an hour.

Overall elevation drop? From the 943 feet (mean sea level) of Breckenridge–Wahpeton to Lake Winnipeg's 714 feet.

Watershed size? About 45,000 square miles (excluding the Assiniboine River basin, which drains into the Red at downtown Winnipeg), or an area Gene Krenz and Jay Leitch—in *A River Runs North*—compare to the states of Mississippi or Pennsylvania.

River width? A stone's throw at the start, *ker-plunk,* to several hundred feet or more, narrowing and widening according to the contours of the land.

No sand beaches, until river's end. No waterfalls.

And rapids?

None on the Red. Unless you call Goose Rapids—between Nielsville and Climax, Minnesota—a rapids, which the old-timers did. Steamboats couldn't get past the Goose's stony shoals, the subtle S-curving drop, and the few pretty islands with intervening riffles barring commerce's deep-drafted way. So those old-timers gave the place a name, called it a rapids, and, under some circumstances, I suppose it might be so.

A SEARCH FOR WHITEWATER

Hal Crimmel

IF YOU HAPPENED TO VISIT INTERSTATE STATE PARK one autumn day several years ago, perhaps you saw something odd: a person scrambling down the rocky banks of the St. Croix River, waving at a kayaker resting on shore beneath the bridge. You might have seen that person borrow the paddler's clammy life jacket, strip to his underwear, climb into the kayak, and shove off into the swirling St. Croix River.

I am a little embarrassed to say that the person was me; the kayaker, a complete stranger; and the riverbank, not exactly a secluded place. But after a long, hot month in Minnesota, searching without success for a whitewater river, I was desperate to paddle again.

On that September day, the rushing St. Croix sparkled in the pale sunlight, and the pungent scent of damp rocks rose from the shadows. Leaves burned with color along the cliffs. As I paddled out into the wave train, I breathed a sigh of relief at having found these rapids. And for the first time, I thought Minnesota might have what I sought.

Before moving to the state, I had lived near the six-million-acre Adirondack Park in New York. There, glacier-scoured mountains plunged to headwater lakes, and dark rivers dropped quickly through wild forest. Kayaking down those whitewater streams was my passion. Then my wife's career brought us to Minnesota. My paddling friends snickered: "It's completely flat out there. Better sell your boat."

As we neared the Twin Cities in our moving truck, the countryside flattened slowly before my eyes. Someone seemed to be letting the air out of the hills, leaving a sea of grass and trees. I wondered if any steep, rocky rivers might flow nearby. Thus began my quest to find Minnesota whitewater.

The first month I looked in vain, though you would think the White-water River a logical starting place. Wrong. No real rapids grace its length.

On the Snake River, I dragged my boat across miles of rocky shallows in the late-summer heat. Several Saturdays of this, and I conceded defeat.

But my visit to Interstate State Park yielded waves and kayakers. Perhaps there was hope after all. I began paddling again.

In November I tried the Vermillion River near Hastings. I found whitewater, but the river smelled like laundry soap, due to phosphorus from fertilizer runoff. And I could hear the clanking of railcars on a spur line and the roar—like a giant furnace blower—coming from the mill above the falls. Pop bottles bobbed in clumps along the banks.

I was unsure if the Gopher State had any hidden whitewater gems. But the hard winter of 1996–97 rekindled my hope. I knew that runoff from the near-record snowpack would make any river exciting. If ever there was a year to paddle Minnesota, this was it. And I hit the jackpot: the Kettle River in Banning State Park had levels above nine feet—big water!

The first rapid, Blueberry Slide, was full of truck-sized holes and eight-foot waves, which were exploding at the top and then breaking like ocean surf. If I tried to plow through them and failed, I would be thrashed around pretty good and come out cold. I eyed these fluid mounds, paused, counted one-two-three, and went for it. The river snatched my kayak out of the eddy, and the current swatted my boat dangerously close to the exploding waves. Head down, I barreled up and over an icy wall of water as it collapsed on me like a rotten roof. Made it!

More excitement was in store that spring. After the trees leafed out, I paddled the lower St. Louis River, a dangerous run filled with steep, quirky falls and weird, razor-sharp rock outcrops. Below the swinging bridge at Jay Cooke State Park, I scouted Fin Falls, a long, violent rapid. A mistake here would result in a bad swim and a severe beating along the rocky riverbed.

But the temptation was great. I knew that if I could skip off the first ledge, stroke through a series of sticky holes, then crash down the final tongue into a narrow cleft with the rapid roaring in my ears and my heart pounding, I would feel a special sort of ecstasy, as if I had absorbed the river's force and made it my own.

One last look and I was off in a flurry of strokes, an imaginary line spooling out as envisioned. The river dropped out from under me, and a heavy fist of water rose up to deal a blow. I leaned hard on the paddle—as a prizefighter might lean back on the ropes before springing into center ring—then eddied out and caught my breath. In this small chasm, water thundering by at eye level, conifers high overhead, I felt a burst of sheer joy, as if the river gods were suddenly smiling on me.

The gods were not always charitable, and I crashed and burned more than once during my kayaking trips. But despite the harrowing swims in icy water, the vicious raps on my helmet, the scraped and torn flesh, the plum-sized bruises, the freezing temperatures and knee-deep snow, the swarms of insects—or perhaps because of all of these things—I started to like Minnesota.

I began to take pleasure in harsh conditions, which lent magic to kayaking here. Once, while lining up to run a small waterfall on Silver Creek near Two Harbors, I watched the sky darken and felt the temperature plunge twenty degrees. Balmy day gave way to raw northern spring. Hail poured down from the heavens, rattling on my boat, tap-tap-tapping on my helmet. Trees bent in the wind, their branches clattering over the river's deep rumble. My companions and I let loose a collective shout into the air, an exuberant bay of emotion, like a pack of wolves howling at the moon.

Such intense, sudden storms seemed an extension of the creeks themselves. Those rivers falling into Lake Superior lead a short, ferocious life, like north woods insects, coming on fast and then dying off. In summer most rivers are just trickles, safely waded by fishermen. In winter they lie dormant under a thick blanket of ice and snow. In spring the streams can explode, sometimes with trees and boulder-sized cakes of ice large enough to smash a boat. To dodge this boreal shrapnel while running a rapid is to feel the mystery and violence of northern rivers, and the wildness of the forests they spring from.

Kayaking connected me to Minnesota's rivers, forests, and skies. But there was one puzzling piece: how to make sense of the big lake—Superior? Like it does for many paddlers, it drew me, perhaps because the best kayaking rivers flow into it. It is also hauntingly beautiful. Along its shores on foggy spring days, conifers stand like dark spirits against ghostly stands of paper birch. Land, sky, and water seem to dissolve into one another.

You might think that kayaking into a large body of water would provide a decisive end to a river trip, a rewarding sense of completion. Many times I boated into Superior on a stream of tannin-stained, sediment-laden water. But then the river's energy and color would fade to nothing. The river never seemed to leave a trace in the lake, which remained clear as gin, as if neither the river nor my descent of it mattered.

One North Shore river intrigued me most of all: the Devil Track. Its peculiar name conjured up images of a place of dark magic and hard labor. When I finally paddled it, I was astonished to find a canyon of its magnitude in the state that first depressed me with its flatness.

The sound of the water in the deep, red canyon told me most of what I needed to know. At the put-in, a slender chuckle hinted at gently falling water, moving slowly in dark threads between rocks. Then came a gargling rumble of bigger water, a choking bass rumble you feel in your solar plexus, one that makes your mouth go dry and your stomach cramp; it's a place where you just might want to go ashore, put the boat on your shoulder, and keep on walking. But no. You paddle it instead.

I slipped over the first falls, sinking in as smoothly and cleanly as if diving into a cool lake in summer, entering a sweet marriage of flesh with water. The next horizon line waited, and a thread of current was all I had to go on as I took two big strokes and launched into the air. This sensation was profound: the feeling of skating on a frozen northern lake, whirling across a sheet of ice under a clear star-filled January sky, blades biting into the ice, wind at my back pushing me along into the night, feeling weightless, as if with just a little more speed I might lift off and rise to the stars, mind skipping between heaven and earth. At such a moment, I knew I had found, briefly, the right relationship between self and place.

Last July was the last time I ran a Minnesota river. Today I stand on the sun-baked shores of Great Salt Lake, not far from my new home on the edge of the arid Great Basin. The cool Minnesota forests and streams are but a memory in the shimmering desert heat. Yet I feel their power as surely as if I stood at the mouth of the Baptism on a foggy April morning, watching the river vanish into the big, cold lake, and listening to the muffled slap of waves on polished stone. It is easy to summon up the spirits of these rivers, and when I do so, my heart quickens and my stomach tightens. I feel their pull here in the desert air, their memory a bracing tonic in the blazing western sun.

If you ask, I will tell you that good rivers are everywhere. All we have to do is find them.

RIVER PASSAGE

Janet Blixt

 NEARLY HOME TO DULUTH on Interstate 35, I see familiar land-marks. The exit signs for Carlton and Jay Cooke State Park appear on my right. To my left, a casino blinks orange and red. Ahead, the white steam of the Cloquet paper mill clouds the horizon.

The highway makes a wide sweep to the northeast and crosses the St. Louis River. Out of habit, I glance downstream at the current as I drive over the bridge. Here, nearly twenty years ago, I first explored the rap-ids of the St. Louis in my whitewater kayak. That was a day I remember well—memorable, as firsts and lasts, beginnings and endings, in one's life tend to be.

One bright May morning, a handful of kayakers paddled down a sec-tion of the St. Louis River none of us had ever seen before. Its rapids and waterfalls had recently been mapped by other paddlers. I remember put-ting on my helmet, climbing into my boat, and stuffing gum into my dry mouth. Every time I paddled this river, it would be with a mix of excite-ment and trepidation, but never so much as on that first trip.

At the start of the run, the river ran broad and smooth, a quarter mile across. The river changed character frequently as we descended toward Lake Superior. The current spread out through wide boulder-bed rapids and funneled into several canyons where the water converged into chains of waves.

Twice, the river split around wooded islands. Among the spruce, birch, and aspen, an occasional white pine rose above the shoreline. We spotted eagles and great blue herons. Almost-vertical piles of gray slate cropped up everywhere, forming ledges, waterfalls, and rapids. With the exception of a water level station and a power line that crossed the river, we saw little sign of humans.

As I paddled, I often wondered: Who else has been here? What was their business? What set the rhythm and purpose of their day? I knew that the St. Louis had been a major waterway, connecting the Great Lakes to the interior of North America, used for hundreds of years by the Ojibwe and Dakota, French and British fur traders, missionaries and explorers. French explorers in the 1700s had named the river for King Louis IX. The Ojibwe called the river *Kitchigumizibi,* the Lake Superior River.

As I floated down the river, tucked snugly in my boat, I could imagine Ojibwe Indians and French Canadian voyageurs lugging packs and canoes through the woods to avoid the very rapids I was paddling for adventure.

These long-ago travelers trekked the Grand Portage, a nine-mile detour circumventing the waterfalls and rugged terrain of the St. Louis River. In good weather, the portage would take three to five days; in bad weather, a full week. This route linked the St. Louis River and Lake Superior with the Mississippi River and Lake Vermilion.

The Grand Portage was broken up by nineteen *pauses,* or rests. Each voyageur, carrying roughly two hundred pounds, would make several trips back and forth between these rests.

Maple Pause, one of these now-overgrown ancient rests, was located in a sugarbush area about a mile west of the river. Travelers on the Grand Portage described its location as nearly opposite the highest falls—what paddlers now call Electric Ledge—a challenging riverwide drop where the current roars over tilted ledges of slate and into turbulent pools below. I could understand why travelers in birch-bark canoes worked to avoid the falls.

For kayakers, the only place to get safely down the falls was right of center on a tongue of water about as wide as the length of my boat. Paddle too far left and you encountered more rocks than water. Too far right, a churning hole would toss your boat around and spit it out like a toy.

Huddling in an eddy above the falls that first day, I watched each paddler drop over the edge and disappear. A log sticking out of the channel marked the spot where I needed to go. "Paddle like hell," I muttered as I windmilled toward the edge. I glanced to my right as I slipped down the chute. I saw a powerful vortex of black and foamy water, turning over and over on itself. "Paddle like hell," I chanted, making it upright to the bottom of the falls where grinning fellow paddlers clustered in a calm pool.

Often, I would make it down Electric Ledge, only to be flipped over by the waves. Struggling upside down in the surging water, I would pop out of my boat. I could feel the rocks underwater poke at my legs. I would hold on to my boat and paddle as I kicked over to the big eddy, working to keep from going downstream to more rocks and rapids. Electric Ledge became my tension point in the run.

Eventually, I learned to trust the power of water and use it to my advantage. I learned to stretch out low over the moving water with my paddle and lean on it. Using my knees, I would tilt my boat in the same direction. Head down on my shoulder, I pushed off the water. It was a commitment to something I didn't quite believe would work. I did it anyway. In a matter of seconds, I could feel the solid water pushing me back up. That quick movement became an automatic, necessary part of my whitewater paddling.

Sometimes my brace didn't work. The water at the bottom of Electric Ledge was too frothy to hold me up. Over I would go, my heart pounding. One of the goals in paddling whitewater is to stay in your boat; it's much safer than swimming. I knew how to roll; I had the technique down pat in calm water; I had taught others how to do it. But hanging upside down in murky water, knocked about by the current, I would bail out. I had to work to keep a level head and dismiss the panic in order to stay in my boat, set up my paddle, and sweep back to the surface.

At Electric Ledge I did my first combat roll—knocked over by a wave and then reaching up with my paddle to twist back to daylight. A photo in my office reminds me of these struggles: It shows a blue-sky summer day; I am sitting in my kayak in an eddy at the bottom of Electric Ledge, holding my paddle high in jubilation above the silver shining river.

. . .

Nowadays, my whitewater kayak lies in semiretirement in my backyard. Though I haven't paddled the river in years, I still enjoy it on foot. My friends and I have a fall tradition of hiking the St. Louis, then feasting on an extravagant potluck. We gather at a house in Thomson near the river, cars pulling in from the Twin Cities. Expectations of a relaxing day and good company season the air with high spirits.

Following the trail, sometimes hauling wide-eyed babies and tiny dogs, we make a chain of laughter and talk. After crossing Otter Creek near the old railroad bridge, we climb up along the south riverbank. We always pause at the first high rocky ridge, where we pick wintergreen to chew, admire the view, and wait for stragglers.

Looking down, I see the river turn eastward, making a broad bend that builds up to another set of rapids that churns under the swinging bridge in Jay Cooke State Park. The river has miles to go before it meets Lake Superior.

Watching the river flow, I miss riding low in the water, immersed in the fast-moving current, waves hitting my face, a knot of excitement in my stomach for the always unpredictable wildness ahead.

The river, of course, is oblivious to my nostalgia. My affection and regard for this river began on my first trip. It was here I learned to paddle well. I learned to trust the power of the water, for its current would work for me or against me. I made lifelong friends on this river, our adventures creating a common history. And as I paddled, my imagination and curiosity were sparked by stories of earlier travelers.

Sometimes, a day on the river would expand to fill a year with its intensity and richness. The river's wildness seemed to slow everything down, a counterpoint to the fast-moving current. Every time I pulled my boat out at Thomson Dam, I ended my passage into a space and time that seemed somehow set apart from the modern world.

KAYAKING THE WILD SHORE

Greg Breining

 THAT NIGHT I CRAWLED into my sleeping bag and saw water rising around my eyes. *Oh, God, don't let me dream about drowning.* But the next time I opened my eyes, I heard the voice of the white-throated sparrow.

I pushed off early and soon crossed over into U.S. waters and cleared Pigeon Point. I glided among the Susie Islands, the last islands of significant size or number I would encounter along the North Shore. The Susies were the end of one shore and the beginning of another: the archipelago of the Canadian shore gave way to the straight, singular shore that stretched to Duluth.

Past Grand Portage, a smattering of houses and mobile homes lined the shore. A near-mansion overlooked the lake from the bluff across the road. On some lots, the forest had been cleared for a lawn, where saplings were planted with geometric precision. Of course, that's what you do to some craggy, beautiful place: you make it over into a suburb.

Traffic roared by on U.S. 61, which ran within a couple of hundred feet of the lake. The presence of traffic took much of the apprehension out of travel. What could happen? I would swim to shore and climb to the road to hitchhike. I began to conceive of the unlikely story of a man who kayaks through the wilderness of Canada, only to drown as traffic speeds by a hundred yards away.

The rest of that day and the next, I continued west toward Grand

Marais, passing more cabins than I had believed existed along Superior. The view from the highway is misleading, because many properties are screened by trees. The vantage from the lake is different: I might as well have been paddling along a shoreline in a Twin Cities suburb. Spoiled by the wild, island-studded coast of Ontario, I was losing interest. What makes travel interesting is crossing gradients, whether gradients of topography, culture, or weather. I was plodding along a single contour, all the while thinking that the really interesting things were *up there,* on shore, while I was *out here,* as though closed off by a wall. Somehow, I had to make this shore more interesting.

So when I reached Grand Marais, I called for a ride and went home.

Highway 61 had done its job. Built during the 1920s, it transformed the quiet home of a few hundred Ojibwe Indians and Norwegian fishermen into a tourist destination. In the process, the road and the development that followed have diminished the very qualities that attracted people to the shore. Who was hurt? Some fishermen, some woodsmen, and a few snobs who can travel the wilder shores of the lake by boat. Who benefited? Millions of tourists who enjoy an undeniably pretty drive. Viewed in those terms, preservation is hopelessly elitist.

The die may have been cast with the construction of the road, but the crush of tourism and development is more recent. I remember a distinctly wilder place, even thirty years ago as I searched the hills for trout streams. I recall driving into Tofte one day to ask directions at a gas station. For all I could tell, the gas station *was* town, and its entire population a grease-covered kid who laconically pointed me up the Sawbill Trail as flies buzzed around the station. A comparison with Appalachia was not out of line. What is Tofte like today? Holiday Stationstore, Holiday Inn Express (for people in a hurry), banks, shops, restaurants, Bluefin Bay resort, townhouses, condos. And Tofte is not the only community spawning this kind of development. It is happening from Duluth to Hovland. Meanwhile, up to 70 percent of the septic systems along the shore are failing.

And the highway? It has been widened and straightened. Multimillion-dollar tunnels have replaced the precarious cliffside curves. The improvements have worked so well that now highway engineers use computer models to determine how to make drivers go slower.

I wanted to find traces of the North Shore I had known years ago. I owed it to myself and to the shore. Of the three transcendent moments I have experienced in my life, one occurred here, in the canyon of the Kadunce River. While fishing, I had wandered up the small stream until I climbed over a waterfall and found myself in a narrow canyon. Mosses and ferns spilled down from the rocks, and light drifted in like snow. At that moment, it seemed that nothing at all existed but the rock, the looming shadow, and the strangely important rush of water.

I decided to start my exploration in Duluth. Were San Francisco not many times larger and already in possession of the name, Duluth might be known as the City by the Bay. Tucked snugly in the hillside at the west end of the lake, it is one of my favorite cities. I had lived there for two years when I worked on the city newspaper. The job put me in touch with the gritty, industrial side of town, a nexus of transportation. Grain trucks farted down the long hills to the lakeshore. Ore trains rumbled along the hillside to loading docks in the West End. The deep foghorns of freighters and ore boats cleared a path from the harbor to the open lake.

All things met at the harbor. Twenty years ago Canal Park was a grungy agglomeration of factories, warehouses, and workingmen's bars. Today, the warehouses have been refurbished with shops, apartments, and studios. The streets are covered with pavers, and the sidewalks are landscaped with young trees.

I was meeting environmentalist Janet Green in a sandwich shop in the basement of the DeWitt-Seitz Marketplace. We had never met in person, and she surprised me with her cherubic appearance. She had a soft, round face, bifocals, white hair, and pale blue eyes. She had just come from the demolition of the old Flame Restaurant, future site of the Great Lakes Aquarium, a museum of ecology and natural history.

Green and her husband, John, attended graduate school at Harvard. Forty years ago he took a job as professor of geology at the University of Minnesota–Duluth. Compared to the Maine coast, where Green had sailed with her family, the North Shore was a disappointment. On Penobscot Bay there were islands to explore; here, just the unrelenting shoreline. "That's why I've become a real landlubber," she said. "There's a lot more to explore on the shore."

Bird-watching became her means for exploring the North Shore. Over time, she wrote several books on birds in Minnesota. She served as president of the local Audubon chapter and sat on many conservation committees and task forces, including, most recently, the Minnesota Forest Resources Council, a board set up through state government to mediate forest issues on public land. "It's a form of arm wrestling," she said. "I felt that if you were interested in nature, you should be interested in conserving nature."

Development along the shore fragments the forest with roads, buildings, and clearings. The greater danger, Green said, is the transformation of communities in ways that, taken as a whole, no one wants. Money appears, land prices soar. Locals can't afford to live in their own communities. "It's a struggle for a community such as Grand Marais to maintain its identity," she said, especially when the habit of independence-minded locals is to let things go as they might and to allow everyone as much freedom as possible. The result is the same kind of strip development you might see in any American suburb.

The North Shore highway, she said, "is no longer your scenic highway; it's just a place to go fast to get to where you want to go. It brings a type of person who doesn't care."

Driving the so-called scenic highway from Duluth to Two Harbors, I passed new houses, gift shops, and wide lawns. There were a few touches of the old North Shore, such as the cluster of fish shops at Knife River, with smoked whitefish and lake trout. I spent the night at Tettegouche, largest state park along the Minnesota shore. Early the next morning, I launched my kayak in the estuary of the Baptism River. I dawdled in the rugged gorge and then powered over the shallow gravel bar at the river mouth and paddled into the lake.

During the last several years, kayakers have worked with the Department of Natural Resources to develop a "water trail" along the North Shore, a series of closely spaced sites allowing paddlers to travel and camp without trespassing. To date, the trail runs about forty miles from Two Harbors to the Caribou River. Some of that reach suffers the same shortcomings I had experienced in paddling down from Grand Portage: a straight shoreline, the constant whir of traffic, and the unrelenting parade of homes. But some sites along the trail are stunning, such as the long, winding estuary of the Gooseberry River, and the lighthouse atop the cliffs at Split Rock, easily the most imposing and beautiful lighthouse on the lake. I hoped to see another interesting stretch today.

The shore had a hint of Canada, with rugged rocks and cliffs. Paddling southwest, I saw a young boy playing among the boulders along shore. Dressed in a T-shirt and jeans, he might have been me more than thirty years ago. I quickly reached the Palisades, which rise abruptly from the lake some two hundred feet. I paddled through a little sea arch. Swallows swooshed through the opening and scattered to the sky.

I doubled back toward the Baptism River and followed massive Shovel Point far into the lake. Looking up the shore, I saw a steady procession of headlands, long fingers that fell in gradations from green to gray and faded into the distance. As I paddled, I passed points and cliffs riddled with small caves and arches, including one opening that had the organic shape of a ventricle. I could hear the buzz of traffic. But unlike the stretch near Grand Marais, with its gradual shore open to the highway, the cliffs here were visible only from the lake. At the very least, by being out here, I was seeing something I otherwise could not.

The mouth of Kennedy Brook tumbled twenty feet from a cliff, splattered on the beach and seeped through the gravel several yards to the lake. As I rested, I spotted a peregrine falcon as it flew from a cliffside nest, its location marked by white streaks of excrement on the rock. It landed in a nearby tree as a second peregrine soared overhead. Peregrines vanished from the North Shore—indeed, from the entire Midwest—during the

1960s and '70s, victims of DDT contamination. Since the pesticide was banned and peregrines were reintroduced, they have returned to nest in the lofty crags along the lake. The peregrine in the tree scolded me with the sound of a coarse file over hard steel.

Finally I heard the roar of a waterfall and cleared a point to see the Manitou River spill thirty feet over a cliff, as though it poured directly from the rock. The falls was a stunning sight, but as if to gild the lily, the current flowed into Superior in the embrace of a sea arch. I paddled to within casting distance of the arch and pulled out my fly rod. It was a flawless scene. The falls, the arch, deep water the color of emerald. A silver, blue, and white streamer hit the water. Wouldn't it be perfect, I thought, if a big fish hit right here. In that instant I saw a dark shape and a flash of silver. It hit the fly and ran deep. For fifteen minutes I battled a fish I could not see. I paddled with one hand and held the rod with the other until I was able to land on a patch of gravel among the cliffs. In another ten minutes I was able to bring the fish close and scoop it onto the gravel. Twenty-six inches by the measure of my outstretched fingers, the fish was silver and spotted, bullish across the shoulders. Anadromous trout are hard to distinguish. One by one I eliminated species: not a Pacific salmon, not a steelhead, probably not an Atlantic salmon. I finally settled on brown trout. I had no way to eat the fish or to keep it, so I unhooked it and cradled it in the water at my feet until it swam into the deep shadows.

I wish I could say I packed up my rod and paddled back to the car in a state of complete contentment. But I didn't. William Blake may as well have been talking about fishing when he wrote, "You never know what is enough unless you know what is more than enough." I beat the water for another half hour until I paddled up the last few feet of river, then spun and paddled through the arch on my way back to the Baptism.

Standing at the bridge over the Devil Track River, just off the Gunflint Trail, I watched the amber water dance amid the boulders and shadows as it raced downstream. The rushing water generated feelings of dread and anxiety, recollections of kayaks flying over impossible falls, surging current flushing through narrow canyons, an unrunnable waterfall waiting at the narrow waist of the gorge. It had been the first time, as far as I knew, that anyone had paddled so deep into the canyon. It had been the most frightening river I had ever paddled, and I never paddled it again.

Today I was equipped not with a kayak but with a fly rod, a much better choice if you're alone and forty-something and out of practice. The water was low. I enjoyed the pools of water and light, shadows and brightness, the lively green of trees and the sparkling sun. I stumbled among the slick rocks, looking for pockets of calm in the river's swift descent. To a fish, depth is relative; in this case, a pool with two feet of water was more than enough. Brookies flashed at the drifting fly. In such a small stream, ten-inch trout seemed large. There is no fight to such a little fish, just the wild vibration of fright. The thrill is coaxing them from their hiding places, the surprise of seeing such a tiny stream, with such transparence, offering up something live.

I decided to drive down to George Crosby Manitou State Park. It was a backpacking park: no cars, no roads beyond the parking lot. I grabbed the rod, fishing vest, some water and, well into the afternoon, set out on Middle Trail, through a grove of mature birch and maple, toward the Manitou River.

Like the Devil Track, the Manitou was named for spirits. Unlike the Devil Track—a name transmogrified from *Manido bimadagakowini zibi*, "Spirits' walking place on the ice river"—the Manitou retained the simple brilliance of the wonderfully elastic Ojibwe word for an array of qualities: spirit, mystery, the unseen nature of existence. Indeed, the Manitou had always seemed to me a magical place, of white water and black rock, the colors of basalt and rapids, of birch bark and the night sky.

The water was low, and I jumped from rock to rock, pool to pool, picking pockets for brook trout. The fish were few, and they were small. As I reached the entrance to a deep gorge, I decided that while this may not be the best trout fishing in the world, it may well be the most picturesque. For that reason alone it may be the best.

The gorge became more constricted, and the canyon walls grew steeper. Soon I gave up fishing and began scaling a bluff to find easier walking. Picking my way across talus and the raw soil of a recent rock slide, I realized I was a good one hundred feet above the river on a loose slope. What was I doing scrambling around like a mountain goat? Then I thought of spending the night with a broken leg. I have a morbid fear of struggling out of a place at night. This hike suddenly seemed far riskier than what I had been doing out on the lake in a sea kayak. When I finally eased myself back down toward the river and reached the trail, I recognized that one measure of wilderness is its effect on the heart. At least this much wildness remained along the North Shore: the single moment of panic in the breast. It is a place where, if you look, you can be lost and alone.

DOWN AT MILLER CREEK

Shawn Perich

 MILLER CREEK DOESN'T LOOK LIKE MUCH where it runs through the concrete culvert beneath Anderson Road. Spring, when the stream runs strong and boisterous, is about the only season when you might notice it. In summer a modest brook flows shaded and cool beneath a tangled alder canopy, hidden from passing traffic.

The summer morning air was still chilly enough for a light jacket when we'd pedal our bikes the mile or so to Miller's (as we called it). Our fishing rods were taped to the crossbars. By the time we'd hidden our bikes in the dew-wet grass along Anderson Road, we were soaked from the knees down. It didn't matter, because we'd soon be splashing and squishing along the creek. We fished so often during the summer that our sneakers never really dried out anyway. Our quarry was brook trout—tiny, speckled jewels that inhabit the creeks coursing through Duluth. Although we pursued them with the sort of relentless zeal possessed only by twelve-year-old boys, there seemed to be an endless supply. At our house, fresh trout were frequently on the menu.

Miller Creek was a favorite among our fishing repertoire of neighborhood brooks and ponds. The creek belonged to kids. The muddy paths along the banks were worn deep by generations of trout-fishing delinquents. My grandfather had swum and fished in this creek shortly after the turn of the century. He used to tell me how he and his friends had carried buckets of Miller Creek brookies to the Twin Ponds along Duluth's Skyline Drive. Grandpa said that several years later a neighborhood fisherman discovered the Twin Ponds trout, which by then were trophy-sized. The fisherman kept his discovery to himself, covertly fishing in predawn darkness. Eventually, word got out. It always does.

We never caught trophies, but we always caught trout. Downstream from Anderson Road were several pools where hungry but cautious brookies lurked. In a couple of places, you could sneak up to large rocks, peek over them, and see the trout swimming below. Some kids tried to catch these trout in their hands, but we always used a hook and line—it was more effective.

The best place to fish was a foaming, well-oxygenated pool where the creek tumbled over a five-foot waterfall. Quite often we'd see trout leaping like tiny salmon as they attempted to scale the falls.

In August the creek's water no longer felt cool to the touch. Fishing was difficult, because the sluggish trout were struggling to survive in the warm water. The cool, dark culvert beneath Anderson Road drew the heat-stressed brookies like a magnet and became a fishing hot spot. We spent hours wading through the culvert, casting with short, ultralight fishing rods.

Kids who get wet and muddy intuitively understand how nature works. Despite their apparent abundance, we knew that Miller Creek's brook trout had a tough go of it. And we knew why. Brook trout don't ask for much other than springs and shady banks to provide a constant flow of cool water, but some folks didn't see the bogs and brambles along Miller Creek the way we did. We saw a wondrous, wild world populated with trout and frogs and snowshoe hares. They saw parking lots.

As I was growing up, progress came to the Miller Creek watershed. A new airport was built up on the headwater springs, and a nearby forest was clear-cut for an industrial park. Farther downstream, tributary creeks were ditched and the meandering creek was channelized to accommodate roads and suburban growth. Retail blight spread like fungus along the stream.

Upstream from Anderson Road today, shopping malls cover places where twenty years ago you could hear grouse drum. Instead of cool water from alder swamps, Miller Creek now receives the polluted gutter wash from parking lots.

Recently, developers built a retail store on a site that has the creek's last cool springs, and they're planning yet another shopping mall expansion. Fish biologists fear habitat loss to development has reached a critical mass that could be the brookies' coup de grâce. Duluth's zoning requirements are not sufficient to protect the trout.

It's hard for a trout angler to watch a stream die. It's especially hard when those waters were such an important—make that formative—part of your life. Below Anderson Road, the creek will still tumble through backyard brambles, but without brook trout it will be just a lifeless, feral ditch. Future generations of kids in my old neighborhood will be denied the simple adventure of hopping on their bikes and going fishing. I suspect they'll grow up to be very different from me.

Embracing Winter

BOUNDARY WATERS WILDERNESS: JANUARY

Laurie Allmann

"I THINK I SAW A WOLF LAST NIGHT." I crack a salted peanut, drop the shells into an ashtray. Peanuts and coffee are the closest thing to breakfast that Gladys, owner of this small roadside northern Minnesota bar, has to offer. Gladys nods in response. It's mostly wolves around here, she says, and where you find wolves you won't find many coyotes. She goes into a back room and comes out with a wildlife book. She opens it to a page that compares the two, sets the book in front of me, tops off my coffee. Coyotes, according to the text, are a quarter to half the size of wolves; their ears are larger relative to their body size, their noses are more pointed, and they tend to carry their tails curled downward as they run. I look up. "It was broad across the chest. Big. Held its tail high." Gladys nods again. Smooths the page. Says she likes to look at the book when things are slow. The pages of the book are worn soft as cloth.

Gladys grows distant, caught in her own thoughts as she turns to put the book back in its place. Left alone, I return to the night before, to the white oval of a frozen lake illuminated by refracted starlight. It is plenty bright enough to make my way. My snowshoes break the crust of snow into jagged plates, the kind of crust that will shred the shins of a moose, ring its tracks with blood. A pine-hushed arctic wind pours out of the Quetico. Beneath the snow, the lake ice makes sounds: booms, groans. Sometimes a high-pitched keening like the singing of whales. When I pause, my breath rises in a vapor cloud that stiffens my eyebrows with frost.

On satellite photographs of North America taken at night, in which all the city lights shine like constellations, this is one of the blessed black spaces. Sprawled in the darkness before me are millions of acres of wild country, from the Boundary Waters Canoe Area Wilderness on into Canada's Quetico Provincial Park. Red and white pine of the temperate forests are joined at this latitude by upland spruce, balsam fir, and jack pine in the first glimmers of the great boreal forest that will begin in earnest to the north.

Thousands of lakes lie here in the beds made for them in the Canadian Shield's bedrock by the scouring of the last ice age. The shape of each body of water is a singular record of yielding. Long, thin lakes follow fault lines of the rock and lie in parallel valleys where glaciers raked out the ancient muds of the Rove Formation from between stronger blades of diabase. Lakes of wandering shores, irregular as Rorschach blots, fill depressions where glacial ice encountered instead more uniformly resistant rock such as gabbro and granite.

Low black hills surround the pool of light that is this lake. In silhouette, a monarch white pine lifts its arms up above the other trees, both gangly and graceful, the tall child in the school photograph. I pick out the slight saddle in the horizon that hints of a stream-carved passage to another lake. In spring, summer, or fall, it is a place I would paddle toward in a canoe, where I would find a narrow trail, the portage. Along it would be lady's slipper orchids, twinflowers, bluebead lilies. A caution would ring in my thoughts as I crossed over patches of bare bedrock with the canoe on my shoulders: *Watch for the nighthawk cryptic on her eggs, feathers mottled gray like the rock, who would not move even as your boot descended upon her.* None of it matters now. Not the turn of the paddle blade on the recovery stroke to slice without resistance through the air, not the swing of the wind toward the east that would give warning of a wave-kicking squall, or the distance kept to give a loon peace. These are all useless on this winter night, the foreign coins left over from a trip to another season.

. . .

I seek out Aldebaran in the sky overhead, the eye-star of Taurus grown big and red with old age. In the clarity of the bone-dry atmosphere, the stars seem to have drawn nearer to earth: descended, perhaps, to peer at the peerless irony of humans who would give the name "canoe area wilderness" to a land that more than half the year is locked in ice.

This border lakes landscape is closer to the North Pole than to the equator. Its climate is for the most part untempered by the Great Lakes, and zero is a height that winter temperatures often observe only at a distance. But more than cold, the region would better be thought of as *lean* compared to lands at more southerly latitudes. Begun with little till atop bedrock, the soils have had less time to develop since the departure of glacial ice, and have been slow to build under the conifer-dominated forest that came to establish here. Plants experience essentially drought conditions while surface waters are frozen from late September through April. The lakes are clear and beautiful but low in fertility. And the oblique angle of the sun's rays means a lessening of energy coming into the natural system. From these finite accounts must life be drawn.

Accordingly, the more cold-tolerant and less energy-demanding conifers are favored over deciduous trees. Many species of wildlife enter a period of dormancy for part of the year. Those that can—including 80 percent of the summer population of breeding birds—migrate during the months when there is a decline in availability of their traditional foods, such as fish or insects.

What hearts, I wonder, can the snowy owl hear beating on this mid-January night? It would be quiet compared to the cacophony of the growing season. There would be those of moose, lynx, woodpeckers, beaver, and otter, of shrews and voles in their snow tunnels, and fish making slow turns beneath the lake ice. There might even be, I realize, some hearts newly emerged into the world.

I smile to think how good are the odds that I share the passing minute with a black bear somewhere nearby in her den giving birth to cubs. She will be curled into a sandy bank overlooking a cedar swamp, or snugged up against a fan of roots in a hollow she has dug at the base of a downed tree. The calluses on the pads of her feet will have begun to wear off during her dormancy, revealing smooth new skin beneath. She will be smaller, and will likely have one or two rather than the three to five cubs of the sows fattened on the blackberries and acorns of richer habitats to the south. But the mature virgin forests that comprise half of the wilderness area will have provided enough dogwood, beetles, blueberries, and wild sarsaparilla to sustain her, just as they have provided the boreal owl with a nesting cavity in an old aspen, and the pine marten with woody debris on the forest floor where it may rest under the snow and hunt its rodent prey. These animals are among the living, breathing products of what some would call an unproductive forest.

I have stood still too long. The cold presses down like a weight. Not prepared to spend the night, I flip first one, then the other snowshoe around until I am headed back toward where I began. The trail of shallow craters made by my snowshoes has begun to drift in with the fine snow that skates across the lake's wind-packed surface.

The time would have been somewhere past midnight when I made my way out. The wolf emerged from a curtain of trees, crossing over a narrow road that dead-ends into the wilderness. It looked back—once—over its shoulder to the place where I stood. Then it slipped again into forest. Its tracks already felt cold to the touch when I knelt beside them, only seconds after the wolf had left them. Maybe they had never been warm.

I leave a stack of quarters on the pine planks of the table for Gladys. Downing the last swallow of coffee, I step outside into a morning just about bright enough to shatter an eye. A raven atop a spruce lets loose with a string of quorks, trills, yells, knocks, pops, and bells. I nod in agreement with whatever it meant to say.

BRITTLE BEAUTY

Rick Naymark

 ABOUT 10 A.M., RIGHT ON SCHEDULE, a steel gray Suburban drove up to the front door of the Gunflint Lodge. The driver, a jolly man bundled in a puffy down jacket, hopped onto the frozen, snowy porch and hurried inside.

Shaking off the cold, he welcomed us to our cross-country skiing adventure along the Banadad, a nineteen-mile backcountry trail that began a few miles from the lodge door on the edge of the Boundary Waters Canoe Area Wilderness.

My longtime friends Linda, Lois, Earl, and Dave and I were dressed in cross-country ski clothes, our skis waxed and ready, sitting on duffle bags stuffed with overnight gear. We were excited but also wary, given that the outside temperature had plunged to thirty below zero.

The driver assured us we'd be warm enough on the trail and in the small, canvas-walled hut called a yurt, where we'd be spending the night. Then he loaded our gear, and we piled in. He drove us along a short stretch from the lodge to the Gunflint Trail road, turned left, and went another mile to the ski trailhead.

The driver threw the Suburban into park, jumped out, and helped us step down onto the snow-packed road. The subzero snow under our boots squeaked like Styrofoam.

"Have fun," he said. "I'll deliver your sleeping gear to the yurt. It will be waiting for you. We'll have some hot tea ready too."

With that, he climbed back in, threw it into gear, and drove off, his tires crunching loudly and his engine growling.

Suddenly, everything was perfectly still. The isolation of the near-wilderness loomed. We stood with our skis in the frozen silence, eight miles from our next shelter. Before us stretched a long, straight trail across the indifferent terrain of northeastern Minnesota. We began to understand why this trail had been named Banadad, Ojibwe for *lost*.

We soon realized the air was too cold for us to stand and ponder our situation. Shaking ourselves from our momentary shock, we pulled on our backpacks, latched on our skis, adjusted our pole straps, and tentatively began to ski. Before long, we all found our pace and began to enjoy the rhythmic, almost hypnotic stride that would take us along the tracked trail.

Our plan was to ski at a steady but not fast tempo. We wanted to generate enough heat to avoid frostbite, but not so much as to begin sweating. Sweat increases the penetration of the cold. We knew that if we kept moving, the temperature would be tolerable.

In fact, it was more than tolerable. It was magical. At minus thirty, the air is condensed. Senses seem heightened. Sounds amplify and carry farther than normal. A crystalline halo forms on the horizon, and the brittle sun becomes a pale yellow.

Amid this beauty, awareness of risk made us both careful and present in the moment. After all, we were at the very northern tip of our very northern state, a stone's throw from Canada, on one of the coldest days, in the depth of winter, when bitter nights are long and the wind can suddenly pick up and shear you like frozen sandpaper. In arctic temperatures, any problem must be remedied immediately, because trouble begets trouble. If your fingers or toes grow numb, you cannot ignore them. It's imperative never to be alone, because if you are rendered helpless by an accident, you could freeze to death.

The Banadad trail is mostly flat, bordered by frozen marshes and occasional stands of birch and pine. Except for the sounds of our labored breathing and the scrunch of our skis, it was absolutely quiet.

The combination of beauty and bitter cold seemed to mesmerize us. We kept together, but stayed silent as though in some state of reverie.

At a moment of rest some two hours into the trek, Linda pulled out brownies from her backpack. They were hard as frozen candy bars. We tried to chew them, but our jaws were stiff from the cold.

All afternoon the sun hung near the horizon. Its meek light offered little warmth. In all directions we saw a broad blanket of snow, with only a faint whisper of dried grasses in marshy places and the arc of an occasional bird darting from one cedar to another.

In this solitude, aware of our dependence on one another, we felt a strong bond—unspoken, but clear as the air.

In late afternoon we arrived at a bend in the trail and saw two yurts just off to the left. The structures, patterned after shelters used by nomadic Mongolians, were constructed of white canvas stretched over a wooden frame shaped like half a melon. Their rotund shape makes them resilient to heavy snow and winds, and they retain heat with some efficiency.

The driver—also the yurt keeper—opened the door of one yurt and greeted us. He had tea waiting, and our luggage sat neatly in the center of the wooden platform floor. He went outside and returned with an armful of split logs, which he tossed onto the coals of a wood stove. The indoor temperature soon climbed to an acceptable fifty degrees.

Bunk beds lined the sides of our lodging. We set out our sleeping bags, pulled off our trail clothing and ski boots, and dressed in dry, warm flannel and down. It was only four o'clock, but the sky was already turning a deep, dark blue as the last weak rays of winter sun seemed to evaporate.

The yurt keeper had gone to the other yurt, about fifty feet away. When he came back, he invited us to have dinner with the family staying there. As we sat down and introduced ourselves to the family—a mother, father, and two grown sons from London—the yurt keeper began preparing a Mongolian feast.

Around a large, metal pot of boiling chicken broth in the center of a picnic table, he laid out platters of raw meats and vegetables. The idea was for each of us to load up the tines of a long fork with raw food and submerge it into the cauldron, called a firepot. In a few minutes, the freshly cooked morsels could be deposited on a bed of rice and dinner would be ready, Mongolian fondue style.

"Very delightful," said Victoria, the mother. "Similar to that feast we had while crossing Iceland, wouldn't you say, Rex?" Her husband nodded.

"Have you had Mongolian before?" Victoria asked me.

I shook my head. "We did buy a fondue pot at a garage sale, but we used it to melt wax for dipping pine cones."

"Pine cones?" Victoria asked, startled.

"Yes," I said. "You dip them in wax and then sprinkle glitter on them. They make great Christmas gifts as fire starters."

She gave a smile, cold as the outdoor air. "How clever," she said. "I suppose that's what you call American ingenuity."

One son, Reginald, tried to resuscitate this impromptu social event. "I say, do you get around much, doing things like this trek?"

I had to think a minute. "Well, we stick pretty much to home." How could I impress Reginald? I thought I'd tell him about our Aquatennial celebration. "In the summer we make rafts out of milk cartons and race them. And we fill a swimming pool with Jell-O. I think we hold the world record for Jell-O."

Reginald turned to his brother and winked. Then he addressed me. "We've rafted the Amazon River. And we've been to tremendous restaurants in Paris and Rome. I think I did have Jell-O once. I was in a Nairobi hospital, recovering from a tusk wound from a wild elephant during a horrific safari."

Thus went the dinner conversation. As soon as we could, we excused ourselves and went back to our own yurt.

One last chore remained—to use the outhouse. A bone-chilling outhouse encourages one to be efficient. That accomplished, I darted into our yurt, crawled into my sleeping bag, and stared at the ceiling, a scant foot above my nose. Were we really in a yurt, in the middle of nowhere? Or was this a dream? Nothing more than a layer of canvas separated us from air more than sixty degrees colder than a refrigerator.

. . .

In the night I awoke to the wailing and hooting of wolves. I quietly pulled on some clothes and a jacket, edged off the bunk, stepped into my boots, and tiptoed outside.

I was awestruck. A canopy of brittle, blinking stars arched above the dark silhouettes of trees. The air was still and cold—so cold that I felt frozen in time, as if I were trapped in amber like an ancient insect that is worth nothing except for the beauty that surrounds it.

Indeed, for this night, we were trapped—at bay in beautiful and harsh country, where the elements were so crystal clear that we could glimpse the sheer beauty of the universe.

I have not been on a safari or eaten in the best restaurants of the world. Yet this night in northern Minnesota, I was at the center of the universe, and no other beauty could rival what was before me—the stars, the howling wolves, the muffled snores of my companions, the crackling logs in the stove, the utter and precious stillness and darkness. I was filled with a deep sense of peace.

This gift of perspective awaits any adventurer, especially one willing to ski the Banadad—the lost—trail. In being lost to civilization for even a short time, we five trekkers found much strength, joy, and humility to bind us together in this memory for a lifetime.

LAKE SUPERIOR, WINTER DAWN

Gustave Axelson

"COME, LET'S GO DOWN TO THE LAKE to see the sunrise."

The words wake me from contented early-morning slumber. Opening my eyes just slightly, I see that predawn light has cast silhouettes of the dresser and chair, strewn with winter clothing, on the bedroom wall.

"Come on, I've got some coffee brewed. If we leave now we can still catch it." This time the words are accompanied by the frosty fog of the speaker's breath. That tells me it's cold in the cabin. Damn cold. And, no doubt, colder still outside.

The speaker is my friend Ruurd, who along with his wife has joined my wife and me for a weekend getaway. The lake Ruurd speaks of is mighty Superior, notorious for frigid waters even in July. In December it lashes out with a frozen arsenal of snow, ice, and gales that penetrate even the thickest pair of long johns. The day before, with the sun at full mast, I went down to the lake and came back with my nose hairs frozen and my eyelids nearly sealed by frosted lashes.

"Well, you can stay here and sleep if you want, but I'm not going to miss the sunrise," Ruurd whispers with just a hint of annoyance in his throaty Dutch accent.

I'm now awake enough to fully appreciate how warm and snug I am under my blankets, my wife's head buried in my shoulder. She yawns, rolls over on her side, and nestles her head deep into her pillow for a few more hours of sleep.

In one hurried motion, I pull back the covers and leap out of bed. My bare feet hit the wooden floor with a resounding slap and report back that the cabin is indeed quite cold.

Ruurd seems pleased with my decision. "There you go," he says. "You won't be sorry. Now get dressed, let's get going, we don't have much time."

Moments later, I'm swishing down a wooded ridge to the lakeshore. I don't really remember getting dressed, or stepping into my cross-country skis. I do remember the thermometer's reading on a tree outside the cabin—minus twenty degrees.

At this point, all I'm aware of is the stinging numbness of my cheeks and nose. With a stiff arctic wind, the lake warns me to turn back. Cold air fills my lungs, and they protest with a choking cough. I momentarily stop to lean against a tree and regain my breath.

"What's wrong? Are you all right?" Ruurd yells from fifty yards ahead. "Let's go. We're almost there."

The last stretch down the ridge drops nearly two hundred feet. It requires little effort from me, other than keeping my skis in Ruurd's tracks. But the brisk pace of coasting downhill amplifies the wind chill. My teeth are chattering as I reach the bottom of the ridge. Ruurd mentioned none of this when he asked me to go see the sunrise. Then, I find out what else he failed to tell me.

He didn't say anything about the magnificent diamond sculptures the lake carves along its shore. Each sharp point of rock is perfectly rounded by several inches of ice. Shafts of ice the diameter of a baseball bat shoot down from the rocks, forming spectacular icicles.

He didn't mention the ice-glazed birch trees that face Superior, with their thin branches bowed by heaps of snow. Chickadees and nuthatches and downy woodpeckers flit among the trees as they carry on their morning business. I'm sure they've something to say, but their chatter is muted by the relentless crashing of the lake's waves.

Ruurd never said a word about the giant, jagged boulders of ice floating in the lake. The bergs collide with a brittle crack each time a new wave readjusts them. Above all, he is guilty of not telling me about the sun's lakeside magic—the rays of glorious rose and orange and blazing gold.

The rays refract through the ice on the trees and rocks, filling my eyes with brilliant, piercing white sparkles and glints.

"Care for some coffee?" Ruurd offers. "I made it with steamed milk and chocolate, just like we used to do in Holland."

I take off my gloves so my chilled hands can feel the toasty steel thermos; the steam rising from its mouth looks as inviting as a roaring fire. I hold the thermos close to my face for a moment to thaw my cheeks before taking a swig and feeling the coffee's pleasant burn roll down my throat.

"Is it too strong?" he asks.

It is on the bitter side, despite its milky shade of brown. But it's also hot. And my teeth are no longer chattering.

"No, it's perfect," I say.

We speak in hushed tones. Amid this crystalline palace, it almost seems inappropriate to speak at all. I take a second sip of coffee, then remove my hat and untie my scarf. The stiff wind blowing off the lake has mellowed into a gentle breeze.

Ruurd points out the tracks of a timber wolf that wind along the tree line on the shore. A former wildlife preserve director, he knows about the north woods and its inhabitants.

"You see how wide the wolf's paws are, how his tracks only depress a few millimeters into the snow? Their paws are designed to give them excellent flotation," he says. I nod in agreement, though I don't think he noticed.

"Now you see these deer tracks? Look how their hooves sink so deep. They don't have a chance, struggling through the snow while wolves run on top of it."

He pauses to stare out at the lake for a moment.

"Then again, deer don't really belong this far north. This is supposed to be caribou country."

I listen to Ruurd's story about the hardships of timber wolves and deer in winter. Then our conversation wanders to other topics—the canoe trips we hope to take this summer, what a great life it would be to work as a sailor on a Lake Superior freighter ship, how we met our wives.

As the talk dwindles, I notice the coffee thermos is empty and I have taken off my jacket and balled it up under my head as a pillow. I'm reclining on the icy rocks just as if I were at home on the couch, watching football on a Sunday afternoon. The only chill I feel is at my fingertips, wrapped around the thermos that is now filling with falling snow.

"Well, we better get going," Ruurd sighs. "The girls will be up soon." My jacket and hat, gloves and scarf, feel heavy now. The sun has been sucked into the gray, snowy clouds that have moved over the lake. I push on my pole to start the ski back to the cabin, and a gust of wind sneaks down my collar to send a shiver down my back. A few swishes of my skis, and my cheeks are numb again.

RIVERING ON THE ONION

Stephen Regenold

MAXWELL FROST WAS NOT A SKIER. Yet there he was side-stepping down a frozen waterfall, ski edges slipping on ice under thin snow. Below him was an open pool of black water.

"I told you, I'm a snowboarder, man," Frost said, smiling, poking a ski pole for balance on a shelf of exposed stone.

Wind raked the snow at Frost's feet. Gear jangled on the climbing harness around his waist.

"Point the skis and go!" I yelled from above.

We were halfway down the Onion River, a twisting gorge of red rhyolite stóne and falling water that snakes from the Sawtooth Mountains to Lake Superior. It was mid-February, late afternoon on a Friday, and a few degrees below zero. Frost, five other skiers, and I had set out early that morning to explore the icefalls and deep ravines of the North Shore on a guided trip led by the Recreational Sports Outdoor Program at the University of Minnesota–Duluth. I'd been invited by outdoor program directors Tim Bates and Pat Kohlin to ski with Frost, a twenty-five-year-old art-education student, and three of his classmates.

Like many rivers in the region, the Onion is all but inaccessible for much of the year, a canyon of torrential whitewater funneling through cliffs toward Lake Superior. But under winter's grip, the Onion morphs to a navigable track of snow and ice, rushing water clamped under thick ice sheets that crack and buckle like dry earth.

Rivering, as locals call it—also known as *rivereering* or simply river skiing—is a hybrid sport involving skis or snowshoes, ropes, climbing equipment, and some canyoneering savvy. Rivering on the Onion is a bipolar experience, starting with a quiet ski through winter woods in the flat and forested upper reaches of the river and ending with a dramatic plunge toward Lake Superior.

Our trip on the Onion began at the Oberg Mountain trailhead, where a cornice-topped outhouse sat watch over a deserted parking lot. There were two cars but no people in sight as we geared up.

"We'll head to the river on this trail," said Bates, pointing with a pole into the woods.

We skied among tight trees, kicking and poling, trying to maintain direction on an untracked trail. Birds scattered from branches as we came through. Skis scraped along. Otherwise, there was no sound.

I was bundled four layers deep—polypropylene long underwear, wool sweater and pants, fleece jacket, all wrapped in a Gore-Tex shell. Air was sharp on the inhale, my nose tight, frozen inside to out.

I was breaking trail in the lead, kick-stride-glide, kick-stride-glide, coasting some even in deep fluff. "That should go downhill to the river," Bates yelled ahead to me, referring to a turn in the path. Then, the woods opened up. There was a final drop to a rocky bank. I pushed off and slid, tracks cutting clean through a V of birch, deep snow knocking shins until I slowed at the far bank on the creek.

"Which way is downriver?" one of the students asked from behind.

The Onion cut left and right, a winding boulevard of white bordered with soil banks and shaggy roots. The pinprick footprints of little birds dashed clean snow at my ski tips. Then we approached our first signifi-cant drop in elevation.

"Time for the descent!" Bates said.

"Here it goes," Frost yelled, hopping to turn his skis downhill. He crouched like a monkey, poles limp, gloves nearly dragging in the snow. But he cut a line in the snow nice and easy, then stopped—standing up-right beside the base of a cliff.

"Nailed it!" he yelled. We were two-thirds of the way into our three-mile journey down the Onion. The final mile dropped fast—cutting south to lose five hundred feet of elevation in a plunge. Rocks lining the river's edge were the first sign of the steep section. The compass needle spun to aim at my chest, and as I headed downhill and to the south, the sky ahead opened strangely where before it had been choked with trees.

"Watch this section," Bates yelled back to the group. "The ice is getting thin." We had reached the mouth of a small ravine, rock walls towering and frail.

Upriver the Onion had been frozen thick and safe. But with the steeper pitch, water pinched between cliffs and moved quickly, so ice had trouble firming up. I skied second in line, hugging the rock wall on the right bank. Water bubbled and swirled through a dark window of thin ice midstream.

Most North Shore rivers run low in the winter, with knee-deep water flowing under ice. Some are dry or frozen clear through. But fast water and deep pools on rivers like the Onion pose serious risk of hypothermia and drowning for those unlucky enough to fall through. Bates carried a full extra set of clothes in a pack, plus fresh socks and boots for wet feet. "Just in case," he said. Frost had climbing gear in his pack. We used ice screw anchors and ropes on steep river sections where skis couldn't cut it.

"Come through one at a time," Bates shouted upriver after I emerged out of the rock ravine.

A quarter mile from the end at Lake Superior, where the waterway drops eighty feet in two rolling falls, our group paused to talk strategy. The face below—hard snow over rocks and ice—was as steep as a black diamond downhill ski run.

"Will my edges hold on this grade?" Frost asked, looking down at the backcountry cross-country skis with metal edges that the guides had provided him.

I dropped in first, skiing perpendicular to the flow, metal edges biting clean in hardpack snow. A bent knee, a little hop, and I spun back to carve another turn across the face.

"It's perfect!" I yelled up.

Fifty feet below, there was a pool of open water. Rocks and deadfall trees on the right blocked another route to the bottom. But the Onion's white path opened to the left, a ramp skirting the waterfall, providing passage downriver and out of sight, around a bend to the deep canyon ahead.

Highway 61 came into sight ten minutes later. Then, the group was on Superior's shore, skis in hands after crossing the road, the mouth of the Onion gushing in a slot coming out of a culvert. I dipped a ski pole in the lake, sending little waves rippling, to signify the end of the journey.

ME AND JOE

C. B. Bylander

 SOMETIME THIS WINTER, when my wife is in the mood for walleye, I will slip fillets from the fridge, dip them in egg, dredge them in special seasoning, and plop them in a pan of spitting-hot melted butter and oil.

Then I'll stand guard, spatula at the ready, as they brown on the outside, turn flaky white on the inside, and proffer an aroma that could only smell sweeter if it rose from a pan atop a campfire on some distant shore.

Next, I'll pour two glasses of wine. Ferry the remaining fare to the table. And as we dine, the world will be fine. It always is when the fish on your fork comes from a hole in the ice rather than a freezer at the supermarket.

As we savor our meal, I will relish the fishing trip too. This will be especially true if our repast begat from a journey to Joe's. Joe is my ice-fishing buddy. He lives on the north shore of Mille Lacs Lake. We have fished together for years. We do not wet lines a lot, but we do always launch a foray each winter from the harbor in front of his home. I look forward to these ice-fishing trips. They're great.

I look forward to them because Joe is so many things—a caring curmudgeon, a prince of a pal, and a perfect paradox. A self-described recluse, he is lousy at this for his phone is often abuzz and his solace sought. Likewise, his cherished simple life is constantly in conflict with his pit-bull pursuit of bones of fact. His kitchen table, for instance, is a sea of the flotsam and jetsam of an ardent angler and former fishing guide—the latest lures, unwanted line, photographs of fish—yet it also contains the *Atlantic Monthly,* the *New York Times,* and tomes heavy in substance, stature, and weight. As a result, I never know in which direction Joe will cast a conversation. But I do know that eventually it will land on angling tactics, techniques, and the weather.

That's because Joe knows fishing, especially at Mille Lacs. And he knows that a discourse on the day is de rigueur. Joe will wax about the wind, the state of the fishery, and the latest reports from reliable sources, such as Barneveld, The Prince, and the Cheers-like gang at Phil's Myr-Mar, a marina restaurant and saloon across the puddle where patrons often greet Joe as though he were Norm.

These prefishing prognostications are kin to the kind of commentary kicked about on television pregame football shows. We talk about offense: Will Ivan's latest lure be the hot ticket? We talk defense: Will the cold front shut down our plans and force a change in strategy? We talk intangibles: What if late-arriving louts drill holes near our shack right during the witching hour, that precious fish-feeding time as the sun slips behind Garrison? What should we do? Such invention and grousing are good fun and entertaining to boot. It is why ESPN broadcasts pregame football shows even when it does not air the game.

But I digress.

In time, Joe and I will don our fishing duds, strap on our boots, and hoof to a fish house not far from shore. This shack is adequate but spartan. It is essentially two holes in the floor and nothing more. There is no table for cribbage. No bunk for a snooze. No electronic tomfoolery or color TV. Just two holes, a couple of coat hooks, and small gas stove that sputters a soft light and toasty warmth. This piscatorial palace is mostly a thin skin of tin.

Palace? Not really, but it seems like one. I say this because within its confines, Joe and I, like others of our ilk, assume the airs of the philosopher-king. With stocking hats as crowns and plastic pails as thrones, we rule the rock rubble. We become sultans of the sand. We are temporary lords of the lake—well, at least lords of our small slab of ice. We exercise this sovereign responsibility by making pronouncements on all things important and many things that are not. We do this until a fish breaks our stream of consciousness or, in rare instances, our line. Northern pike—crocodiles, as Joe calls 'em—are the worst line breakers. When we spy them below, we try to banish these bums to other parts of the lake, but they frequently disobey our orders. The eelpout heed no better.

We often fish fairly close to shore. This near-shore winter fishing—"viewing," Joe calls it—is always fun and fascinating because fish, frankly, are as unpredictable as pups. Hunkered over my hole, I have watched a walleye slam into a Swedish pimple. Other times, the darn fish swims up cautiously, snuggles its snout to within a whisker of the lure, and then fins away without ever opening its mouth.

Different again is the walleye that sees the bait, cruises past like an aimless torpedo, then circles back to mash the minnow that seconds before it chose to ignore. I do not know why walleyes do this. Was the temptation too great? Was the jigging just right? Who knows? It is just fun to behold.

Joe and I usually chew the fat for most of our trip, but there are times we simply sit in silence. We listen to the wind, which sculpts the snow into desertlike patterns. We listen to the ice, which booms and groans as it heaves its mass from shore to buckling shore. And we listen to our own thoughts and the internal voices of those who are important to us. I've often found that ice fishing is a great way to get away and meditate. Granted, a shack on Mille Lacs is not a monastery in Katmandu, but it can do. And it is a lot closer.

Sad to say, I cannot report that I have ever caught a huge fish from Mille Lacs during a trip with Joe. However, I have come close. It happened years ago, while Joe and I were sitting side by side during the evening bite. We were twitching jigging spoons tipped with a minnow. Joe, as usual, had been outfishing me and at some point gave me his rod because his lure was hot and mine was not. Joe's jigging stick was little more than a glorified dowel, a short shank of fiberglass rod, and a pair of pegs on which to wrap line. As I was fishing with this stick, I looked down the hole and spied a "whale," a word we reserve for only the largest of fish.

"Whale, Joe!" I exclaimed.

"What's it doing?" he replied.

"Just looking."

"Still there?"

"Yup," I said.

And then the whale opened its mouth and the fight was on. It was a brief battle but memorable nonetheless. As I set the hook, the rod arched as though I were trying to heft a boulder from the bottom of the lake. Joe, noticing the bend, popped off his pail and dove to his knees so that he could help snag the fish when its head poked up the hole.

Well, the whale was not particularly interested in meeting Joe. First, it took a run toward Isle. Then it circled back toward Malmo. Finally, as I was steering its snout toward the hole at my feet, the fish plain missed its exit and disappeared into the great beyond. Instead of a fish, I was left with a length of slack line in my hand. The only heft was that of a fishless spoon.

Joe and I, of course, mused about this episode for quite a while. Then, after a fitting period of time, I asked the question for which I was confident Joe would know the answer, because his eye for fish length and weight is as sharp as a dorsal spine.

"You saw the whale. Almost grabbed it. How big was she?" I asked, knowing the largest of walleyes are always female.

"Eight. Maybe more," said Joe.

"Good to know," I said, a twinge of dejection snagged to each word.

Since then I have never seen such a large fish on a trip with Joe. Yet that is fine. There are more trips in our future. More opportunities. And meanwhile, the memories are good in and of themselves.

It is usually dark when we leave the lake. The stars, tiny pinholes of light in the fabric above, shine down on us. So does the moon. And beyond, on the roads that circle the lake, the headlights of cars flicker and fade. I suspect some people in those cars might see me and Joe and think we are crazy as we plod off the ice with sled in tow. And they might be right. But then again, they've likely never seen a whale whack a lure . . . or even better, the smile of a spouse over a pan-fried walleye, freshly drizzled with lemon, on a winter night.

FISHING THE ICE

John Brandon

 "DON'T FORGET THE COOKER, DAD."

My son Joshua was squinting at me, curious and full of questions. He was pulling wool trousers over thick socks, pretending not to struggle. "The cooker?" I asked.

"You know, that thing." He grinned, struggling to communicate. "The fish cooker. We might need it!"

Joshua was a sturdy six-year-old, a miniature version of his dad with big hands and broad shoulders, a shock of blond hair, and a big smile. Today, he was going to "fish the ice" for the first time, a new and exciting idea.

"Mom will cook the fish at home, son, but we have to catch them first." Joshua frowned and stared at me. Just one year ago, he had been diagnosed with central auditory processing disorder, which means he has trouble understanding new information and processes instructions slowly.

The wheels turned.

"Oh, I get it!" he yelled, standing with trousers pulled snug. "Mom cooks the fish! We don't need to bring a cooker."

He raised his arms and pushed them through his sweatshirt sleeves. I looked outside. Skeletal trees partially blocked the view of multicolored icehouses just below Joshua's bedroom window. The sun arched over the lake as a light snow fell, then billowed in lazy curls. The morning began like a slow, wide yawn.

We packed lightly. Hand auger, ice skimmer, salmon eggs. Peanut butter cookies and a thermos of steaming cocoa.

"When we get there, can we eat the cookies right away?" he asked.

The cookies—they helped Joshua focus when everything around him was moving too fast; they pumped extra fuel into his brain. Over time, he will learn how to cope with all the mixed-up sounds and garbled words, a cacophony of noisy confusion. Now, all we had to think about was how to get across a cold lake and find a place to fish.

"Dad? When we get to the spot, will we have to cut a hole in the ice? And how do you get the fish to bite—do you jig it?"

"Yes, son. We cut the hole, and then we put the hook down there to catch the fish. You can jig it if you want. Joshua, did your mom buy you a new hat? We need to stay warm."

"Mom said it would get cold." He grimaced and shivered, then started down the stairs to look for his winter coat and new hat.

We assembled all the gear, pulled on our boots, and stepped out into the frigid air. A short walk down the hill, and we were trekking onto the lake. Wind touched our faces and spoke in whispers.

"I'm going to fall through!" Joshua said, and we stopped for a moment. Sometimes, new sounds and experiences cause Joshua to panic slightly—at least until he can unravel and digest his surroundings.

"Son, the ice is at least ten feet thick. See the trucks over there? None of them have fallen through, have they?"

"But we *are* going to fall through, Dad!"

I smiled, shaking my head "no" and took Joshua's hand. We decided to go back to the shore for a short rest. In the tranquillity of winter, we drank hot cocoa and ate cookies, waiting for the wind—and Joshua's fears—to dissipate.

Daylight opened her fragile hands as the sunrise gave way to midmorning calm. A distant crow screamed, the ice beckoned. Joshua was ready.

We headed for a spot on the north side of the lake and plunked ourselves down in the lee of two or three icehouses. The auger bored down easily through the ice, opening a portal to the depths. Joshua immediately forgot about falling through. Thinking about panfish and hoping for wall-eyes, I slipped the salmon eggs onto Joshua's hook. He dropped the line down, mesmerized.

"Jerk it like this," I told Joshua, motioning slightly. Fishing was the perfect panacea for his disorder, a simple act with simple results. Fishing rod, line, bait, hook—and fish. In the summer Joshua enjoyed the sport as though he were placing round pegs in round holes. Fishing had a symmetry and straight-as-an-arrow goal. He understood.

"I got one!" he yelled, feeling the anxious pull of a bluegill. It seemed a miracle that you could drop a line and hook a fish deep within the blackness of the lake. Joshua whooped and hollered, as his clumsy hands cranked his reel, and I helped him unhook the hand-length fish.

"What are we going to do now?" he asked.

A lesson began to form. Here was Joshua, struggling to decipher the world, and the fish, struggling up from the murky underworld. Both boy and fish had trouble interpreting their surroundings. I suggested that we put the too-small fish back in the water, and Joshua knew that it was the right thing to do. Somehow, it made sense—the bluegill had a potential that had not been fully developed.

Joshua needed time to learn about auditory processing. My wife, Rebecca, has overcome her own processing disorder. She still struggles to understand and pronounce words like *parmesan* and occasionally hears me say *grille* instead of *girl*. How she processes the words that flow into her brain is a complex mystery, one that scientists will probably never understand. The circuitry will always be slightly disconnected.

Joshua will also learn the technique of listening to patterns, patiently deciphering the words, and slowly connecting the dots of language so that he can communicate at a more advanced level.

My daughter Hannah has also had to retrain her mind for auditory processing. When she first started school, she used some words only her parents understood, and we could converse with her in this native tongue. Now in second grade, she speaks with more eloquence than many others her age.

"Can we go home now?" Joshua asked, teeth chattering. A half hour of fishing had become a lesson in understanding my son. In some ways, his auditory processing disorder is the very thing that makes him unique, an imprint from a master workman who gives each of us at least one genetic challenge to overcome in life. It had taught me to speak more slowly to Joshua, to wait for him to connect.

We packed up, threw snow into our ice hole, and waved good-bye to the fish. The walk back was quicker and easier. Joshua had put the pieces together. You walk across the lake, carve out your fishing hole, drop your line. The ice below your feet is nothing more than a passageway, a thick coating on the water that makes winter fishing possible.

Joshua lifted his feet over the snowdrifts, marching like Peter chasing the wolf, and enjoying the hike. I followed him, forming an idea. Ice fishing is about shared experiences, about battling the elements of winter and still enjoying a sport. It's about overcoming obstacles.

When nothing quite settles my nerves, ice fishing provides a mechanism. It is a simple activity that can open the channels to understanding. When we go, I can spend time listening to my son—really listening.

That evening, we ate pork chops and mashed potatoes for dinner, Rebecca brewed more hot cocoa, and we laughed—belly laughed—about fishing the ice. We talked about the cooker, and about sending a tiny bluegill back to freedom. And Joshua understood.

A FLASH OF SUMMER

Jason Abraham

 IT WAS A PERFECT DAY to hunt squirrels. The winter sun, still weak from its slog through much of February, would be warm enough to coax bushy-tails from their dens around noon. My plan was to be nestled under a snowy oak tree to meet them.

I was in the basement piling on heavy winter clothes when I noticed my fly-fishing gear, abandoned in the corner since the last warm days of autumn. A patch of blue sky, brilliant as summer, showed through a window. Something inside me snapped—winter had gone on long enough. I wanted it to be warm and green outside. I wanted to swat mosquitoes and need a cold drink. Most of all, I wanted to wade in moving water and fish for trout.

Until this day, I'd never considered going trout fishing in the winter. I'd fished the spring end of the winter trout season, which runs through March 31, on many streams in the southeast. But that was sans the ice, snow, and cold that make winter, well, winter. Today would be much different. Catching fish wouldn't be a priority; catching an early taste of summer was my goal.

I shucked the heaviest coat for a fleece pullover and grabbed my thick neoprene chest waders, a pair of wool fingerless gloves, and my fly-fishing gear. I headed for Beaver Creek, a small stream that drops 450 feet as it tumbles nearly six miles from its source near Plainview to its confluence with the Whitewater River. The creek shares its name with the village of Beaver, a small settlement that once thrived at the creek's mouth. New

Englanders who settled the area and cleared the hillsides of trees to farm named both—creek and town—in 1854. Most of the village was abandoned by 1906, after a series of devastating flash floods, exacerbated by denuded hillsides, made the area unlivable.

In the years since then, Beaver Creek and its surrounding watershed have reverted to wild countryside. Today, the stream twists and turns through dense hardwood forest, permanently protected in the Whitewater Wildlife Management Area.

I stop my truck and survey the stream from the warmth of the cab. I note the one advantage I'll enjoy on this day—the absence of streamside vegetation, now buried under a foot of snow, should make fly casting a bit easier.

Tossing my fishing vest onto my shoulders, I breathe in the pungent smell of sunscreen and mosquito repellent, returning me briefly to warm days. An icy wind snaps my reverie, and I plunge into my thick waders, hoping for warmth. Opening my fly box, I know I should select nymph imitations, since trout feed primarily on insects in nymph stages in winter. I should also pick some heavily weighted fly and focus on fishing deep holes, where lethargic fish would logically be gathered in winter hideouts.

Instead, in this quest for summer, I tie on a shrimplike scud and a hare's ear—two lightly weighted flies that ride high in the water column.

Snow squeaks under my boots as I walk toward a short riffle, one of the only stretches of the creek not clogged by ice. This fast-moving water is perfect for summer fishing, when trout have the energy to hold in the food-rich current. In winter, however, trout prefer pools, where they have less need to exert precious energy.

I step into the water, which at thirty-two degrees feels much warmer than the surrounding air. Frozen fly line splashes hard in my first cast. The guides of my fly rod clog with ice. Even my flies coat with ice during the few seconds they're exposed to air between casts. On the verge of quitting my reckless rush toward summer, I cast to the head of the pool, the fastest water and least likely place to find trout. The instant the flies hit the water, I see a telltale tug on the line. My arm instinctively flails backward, setting the hook.

I try to bring the brown trout in quickly to preserve its energy reserves, but it's strong and it fights hard. The snowy banks and icy water slip away as I focus only on the flashing fish at the end of my line. It could be summer again.

Oblivious to the cold, I remove my fingerless gloves and plunge my hands into the water to gently cradle the fish. The brown trout's dark red spots and tan body stand in stark contrast to the drabness of this day. I slip my barbless fly from its jaw and watch it swim back to the head of the pool.

I think about that fish as I head home and wonder why it would stay in such fast-moving water in winter. Maybe it, like me, had tired of the winter routine and needed a quick reminder of summer.

A THOUSAND CHANDELIERS

Will Weaver

TO MOST PEOPLE IN THE WORLD, *ice* is a negative word, one with bleak and chilly connotations. "She gave him an icy stare." Or, "The lawyer, in his remarks, was skating on thin ice." And, "At the party, someone needed to break the ice." With roots in Old English, the word *ice* in ancient times was associated with death, sleep, and punishment. And who, in Minnesota, has not felt unlucky to slip and fall, or encounter the dreaded black ice while driving. But northerners like us—indeed, all people around the world who live up where our planet wears its winter skullcap—have found ways to live with, play on, even celebrate ice.

In 1886 St. Paul held its first winter carnival in response to an insult by a New York reporter who likened St. Paul to Siberia—"unfit for human habitation" in the winter. An ice castle was added to the carnival in 1887 and has appeared intermittently at carnivals over the following 120 years. Its glistening towers, colored lights, glassy rooms, and grand ice sculptures out front draw tourists from around the world.

Other northern cities have their own icy traditions. Near Quebec City, Quebec, an ice hotel is erected each winter. It can accommodate eighty-eight guests on beds of ice, covered with deer and caribou furs— with goose-down sleeping bags on top! The furniture throughout the hotel is carved from ice; an art gallery is filled with ice sculptures. The bar—guess what it's made of—serves drinks in ice glasses and cold cuts on ice plates. Who would want to sleep in an ice hotel? Better sign up early for next year: reservations are hard to get.

This for a chilly hotel that exists for only a hundred or so winter days, depending upon the weather.

Which brings us, if you're a true northerner, to the inevitable: Spring. Ice-out time. The ice sculptures of swans and rearing horses, ice castle turrets, ice beds, icicles—all begin to shrink. Droop. Tilt. Fall. Outdoor rinks grow slushy and sad as children turn to skateboards and baseball gloves. Environmentally minded clubs and civic groups sponsor lake cleanup days after a season of ice fishing. Rivers develop smoking spots— black gashes of steamy, open water where the river bends and the current is stronger.

But up north, lake and river ice hangs on almost a month longer than it does in southern Minnesota—and draws more than a few die-hard panfish anglers and snowmobilers to drive to where there is still good ice. However, ice-out time comes to all of Minnesota at some point—April 17, give or take a day, where I live on the upper Mississippi east of Bemidji. Ice-out time on the river is often more dramatic than ice-out on lakes; however, the larger lakes unfold their own spring dramas.

I taught for many years at Bemidji State University, which is nestled on the western shore of Lake Bemidji; and I took great pleasure in watching the daily progress of spring. The beginning of ice-out was the absence of cars parked just off shore. Bemidji State students and faculty make good use of the ice to relieve winter parking problems around the campus; on a bright January day as many as two hundred cars are parked in orderly rows just offshore. Lake parking ends about mid-March, though some diehards persist well beyond common sense. (I always cautioned my students that there was no true honor in being first on or last to drive off the lake.)

Before ice-out begins, Lake Bemidji clears itself of human presence. Empties itself of cars. Fish houses. Snowmobiles. Debris. Then, as the snow melts, the lake ice reveals its own unique palette of colors. Day by day the hues of ice evolve: from dull white to steel gray; from gray to gray green as the ice "rots" or becomes honeycombed; from blue green to a dull, defeated gray. The last change often occurs suddenly—within a short afternoon—as if the spirit, the will to live, has left the ice.

At the Mississippi River inlet on the south shore, the pool of open water widens; a few early diving ducks, such as goldeneyes, appear in the narrow tracts of open water along warmer banks—and hungry eagles sit on the ice, as still as yard ornaments, watching them. On smaller lakes, crappie and perch enthusiasts use planks to get from shore to good ice.

But soon comes ice tectonics: great, shifting plates of ice, some a mile long, slowly separate, break free—then grind and groan against one another. In folk tradition the deep, tormented sounds are explained by the story of the Old Woman Under the Lake, a tale of a spurned lover and revenge. On days when the lake's voice seems so tortured, who am I to dismiss this explanation? It is either the old woman or whales calling to each other, I think to myself.

As the ice begins to move and drift, I sense a quickening, a new spiritedness among people. "It won't be long now," a man says in passing, and everyone knows what he means. Yet for full ice-out, one more factor is often needed: wind.

On Lake Bemidji it is usually a temperate south wind that dooms the ice. The great floes begin to move, crush each other, and pile up two to three stories high, forming a wide, white eyebrow across the far north end of the lake. Open water patches grow to ten acres, fifty acres—until a change in wind direction drives the honeycombed ice back southward onto Diamond Point, just up the shoreline from campus.

On such magical, transitional days, I often walked my freshmen students along the shore to look at the ice move—and to write about it. "You must observe things closely," I harped. "Good writing is always in the details." Such days, the spring sun was warm on our necks and the breath of ice piles chilly on our faces. One of those days stays with me in particular: a gaggle of my students, the supposedly jaded, MTV generation, had their notebooks open and were leaning close, touching the heaping piles of glistening, honeycombed ice as it flexed, shifted, grated, crawled, and tinkled.

"It's like it's alive," one young man said to no one in particular.

"Can you hear it?" another student, a young woman, blurted. She loved poetry and wanted to be a writer.

"Yeah," said another student. "So what?"

The young woman poet looked at us with wonder in her face. "It sounds like a thousand chandeliers!"

At home late that afternoon, I went down to my Mississippi River bank to watch the ice floes moving, rustling, scraping, murmuring. Late sunlight rode trapped and glistening in their porous floes, which passed steadily by with the grace, beauty, and grandeur of exhausted soldiers on a final march.

In the morning the river was totally clear of ice. Its waters lay gray and quiet, as if utterly spent. That afternoon—right on schedule—the first loon came swimming by, head erect, apparently happy to be back.

Doing Science

MEMORIES OF THE LANDSCAPE

Nancy Sather

"HERE'S YOUR BOAT," my father announced early in my four-teenth summer. I couldn't recall having mentioned any boat, but when Dad decided something was the truth, there was no effective counter. So there it was: eighteen feet of heavy rowboat with peeling paint. By decree, its rehabilitation became my summer's task, or, as it developed, my privilege. After hours of scraping and sanding, its warm cedar-strip sides glowed smooth to the touch.

The boat offered interesting possibilities. With it my father had provided a lure to independence I had not thought to seek. A driver's license? Whatever for? To take the boat to Island Lake. An hour of leisure? Whatever for? To explore sinuous shorelines of a whole island, unvisited by boaters who needed amenities, feared mosquitoes, and didn't know the path around the poison ivy on the shore.

Chains of rocks led from the main island to a rocky point. All along these chains the minnows played. Bulrush and horsetail warned away the occasional vagrant motorboat. Yellow bladderwort blossoms punctuated beds of pondweed. Great blue herons fished for frogs. Mine was an uninquisitive appreciation; I was more apt to loll in the boat and watch giant blue libellulid dragonflies diving for mosquitoes than to consider their numbers or names.

Yet it was probably those explorations, made from that hundred-dollar boat, that launched my career as a biologist. Bur oak, basswood, maple, and elm graced the knolls at the island's heart. Hepaticas and bloodroot opened the seasonal procession, and sweet cicely and lopseed closed it with stickers that clung to my corduroy pants. Without the guidance of a developed trail, my feet followed the easiest paths, those made by deer, or by a long-fallen log that left a path through the hazel.

Ostrich fern, lady fern, and interrupted fern formed a fragrant glade in the low swale at the island's northeastern shore. They were joined by a profusion of sedges. Oblivious to the distinction between sedges (have edges) and grasses (are round), I noticed the shapes of their heads— slender arching spangles, miniature balloon pods. Plants whose taxonomic distinctions would become my nemesis in later years were then a mere matter of aesthetics.

Years later I remembered that glade when searching for the cryptic goblin fern. And I remembered the day the water witcher came with his forked stick to help us find a place for a well. He handed me the stick, urging me to feel the tug. I felt nothing, but I noted his sense of ease as he wandered, exercising what my mother called a sixth sense, an intuitive knowledge of a place visited by underground water.

Now I search for rare plants. Haunted by a memory of the island, I return as a botanist to nearby forests looking for the cryptic goblin fern. I remember the shade of the maples, how their fallen leaves formed a spongy blanket on the forest floor. I recall the fungi protruding through the duff: dead man's fingers, jelly babies, coral fungus, and earth tongue. I envision the perfect place to find an inch-high, lime green plant, which more closely resembles a club fungus than a fern. And I find it. Just inland from my island, it is half buried in the winter-whitened maple leaves, keeping company with coral fungus in a little swale nearly bare of the forest's prevailing bellwort and lopseed.

Goblin fern isn't the only plant I've found from childhood memory. Ours were the days when a teenage girl could range the country on a bicycle. One of my favorite rides took me past oak and aspen woodlots, cattle lolling in the heat, and ducks at the open edges of cattail ponds to the leech-infested shores of Poplar Lake. I returned to that route forty years later, seeking Cooper's milk vetch, one of those plants thought to be extremely

rare because they live neither in the forest nor on the prairie. Some ves-
tigial memory drove me to a bank where the winding road overlooks
Poplar Lake. Yes, it was there. Was it the plant itself I recalled from my
teenage forays, or the ambience of the place, the way the bank crumbles
off in a tangle of sumac and open rocky clay? Was it science that brought
me to this place, a professional knowledge of the conditions in which this
species often occurs? Or was it intuition?

Since I've started working with Cooper's milk vetch, I've met many
cabin owners, hunters, and farmers who have their own names for the
plant with the big black pods. "Yes, I've seen that," they tell me. "I never
thought it was anything special. I saw it on a bank by the edge of the pasture." Or best: "When I was a boy, we used those pods as rattles. But when
I was grown I hated them. They rattle when you hunt and scare the deer."
They are not botanists, yet they know this plant in a vernacular sense. It
is an element of the landscape of home. Familiarity.

Now I understand the water witcher's tug on his stick. I like to think
there is an element of intuition in searching for rare plants. I like to think
that it matters that a landscape on earth is engraved on the landscape of
our memories.

We move around in our native landscape often only subliminally
conscious of the things we see. Or hear. Or feel. A certain bird call in
the wetlands. A certain sponginess of the ground underfoot. We carry in
our memories of the landscape a bank of information, both factual and
spiritual, we do not know we know.

ELUSIVE ORCHIDS

Erika Rowe

MINNESOTA has a handful of native plant species with mythic qualities: elusive, rare, revered, endangered, or so specific in their habitat requirements, they are not likely to be seen. Bog adder's-mouth orchid *(Malaxis paludosa)* encompasses all of these qualities. It has proved to be one of the most challenging orchid species to find, partly because of its rarity, but also because it is easily overlooked.

The orchid is small in stature and has a chameleon-like ability to blend into the vegetation and mossy hummocks within its forested swamp habitat. Often, the only sign of the orchid's presence is its delicate inflorescence—rising a scant five to ten centimeters above the moss. Adding to its elusiveness, populations tend to be sparse, often fewer than ten plants at a site and rarely more than twenty.

I did not have much hope of finding this inconspicuous orchid during my summer search for rare plants and native plant communities for the Minnesota County Biological Survey. As an ecologist with the Department of Natural Resources preparing for the 2005 field research season, I put the bog adder's-mouth on my search list of targeted rare plant species. But I didn't plan to spend much time looking for it, given its reputation of being nearly impossible to find.

Minnesota is the only state in the lower 48 in which bog adder's-mouth has been found. This circumboreal species, one occurring throughout far northern latitudes, has also been found in scattered locations in

Alaska, Canada, Asia, and Europe. In central and northern Europe, it is considered less rare, although it is believed to be declining, primarily because of wetland drainage and peat mining.

By most accounts, bog adder's-mouth was unknown in North America until 1905, when H. L. Lyon collected a specimen somewhere near New York Mills in Otter Tail County. Four more discoveries of bog adder's-mouth sites occurred between 1915 and 1934 in Hubbard and Clearwater counties. Nearly fifty years passed before the next discovery of a new population in Beltrami County in 1981. Another site was found in Beltrami County in 2000.

Three of these original seven Minnesota sites of the bog adder's-mouth have not been found again, despite extensive searches. Many factors, such as a lack of reproduction or loss of habitat, could have led to their demise.

When Tim Whitfeld, a Minnesota County Biological Survey plant ecologist surveying nearby Clearwater County, told me that he was going to spend a few days looking for bog adder's-mouth, I was amazed at his ambition. Several botanists called his plan a "wild-goose chase," and one offered a sarcastic "good luck!" But he wasn't dissuaded; instead he recruited DNR botanist Welby Smith and ecologist Michael Lee to help relocate a known population of bog adder's-mouth.

I decided to tag along with the hope that once I'd seen the real thing, I would be more prepared to hunt for new populations of bog adder's-mouth on my own. Photographs and herbarium specimens can only go so far in conveying how tiny and difficult this particular orchid is to see. At the very least, I knew that seeing the bog adder's-mouth in the wild would spark inspiration and excitement. But first we needed to find them again.

On a warm, cloudless day in early August in Clearwater County, the four of us set out for a black spruce swamp. For many people, the word *swamp* conjures images of an inhospitable place, where only mosquitoes thrive and bottomless muck awaits anyone who dares set foot within this realm. Though mosquitoes certainly may gather there in numbers unimaginable, black spruce swamps can be magical places—rich with the scent of sphagnum moss and serenely cool on a hot summer's day. They provide habitat for many interesting animals and plants, including bog adder's-mouth.

Once we arrived, we didn't have to hike far within the swamp to where the orchids were reported to be. We began inspecting the sun-dappled mossy ground immediately. The search was a slow process, as one might imagine, but time slipped by quickly as my anticipation grew. I found myself scanning every inch of the sphagnum-covered hummocks, being mindful of where each foot was placed for fear of stepping on the one bog adder's-mouth orchid that we might have overlooked.

Being familiar with the common plants of a community is essential when searching for rare plants. When something differs slightly in texture or color, it's much easier to notice. I was the one who noticed the first orchid, just different enough from the typical vegetation that it caught my glance.

Before I called out to the others, I stooped down for a closer look. I tried to control my excitement as I yelled for Welby Smith to come over and confirm what I already suspected was a bog adder's-mouth orchid. "Yes, that's it!" he said.

I couldn't believe how incredibly tiny the flowers were and how well the orchid blended in with its surroundings—it was almost exactly the same shade of green as the sphagnum moss. After the first orchid, we found it somewhat easier to see the other scattered individuals nearby, twelve total.

The following day in Becker County, using an aerial photograph of a tamarack swamp, I located a small area dominated by black spruce. It seemed to have the right characteristics for bog adder's-mouth habitat, and I set out hiking. After an hour and a half of slogging through wet, hummocky terrain, my initial confidence was wearing thin. I began to wonder whether this long, arduous hike was to be worth the exertion.

Several plants repeatedly caught my peripheral glance. Two such plants were the delicate flowering stems of naked bishop's-cap (*Mitella nuda*) and round-leaved sundew (*Drosera rotundifolia*). But then I spotted green adder's-mouth *(Malaxis unifolia)* and small northern bog-orchid *(Platanthera obtusata)*. The presence of these latter two orchids indicated that I was in the right habitat for bog adder's-mouth. I decided to walk over and take a closer look to make sure that they were the orchids I thought they were. Then something else caught my eye.

Just above the sphagnum moss, I spotted four bog adder's-mouth orchids clustered together. Shocked, I stood there for what seemed like several minutes, all the while contemplating the actuality of having found a new population of bog adder's-mouth orchids. I eventually came to my senses and proceeded to find ten more plants within two acres.

By the end of the field season, Michael Lee and I had discovered five new populations of bog adder's-mouth, all in Becker County.

The 2006 field season proved equally fortunate, as we found four more locations in Becker County and one in Hubbard County. Tim Whitfeld also found another in Hubbard. These new records have extended the known range of bog adder's-mouth and nearly tripled the known records in Minnesota to seventeen locations.

As the Minnesota County Biological Survey expands farther north and east in upcoming field seasons, we hope to find more bog adder's-mouth populations, expanding their known range. Maybe I'll be a part of those future searches for this most elusive of orchids in Minnesota. After all, now I know what I'm looking for.

A GREAT SMALL UNIVERSE

David Czarnecki

 I LIKE BIOLOGY, always have, and always will. I'm especially
intrigued by little creatures, mostly those that live in or around
water and can only be observed under a microscope. I find almost everything about them interesting. I really don't know why
for sure.

I experienced a rather unremarkable suburban childhood, yet one
enhanced by summer visits to my grandfather's lake home near Remer.
My grandfather was an avid hunter, birder, and angler. He loved his walleyes and lake perch and disdained nearly everything else. Sunfish, large-
mouth bass, and northern pike, he said, preferred warm "dirty" waters
and should be caught (and eaten) only as a last resort. "Avoid the weeds,"
he would say. "Fish caught there'll taste muddy."

Over the years, however, I found that I caught a lot more fish and got
to see a lot more stuff in the waters of the weedy, shallow lake across the
road from his clear, cold lake.

Later, as an undergraduate at Bemidji State University, I found to my
delight that some of my teachers could relate to that same stuff, and they
had microscopes to see it up close. During one very cold winter, I saw
something in a few drops of water that turned my usual lackluster observations into a solar flare of pure astonishment—a live diatom, a freshwater alga, collected from a depth of about twenty feet of water under
four feet of ice cover!

How could anything look so healthy under such conditions? I was immediately smitten and have been ever since. Of the million or so drops of water I've examined under a microscope, very few have failed to enlighten and amaze me.

The majority of life forms exist beyond our immediate recognition. The unaided human eye can resolve a dimension as small as about 1/100th of an inch; and except for just plain size, little else can be interpreted at that scale. Equipped with a decent compound microscope, however, a person can see a dimension a thousand times smaller. This is the world of algae, bacteria, protozoa, and myriad microinvertebrates—literally the world of cells. To me, this microcosm is at least a thousand times more interesting.

A few years ago at Itasca State Park, I had the good fortune of encountering a microworld brought to my attention by my youngest daughter, who was swimming at the time.

"Hey, Dad, what's this green, slimy blob stuff floating everywhere in the water?"

A glance through the microscope showed me a colony of slime-producing protozoans known as *Ophrydium*. Though rarely abundant, *Ophrydium* is not all that uncommon in northern temperate freshwaters. What I found odd was the large size of some of the colonies—some bigger than a tennis ball—and the diversity of diatoms within the slime.

I collected several of the blobs so that I could identify the diatoms. For the next two summers, I collected and characterized more colonies from area lakes and ponds. Interestingly, I discovered that the diatom inhabitants were associated primarily with their lake or pond, rather than collectively associated with *Ophrydium*.

I also uncovered two mysteries. First, one of the species of diatoms I encountered, *Nitzschia flexoides,* was originally described from Lunz Lake in Austria and, to my knowledge, has not been found elsewhere— except Lake Itasca, where it has appeared in every colony I have observed. Second, at the end of the growing season, the colonies break up into individual cells, and the slime disappears; yet I have not encountered *N. flexoides* in any other of my numerous diatom collections from Lake Itasca.

I wonder how and where these diatoms live when the slimy colonies are not around.

Another small wonder I've studied is the "lake ball" of Lake Bemidji. *Cladophora aegagropila* (more recently classified as *Aegagropila linnaei*) is a coarse-walled, branching filamentous green alga that forms rocklike aggregates, rolled by wave action along sandy shorelines, much like a scouring pad put in a rock tumbler.

Sponges, mosses, cyanobacteria, cockleburs, chestnuts, and other round forms found along shore may also be called lake balls. But true *Cladophora* balls, like those of Lake Bemidji, appear to be rare or nonexistent elsewhere in North America.

Yet lake balls are common in parts of Europe and Asia, and usually bigger than the ones in Lake Bemidji, which are less than an inch in diameter. In Japan, where they are called *marimo,* lake balls have been given Special Natural Monument status and are thus protected. They are also found in Lake Mývatn, Iceland, where they are known as *kúluskítur.* Strangely, the lake ball populations found in Lake Bemidji, Japan, and Iceland appear to be the same genetically, but they differ from those of Austria, Estonia, Russia, and Sweden.

How much do we really know about the life that exists around us? How many creatures are out there? What are they doing? How long have they been doing it? Why? I doubt we will ever know for sure. But from my standpoint, one of the most gratifying human experiences is to keep looking.

Does our survival depend on other creatures? If so, which ones? Oops, are we sure? Who's to say, since we don't know what creatures are out there or what they might be doing?

My greatest fear is that two classical branches of biology—natural history and organismal biology—could disappear if the patient, often plodding observation needed for such biology is no longer respected as a worthwhile endeavor.

And yet new discoveries are to be found everywhere, even in places one would least expect to encounter them. For example, a few years ago, a colleague and I did biological inventories of several abandoned mine sites and discovered a diatom that apparently had not been previously described. We named the new diatom *Pinnularia* (meaning "feather") *ferro-indulgentissima* ("very loving of iron"). It certainly is one tough critter.

So if you want to have some fun, take time to just look around. Get to know your biotic neighbors, large and small. Take an "ology" course, one that lets you see creatures where they live. Then take a peek through a microscope. A whole new universe awaits you.

A RIBBITING ADVENTURE

Philip C. Whitford

AFTER LONG PERIODS OF STARING into the abysmal darkness of almost uninhabited parts of the coulee regions of southeastern Minnesota, I found the steady beam from the spotlight painfully bright. "Put your hands on the roof of the car, spread your legs wide, and don't move!" said the metallic, distorted voice coming from the police cruiser's speaker. What choice was there? I walked up from the ditch at the bottom of the embankment and "assumed the position."

This just isn't going to be my night, I thought as I awaited the inevitable Breathalyzer test. Some twenty minutes later, I finally managed to convince the police officer that neither drunkenness nor lunacy explained my odd behavior—standing in the drizzling rain with my hands cupped to my ears.

In retrospect, I really can't blame the officer for his skepticism about my explanations. When I told him I was counting frogs, he asked me to show him the frogs. I said I couldn't do that because I didn't see them to count them. Before I finished explaining, I could almost hear him thinking, Do I really want to put this overage, hallucinating hippie into the squad car for the drive to the station?

Finally I succeeded in getting the officer to listen to the sounds of the warm spring night, and I convinced him that I was counting frogs by the sound of their calls from distant ponds. But it wasn't easy. Good thing

I'd had a chance to practice this routine a few nights earlier in another county—same story, different officer.

In my own defense, I would point out that what I was doing that night is considered perfectly rational behavior for a person with a PhD in biology and a tendency toward insomnia.

It all began late in the fall of 1989. I was teaching at Winona State University and looking for ways to involve some of my better students in field research. Just before Christmas I found a notice soliciting proposals for research funds available from the Department of Natural Resources Nongame Wildlife Program. I wrote a proposal to survey frog populations in the southeastern counties of the state. I proposed to try to find places where the rare Blanchard's cricket frog still existed. The research would also provide baseline data about frog populations that future researchers could use to judge whether species and individual populations were increasing or decreasing.

Surprisingly, though numerous inventories of frog species had been done since European settlement, they had produced no data on the numbers of frogs present. Then, in the late 1980s, there was a great hue and cry from the herpetological community that amphibian species were disappearing and populations plummeting worldwide for unknown reasons. But without numbers, biologists had no way to document whether it was true. In March 1990 I got a call from DNR nongame grants coordinator Rich Baker, saying the proposal had been funded and I should begin my surveys immediately.

First, I had to train students to find frogs. That was easy. For several days I had students in my vertebrate biology class listen to tapes of frog and toad calls. Then I selected those students with the best ear for species identification.

Next, I had to define survey routes and sites across the six designated counties. DNR people suggested several routes with sites that a well-known Minnesota herpetologist, John Moriarty, had established based on records from the 1960s and '70s. I carefully marked all the indicated wet areas—ponds, rivers, and small marshes—along nearly six hundred miles of roads in the six counties.

Unfortunately, all the available large-scale county maps dated from the 1950s. And when I first went out to survey the chosen wetland sites, I found that more than half of the sites I'd selected no longer had surface waters suitable for frog and toad breeding. Many of the small marshes had been tiled and drained, and the creeks once fed by them no longer held water—or even existed.

I revamped my four routes so that each had twenty survey sites, including lakes and ponds, temporary wetlands, fast-flowing coulee streams, and slow-moving rivers. I chose the mixture of wetland types to ensure the best chances of finding all the species of frogs in the area. Several of the species I sought were very restricted in their choice of breeding habitats. Frogs and toads were known to be present and calling from the selected sites. Each route covered 140 to 175 miles—a lot of miles to drive and stops to make in a single night's survey.

The survey procedure was fairly simple: an auditory census. Normally, just as the sun was beginning to set, a student and I would climb into my rattletrap Mercury and drive to wherever the night's survey route began. Sometimes, if the student could not make it, I'd run the survey alone.

At the first site, we would face the water and cup our hands around our ears to help screen out other sounds and to pick up the frog songs—such as the high-pitched peep of spring peepers; the long, whistled, vibrato trill of a toad; the soft quacking of wood frogs; the metallic clicking of the cricket frog; or the quavering "ribbit" of leopard and pickerel frogs. We would spend five to ten minutes at each site just listening, then compare our estimates of numbers of each species.

We recorded our final estimates not as actual numbers of each species heard at each site, but as population index values of 1, 2, or 3 for each species. A call value of 1 meant that few enough frogs were present that individual calls could be heard distinctly. A value of 2 meant that calls were frequently superimposed on other calls and individuals hard to locate and isolate. We assigned a value of 3 when so many frogs of a single species were calling simultaneously that calls constantly overlapped and we couldn't distinguish individual calls—implying a veritable orgy of calls and sexual activity.

When we finished one site, we would go on to the next, and the next, finally dragging our tired, bedraggled carcasses home sometime between two and three in the morning. I was not a pretty sight for students at my eight o'clock class.

The next night we'd do another route until all four were done. We did a survey of each route every three weeks from late March through mid-July in 1990 and 1991.

To make the survey worth the drive, we needed certain conditions: little or no wind, warm and humid air, light drizzle or, preferably, no rain. Then a full chorus of males would sing to attract mates—at least those that deemed the water temperature right for breeding. Each Minnesota frog species prefers a somewhat different water temperature, which coincides with peak breeding activity.

Varying preferences provide what is termed in biology temporal behavioral isolation, a mechanism that helps ensure that different species do not mate with each other. Frogs are not terribly discerning about mates, and a male frog will mount any frog in its territorial water. Male frogs produce release calls, which effectively tell an overzealous male suitor, "Hey, get off my back, I'm another male." Females do not have a release call they can use to dislodge males of another species. However, having each species breed at different times of year minimizes the chances of these reproductive faux pas.

Though the females of each species usually show up only for a week or two when water temperatures are just right, hopeful males call for four to six weeks. As a result, several species of males might be calling at the same time from the same waters—complicating the census process, but producing a wonderful litany of night noises, which at times becomes an overwhelming cacophony. Amid this din, the females' finely tuned ears locate the calling males of their own species. The females are deaf to males of other species.

Once she's located a male, the female swims directly to him to breed. The process must work reasonably well: all these species have survived while living and breeding in the same places for thousands of years, since the glacial ice receded.

During our two years of study, we observed many interesting things. We discovered that frogs and toads weren't the only things that mated at night along these little-used roads. Scantily clad humans dodging from backseat to front—followed by rapidly disappearing taillights—were a common spectacle as we pulled up to survey sites. On some warm summer nights, fireflies were out in profusion. Their flickering lights formed new constellations, constantly moving across valley floors and up the ridges, as they too practiced age-old mating rituals. Such nights made it clear that there were several species of fireflies in the coulee region. Different colors and patterns of blinking became evident as we moved from one valley, over a crest, and into another. Whip-poor-wills, owls, and coyotes called to the moon and stars, marking territories and answering neighbors' calls.

We confirmed that our old maps lacked markings for a number of roads, presenting us numerous chances to explore whole new areas of Fillmore and Mower counties. Foggy and cloudy nights offered wonderful opportunities to lose all sense of direction on unmarked dirt roads. It went without saying that one did not drive up to a farmhouse door to politely ask directions at 1 a.m.

Of all that we discovered, the most disturbing thing was this: in two years of listening along a two-mile stretch of a small river near the Iowa border, we never heard a single sound—not a bird, frog, or insect. All these creatures existed in normal abundance above and below that stretch of river. We couldn't help but wonder why there the silence was so complete. I heard only the blood pulsing in my ears as I strained to pick up some tangible evidence of life. It vividly brought to mind Rachel Carson's predictions in *Silent Spring,* the 1962 book that warned of the deadly nature of pesticides.

By the end of our survey, we had found ten species of frogs and one species of toad (the only toad species naturally occurring in this area). We located only three small remnant populations of Blanchard's cricket frogs by our listening, though we weren't able to document any with sightings or recordings.

We never found large populations of northern leopard frogs or pickerel frogs, though we found some of these frogs almost everywhere we went.

Populations of the small frogs—western chorus frogs, spring peepers, gray treefrogs, Cope's gray treefrogs, and wood frogs—all seemed to be holding their own. Thousands called from the flooded flats along the lower Root River near Hokah in April and May. We found fair numbers of bullfrogs and green frogs only in the still backwaters and ponds near the Mississippi River, which was to be expected.

What the future holds for all of these species is uncertain. Additional surveys will give biologists a better idea whether populations are rising, falling, or stable. What I do know is that loss of these species would leave an immense void in the eons-old chorus of spring and summer evenings. I have listened to the terrible, absolute silence where the sound of life should be. The silence seems to whisper a warning—a warning of our own mortality.

MY NIGHT LIFE WITH
THE BOREAL OWL

Bill Lane

I SLOW MY TRUCK TO A HALT, turn off the engine, and step outside. Above me, a curtain of aurora borealis shimmers over the landscape. I move away from the dying pings of the motor and pause in the middle of the road. I can feel the nighttime. It overwhelms me. I take a deep breath and slowly exhale. Ice contracting on distant lakes echoes on the hushed air, like the boom of artillery. I stand motionless, straining to pick up the faintest telltale sound. Then, ever so softly, the harmonic notes I am listening for: the staccato song of the male boreal owl.

For four years, from mid-March to mid-May, I conducted systematic, species-specific nocturnal auditory surveys in Lake and Cook counties in northern Minnesota—that's a long-winded way of saying I went out and listened for singing boreal owls, over and over again. In the process, I tried to contribute to a better understanding of the owl's status and distribution in our state.

A typical evening of surveys consisted of six to eight hours of driving selected routes, stopping for three minutes at half-mile intervals, and listening for the unique song of the male boreal owl. On a bad night—well, there was always the thermos of coffee and talk radio.

Locating and observing an owl on its territory is a straightforward matter. You simply move to its sound. When I identify an owl along a survey route, I take note of its directional bearing from several locations, plot those bearings on a map, and determine my shortest line of approach. The fun begins when I conduct the foot search. Let me rephrase that. The foot search is fun now. When I started out it was sheer terror.

Finding myself removed from the comforts of modern civilization and thrust into the formless black of a northern Minnesota night was intimidating at first. In my mind I pictured beastly carnivores: flesh eaters that lurked in alder thickets, waiting to devour my tender urban-fattened flesh. Sitting in my truck was one thing; leaving my truck to enter the night was another matter completely.

If the singing owl is near the road, I may reach him in seconds. At other times, however, I may walk for more than a mile through unfamiliar terrain, always mindful that this night may be the one when I get lost—again.

One night in 1988 I spent nearly four hours wearily carving a circle through the countryside. At three in the morning, shortly after entering the forest, I'd made *the* major mistake of anyone venturing into the north woods: I decided to trust my instincts rather than my compass. A compass works; instincts don't. By the time I made it back to my truck, the sun was rising, songbirds were singing, and I was exhausted. Some lessons in life are learned the hard way.

My headlamp pierces the black woods, illuminating movement where none exists. My hope is that the owl will remain at his singing perch throughout my approach. If he moves before I get to him, I will recall a stark lesson from the world of field biology: nothing is ever as you want it to be. When I finally spot the singing owl, I sit down, make myself comfortable, and wait for nature to take its course, busily jotting down behavioral observations in my notebook. I wonder if I will witness, as I have many times, the courtship interactions and vocalizations between the male and female boreal owls.

The male owl is a tireless singer. He announces his territory and reproductive readiness with his unique staccato song, which is triggered by lengthening days and warming temperatures. His resolve to lure a female is so strong it allows me, with a less than stealthy approach, to observe his behavior firsthand. As far as the owls are concerned, I don't exist.

The female, on the other hand, remains aloof, nestled in thick conifers and silent except for a few soft calls in response to the male.

His first order of business is to introduce her to a nesting cavity he has selected. He softly calls from the cavity entrance, enticing her into its cozy confines. The male repeats this introduction to the cavity over the course of the next several evenings. To increase the female's resolve to breed, the male must prove his worth as a hunter. He searches for and presents her with a smorgasbord of small mammals and birds. Generally speaking, the more food the male delivers, the more likely he and the female will establish a nesting site.

If all goes well, mating will take place, and the female will lay her eggs within two weeks. After four weeks of incubation, the first of up to eight owlets will hatch, already better adapted to the nighttime in northern Minnesota than I ever will be.

My research to determine the status of the boreal owl in Minnesota began in 1987 with funds provided by the Minnesota Department of Natural Resources Nongame Wildlife Program, the U.S. Forest Service North Central Forest Experiment Station, and the Superior National Forest's Tofte and Gunflint ranger districts. Although there were several records of boreal owl nests in the state, little research had been done, perhaps because of the severe Minnesota winters, the nocturnal hours, and the remoteness of the study area.

As I listen for the mating calls of these unusual birds I have the opportunity to watch and listen as the dying gasps of winter give way to the renewal of spring. Ice-choked streams, their trickle muffled by knee-deep snow, will soon erupt into roaring torrents. Mosses, long dormant beneath the snow, will touch the senses with the sweet aroma of renewed life. Snowshoe hares begin to turn a mottled brown. At sunrise, songbirds seem to appear from nowhere, creating a cacophony of urgent trills and whistles for their mates. All of these signs serve notice that life in the north woods is starting anew.

From 1987 to 1990 I surveyed more than seventeen hundred miles of the back roads of northern Minnesota. In the process I located more than 115 male boreal owls and documented eight nest sites. I showed that the boreal owl can be found in the state, and that it does breed here. Knowing that I have contributed to an understanding of the species is the reward of my study.

Meanwhile, the nights do not seem as dark as they once were, and the sounds are suddenly familiar. I can now enter the woods with a spirit of adventure rather than a sense of foreboding. Now I am hooked, captivated by the boreal owl and my surroundings. I love the night life.

COUNT YOUR LOONS

Eric Hanson

MY WIFE, ANNE, AND I AWAKEN to the laughing tremolo of a loon and a responding wail from somewhere on Battle Lake. We rush out the tent door, filled with anticipation. But we're quickly stilled by the tranquillity of the morning. The deep green of maples and basswoods, softened by a light haze, connects lake and sky. Behind us, the sun slowly rises. A wood thrush's flutelike call echoes through the trees.

I see two distant but familiar silhouettes. The loons leave a wake of ripples as they swim toward a secluded bay.

We are here in central Otter Tail County to help count loons as part of the Minnesota Loon Monitoring Program. For the next two mornings, we will survey a dozen small to medium-sized lakes in search of adult and juvenile common loons.

I am the coordinator of the monitoring program, which began in 1994 with funds from the Department of Natural Resources Nongame Wildlife Program. Anne is one of more than eight hundred volunteers who keep track of loons on 645 Minnesota lakes in six survey regions. Each volunteer surveys one or two lakes during five days in mid-July.

The DNR began counting Minnesota's loons in 1989, when it joined with volunteers and LoonWatch (a program of the Sigurd Olson Environmental Institute) for a one-time survey of more than seven hundred lakes. That count showed that Minnesota provided breeding habitat for about twelve thousand adult loons—more than half the breeding population of loons in the lower forty-eight states.

The goal of the program has been to detect changes in the common loon population and its reproductive success so that problems can be addressed before they become irremediable. Minnesota's state bird faces numerous threats, including habitat loss, recreational disturbance, and contamination of lakes with mercury, lead, and acid rain.

The monitoring program helps point the DNR toward the cause of any decline. The six survey regions were located in such a way that researchers can compare loon populations in various conditions. For example, two survey regions have lakes that are more prone to acidification than lakes in the other four regions. Researchers can compare the status of loons in the three regions where human population is high and most land is privately owned with the status of those in the three sparsely populated regions that have lots of public land.

The pair of loons has disappeared into the cove on Battle Lake, which is actually outside our survey area. Anne and I head off to our first assigned lake, five miles away.

The sun has burned off most of the early-morning fog as we drive up a gravel road toward a small dairy farm. Farm country does not fit my stereotype of loon country—northern Minnesota lakes surrounded by pine forests. The sight of bulrushes tells us we're close to our thirty-four-acre lake.

A two-track lane appears to lead to the unnamed waters, but I question my little Volkswagen's off-road capabilities. We decide to walk. A quarter mile later, we gain a clear view of half the lake and scan it with our binoculars.

After ten minutes at our observation point, we walk around the bend, find another clearing, and take fifteen minutes to survey the other half of the lake. We spot song sparrows, blackbirds, mallards, and grebes, but no loons this morning. We have four more lakes on today's list.

. . .

Next we go to Dane Lake. With a spotting scope, we take in most of the lake from the side of the road. No loons. Studying the topographic map, I realize the far end of the lake doglegs north out of view. We will need to canoe the entire length, and I'm glad.

I ask the landowners across the road if we can park our car in their driveway. Like most landowners I've met, they give me an enthusiastic yes and a five-minute description of the area wildlife, including the occasional loon on Dane Lake.

Anne and I paddle to the bend, lift binoculars, and spot a lone loon on the far shore. It undoubtedly sees us coming. Loons can detect movement around them much sooner than people can. They have keen eyesight and hearing and can sense vibrations on the water.

We stop paddling. We watch and wait. The loon begins fishing, probably for bullheads and perch.

Anne and I ask ourselves a number of questions: Does this loon have a mate? If so, has the pair reproduced? Were the eggs or juveniles prey to a raccoon or snapping turtle?

By visiting the 645 lakes each year, the volunteers are helping the DNR find out where territorial pairs of loons live, how often pairs hatch out young, and which lakes never have loon activity.

The wind has blown us into the wild rice, and still we see no sign of other loons. We mark our data forms for Dane Lake: one adult at the west end, zero juveniles.

Our next lake is only fifteen acres. After ten minutes of scanning, Anne calls the lake a bust, but I would not rule it out as potential habitat. Based on previous surveys, we know that loons use at least 25 percent of Minnesota lakes ten to thirty acres in size. And because most Minnesota lakes are this small, that adds up to a considerable amount of loon habitat for feeding and resting. Most nesting occurs on lakes larger than seventy acres.

Furthermore, finding out which lakes never have loon activity is just as important as knowing which lakes do have loons. By assessing the characteristics of lakes used and those avoided by loons, the DNR might be able to discern whether construction, pollution, and other changes to habitat are harming loons. For instance, will loons abandon or return to a lake if the water quality changes? Are humans interfering with loons' summer breeding as more of us use lakes for recreation and home sites?

Anne and I check out another small lake surrounded by pasture and a bit of forest. We see an adult loon smack in the middle of it. Since all surveys are to be completed by noon, we quickly move on to our last lake.

Before we begin paddling, I spot a floating object about a mile away. It could be a loon, but cormorants, gulls, and even driftwood have tricked us before. We stop often to scan the lake with binoculars. I've seen many loons pull disappearing acts after a single initial sighting.

Finally, we enter a bay. The dot I saw earlier has moved into the bay and transformed into an adult loon with a three- to four-week-old chick. We spot another adult and chick up ahead. We marvel at the picture-perfect family scene. The chicks receive fishing lessons while we witness grace, beauty, and peace.

We speculate about where the parents nested. Most likely they nested on the lake's aspen-covered island, where they're least likely to encounter predators.

I think of the journey this year's young will make in the fall when they migrate to the Atlantic Ocean or Gulf of Mexico. Luckily, these chicks have another three months to grow a good set of wings.

The loon family has moved on—and we realize we should also. As we paddle to the boat landing, I think about the hundreds of volunteers exploring lakes with friends and family on these hot July days. Why have all these people decided to help monitor Minnesota's common loon population? I'm sure there are many reasons. To natural resource managers, the loon is an indicator of the health of our lakes and our environment as a whole. To many people, the loon is a symbol of wilderness, a powerful connection to the natural world. The thought of a loon frees us from our everyday concerns. Maybe this is why the lonely wail of a loon resounds in our hearts.

SOLO SOJOURN

Joan Galli

 IT WAS A DARK AND STORMY NIGHT. No, not really. Thursday, May 22, 2003, actually began like any other day in the office, with too much work, too little time, too many telephone calls. Yes, it was raining. The day would have been too boring to even mention until the phone rang once again.

I answered and heard Bob Fashingbauer, assistant manager at Carlos Avery Wildlife Management Area, say, "Hey, Joan, a woman from some national crane research group called. She tracked one of their whooping cranes to Pool Nine at the Avery last night."

I was momentarily stunned.

To jump-start a birder's otherwise mundane morning, there is nothing like being told that one of the rarest, most endangered birds on the continent is less than twenty miles away.

Bob was short on the details. "I called her back, but her cell phone was breaking up," he said. "I'm going out to meet her at Pool Nine in half an hour. Do you want to track the crane over the weekend if it stays around?"

By this time my brain had kicked into overdrive and was racing through a series of thoughts and questions. "He must mean the International Crane Foundation. Could it be that one of the cranes from the reintroduction is back from Florida and here in Minnesota instead of at Necedah National Wildlife Refuge in Wisconsin? Oh, wow! Yahoo! We're going to have whooping cranes back and nesting in Minnesota one of these days." The last recorded nesting of a whooping crane in Minnesota was in Grant County in 1876.

I declined the tracking assignment, thinking about all the other work to be done. As I hung up the phone, it struck me: Jeez, girl, you just passed on the opportunity of a lifetime to participate in what you think is one of the greatest ornithological adventures to span three centuries. You've always been intrigued by the struggle to save the whooping crane from extinction. You just blew it big time!

I realized my venture into ornithological history might yet be redeemed if I could at least go see the bird before day's end. I was glad to know that the crane foundation people expected the day's rainy weather would keep the bird grounded.

Mindful of Bob's words that International Crane Foundation staff wanted the crane sighting kept quiet while the bird was still around, I reported the news only to my colleagues in the Department of Natural Resources Nongame Wildlife Program. My colleague Steve Kittelson and I conspired to meet after our morning commitments and go see that bird.

By 1:15 we were on our way to see the crane, we hoped. Because no further word had reached us, the suspense mounted when we left the forest and turned west along the sandy dike road of Carlos Avery Wildlife Management Area. Would the crane still be there?

The rain had stopped briefly, leaving a light mist hanging over the wetlands. Suddenly, far off, we saw a big, white bird. Outstanding against a dark and stormy sky, it lured us down the road for a closer view.

We rounded a curve. Oh, no! There was a maroon minivan in our path. The back hatch was up, serving as a roof to shelter some birder with a spotting scope from the rain. His scope pointed toward the crane. As we pulled closer, we recognized, with great pleasure, a friend—Bill Longley, retired DNR wildlife biologist. My day was saved: I was seeing the whooping crane *and* sharing the adventure with friends.

Together we turned our attention to the big bird. It stood taller by half a foot than the forty sandhill cranes milling around in the meadow. The tallest bird in North America, a whooping crane stands about five feet tall with upstretched neck.

Arrayed in the white plumage of an adult bird, "our" crane was bright and stood out against the rich green, rain-washed grasses and the gray-plumaged sandhill cranes, which blended into the cloudy skyline. This bird was beautiful and also bossy! As we watched, the whooping crane periodically interrupted its foraging to stalk after, jab at, and otherwise harass the surrounding sandhill cranes. We estimated the wading bird to be a third of a mile away on a marsh. Through the scope, we could see a green band on one leg and a transmitter on the other.

An hour later, we reluctantly took our leave.

Back at the office, we searched the Web site of Operation Migration to learn more about the bird. We discovered that the bird was female Number 021, captive-bred, hatched April 12, 2002, from the flock at Patuxent Wildlife Research Center in Maryland. She had subsequently been sent, along with fifteen other whooping crane youngsters, to Necedah National Wildlife Refuge in Wisconsin to take part in a great experiment to reestablish a wild population of migratory whooping cranes in the eastern United States. This multiyear, multimillion-dollar effort is being conducted by a coalition of state and federal agencies and private nonprofit groups known as the Whooping Crane Eastern Partnership.

During the summer of 2002, bird Number 021 had been "in training" at Necedah, learning to follow an ultralight aircraft. In the fall of 2002, the airplane led the "Class of '02" more than twelve hundred miles south on a forty-nine-day migration to Chassahowitzka National Wildlife Refuge on Florida's Gulf Coast.

We learned from her Internet biography that Number 021 had a bit of a rough journey south. She dropped out of the third leg after sustaining a minor injury when she clipped a bare tree branch on takeoff. After receiving stitches, she rejoined the flock the same day and ultimately made it to Florida for the winter.

During the first two weeks of April 2003, bird Number 021 and her cohort returned to Wisconsin. The details of this unassisted journey north can be found on the Web sites of the International Crane Foundation and Operation Migration. Apparently, Number 021 likes to travel: after pausing briefly in Wisconsin, she flew to Minnesota, where we encountered her. Her first visit to Minnesota lasted only one day. In late June she returned and spent the summer near Owatonna and Rice Lake State Park. By mid-September she had flown back to western Wisconsin before making a successful fall migration to her Florida wintering grounds.

As fantastic as Number 021's tale of travels has been to date, the most extraordinary coincidence was revealed a few days after her first appearance in Minnesota. While reading with great sadness about the death, at age one hundred, of Walter Breckenridge, one of Minnesota's most esteemed and beloved ornithologists, it struck me that the day Number 021 had appeared was the day Breck's life had ended.

It seems that even as Breckenridge's death marked the end of an era in Minnesota ornithological history, Number 021 inaugurated a new era for Minnesota birds and birders. The whooping crane was back—with the potential to once again breed in our state.

Breck would have loved such a coincidence, I am sure. He would have been the first to use her appearance to remind us that saving wetlands and wildlife habitat is the responsibility of all Minnesotans—it is our natural heritage and our legacy to future citizens.

In my mind, Number 021 is now, and always will be, "Breck's bird." She symbolizes hope for the restoration of a magnificent bird species to our beleaguered wetlands and marshes. Keep watching. You too may soon see a whooping crane in a Minnesota marsh near you.

LAND USE: A BIRD'S-EYE VIEW

Kim Alan Chapman

 EVERY SPRING WE GET A MIGRATING THRUSH—hermit, Swainson's, or gray-cheeked—in our St. Paul backyard. For a few days, its flutelike song seems to carry the fragrance of cedar and lake water to our door.

Later, near the end of June, I love waking up at 4 a.m. and lying in bed to listen to the urban choristers. First comes the robin, mouth open and shouting. Half an hour later, the cardinal throws his *what-cheer? what-cheer?* against the blue jay's yammer. Then an American crow raucously announces it's awake, while the mourning dove rises with graceful cooing. Grackles and house finches follow in short order. The house sparrow begins a dreary *cheep-cheep-cheep,* and the black-capped chickadee lets loose an indignant scold. Finally, under full sun, the twitters of chimney swifts collide with the bursting *peek!* of a downy woodpecker.

While I lie there hoping for a goldfinch's roller-coaster call, people in the country are enjoying a different aural palette. Near grasslands they hear the slurred whistles of meadowlarks on overhead wires. Phoebes and pewees call their own names from savanna and forest. A pileated woodpecker crashes its bill against a tree as big around as a rain barrel. In the forests, yellow-throated vireos repeat endlessly: *ee-ay, three-eight!* Some thirty bird species, in addition to the city ones I can enjoy, will greet the lie-abed country birder.

What sustains this rich bird spectrum, and how much does it diminish with development? Can we have new homes and businesses without sacrificing the nature that has characterized our region for several thousand years? Such questions had dogged me for a long time. Finally, in 1998, I enrolled as a PhD student at the University of Minnesota and began a study exploring the effect of development on birds.

I started by laying out three hundred research plots of 330-foot radius across the northern Twin Cities—a third of them in three nature reserves, another third in three rural townships, and the last batch in three suburbs. For two springs, in 1999 and 2000, several assistants and I counted birds by watching and listening for all the birds that used each plot during ten-minute periods. I then correlated that information with the types and quantities of trees, shrubs, and grasses in the plots; amount of pavement and building surface; distance to roads and buildings; and other indicators of how intensively the land was being used. The goal: to learn which bird species did well (and which did not) when land around them was used in various ways.

During my two-year study, I felt I was swimming just ahead of a crashing wave. Not only did I see new roads being built and old ones widened, but I also saw new homes appear near several study plots. One day I arrived at a plot twenty miles from the nearest dense suburban development and found an attached garage on it. When I asked the owners why they built so far out in the country, they told me they moved from the city because they wanted their children to have the kind of life they'd had growing up in the country.

I study birds because I love having them around. Their diversity also tells us about the state of ecosystems we depend on for clean water, fertile soil, abundant wildlife, and pleasant surroundings. One could say that bird diversity is one measure of our environment and society's well-being.

Between 1990 and 1997, the rural areas in the seven-county metro region had absorbed new single-family homes on about thirty-three thousand acres, an area larger in size than Boston proper. I hoped our research would give a glimpse of the impact of such growth on bird populations.

In fact, our study turned up some dramatic results. The species of birds in our plots differed depending on land use. Oddly, the suburbs supported more individual birds: we counted an average of twenty-three birds per suburban plot and sixteen per plot in "wilder" nature reserves and rural lands. However, we found that the number of bird species in both nature reserves and rural lands exceeded the number of species in suburbs by an average of 30 percent.

Our study found that some bird species profit from intense development. These *development embracers* are the regulars seen at feeders and heard in a suburban dawn. Mourning doves, robins, grackles, house sparrows, and cardinals, for instance, take advantage of "suburban savannas" of short grass and pavement with scattered trees, abundant nesting places in evergreens and ornamental shrubs, and the nooks and crannies of buildings and other structures, as well as a seemingly limitless food supply.

The same development conditions prevent other species from using the suburbs at all. Ovenbirds, field sparrows, eastern towhees, and several other *development avoiders* shrink from development. In our study more than a quarter of the bird species of typical farm grasslands were missing from suburban "grasslands" such as sports playing fields. Suburban "savannas" supported an even smaller proportion of the savanna species typical of farm country and nature reserves.

What depresses bird diversity is a lack of variety in *habitat types* (such as grassland, savanna, and forest) and *habitat structure* (the various heights of grass, trees, and shrubs). For development avoiders, the vast and uniform suburban landscape means fewer places to nest, find food, and avoid being eaten.

Little known but colorful and vocally inspired birds, such as the ovenbird, scarlet tanager, blue-gray gnatcatcher, eastern towhee, blue-winged warbler, and vesper sparrow, find their best homes in nature reserves. They disappear from suburbs and lands with too much agriculture.

Isolation from human endeavor seems important to these development avoiders, but we found some in large suburban forests, especially those far from buildings and roads. In fact, forests in suburbs in our study had as much species variety as forests in reserves and rural lands. The gray catbird, house wren, and downy woodpecker actually fared better in suburban forests than elsewhere in the region.

Conserving farmlands appears to be key to preserving barn swallows, savannah sparrows, great crested flycatchers, and dozens of other species. These birds are most common in rural areas. They tolerate some development but not widespread and intense suburban development.

Some of the Midwest's most beloved and engaging birds—eastern bluebirds, indigo buntings, and meadowlarks—make rural lands their primary home. So does the less familiar grasshopper sparrow, which keeps in touch with grass-foraging relatives using cricketlike buzzes and twitters. The bobolink, sporting cream-and-white patches, warns rivals away in a fluttering, bubbling descent from on high. The brown thrasher—a bird with a thousand songs—flashes rusty feathers as it springs up from thickets to look around.

Grassland and savanna birds of the countryside are declining in numbers faster than forest birds are. Since 1966 the U.S. Fish and Wildlife Service has been counting birds along highway census routes. Henslow's sparrow populations are shrinking nationwide by more than 7 percent a year. (If Minnesota had lost people at that rate, our population of 3.6 million in 1965 would have dropped to 245,000 today.) The grasshopper sparrow is losing ground at 3.7 percent per year, and the eastern towhee at 1.9 percent. A sense of alarm is growing among ornithologists nationwide as they watch many bird species lose their habitats and head for the endangered species list.

Rural grasslands and savannas have shrunk not only as a result of development but also because the rural lifestyle has changed. Fewer farmers raise livestock. Those who do tend to house the animals and feed them grain rather than pasture them. Crops have shifted to corn and soybeans rather than a mix that includes medium-height grasses, which provide grassland bird habitat. Abandoned hay meadows and pastures are turning into thickets and forests.

Yet I take heart from the diverse rural bird community we found in our study. Eastern bluebirds, ruby-throated hummingbirds, and rose-breasted grosbeaks all thrive, in part because of food and shelter humans provide. Although they were not common enough to statistically analyze, we encountered Cooper's and sharp-shinned hawks, wild turkeys, kestrels, northern harriers, sandhill cranes, and other large or wide-ranging birds in rural areas around the Twin Cities.

I suspect the changes in bird life are going largely unnoticed. If birds dropped out of trees with each new house, there might be an uproar against construction just as there was against DDT when dead robins dropped onto lawns forty years ago. But species loss due to habitat loss and simplification is slow, incremental, and inconspicuous.

If we want diverse bird life, we must protect habitat as our area develops. Then, instead of just watching backyard birds, people could bike or walk to places where they could see and listen to birds such as an eastern towhee, whistling *Drink-your-tea!* A landscape that shelters a diversity of birds will be like a bank account that funds cleaner water, healthier soil, more wildlife, and greater recreational opportunities. And on top of it all, we will hear birdsong, vibrant and various.

Practicing Conservation

ONE SEED AT A TIME

Sue Leaf

ON A CLEAR JUNE DAY, the oak savanna at Wild River State Park is fresh with color and birdsong. Buttery yellow hairy puccoon and bold magenta prairie phlox enliven the wispy grasses. Dusty oaks, singly or in clusters, provide shade. The dry trill of a savannah sparrow drifts out over the grasses. I pick my way through poison ivy, seeking something rare: wild lupine.

Wild lupine is a robust, shin-high plant with whorls of green leaves splaying out like little hands. In mid-June, its showy clusters of blue flowers are at peak bloom. Wherever they grow, a profusion of blues and violets meets the eye.

A classic savanna plant, lupine is at home on sandy soil. It thrives amid prairie grasses in the partial shade of oaks. Wild River's oak savanna was partially cleared for cultivation a century and a half ago. What remained was heavily grazed. Delectable to cattle, the once-common lupine was nearly eaten out of existence.

Oak savanna is a transition zone between forest and prairie, where trees dwindle and grasses take over. In Minnesota, it is the rarest landscape. Only about four thousand acres, or one-tenth of 1 percent of the presettlement oak savanna remains, much of it unprotected.

As some people recall being introduced to a person who would later become a close friend, so I remember the first time I laid eyes on preserved savanna. I instantly recognized it, even while thinking I had never seen anything like it—too grassy to be a forest, but too wooded to be a grassland.

I realized that my childhood home of Roseville, Minnesota, had once been savanna. I had spent many days playing under the dry rustle of rusty oak leaves, in "weeds" I later learned were prairie grasses.

But the sensation of familiarity seemed too rich to be based solely on childhood memories. When I learned that humans had evolved on savanna—Africa's savanna—and show, in psychological testing, preferences for savanna-like settings, I wondered if something more—something ancient—wasn't at work in my psyche.

As a biologist, I find all natural ecosystems brimming with intricacy and beauty. However, only the savanna fills me with emotion that I seem unable to plumb. I return to it again and again, to see what else the savanna has to say to me. I am passionate about its restoration.

The legislation that established Wild River State Park in 1973 required that its native species and landscapes be preserved and restored. A first step in restoration is to bring back the natural disturbance that created the landscape. For centuries before European settlers arrived, fire kept most trees at bay on Minnesota's savanna. Only the prairie grasses and oaks survived cleansing burns. Often a light burn reestablishes savanna.

To decide what to burn, park managers took their cues from old trees. Bur oaks assume a burly form when they have elbow room. Where broad-crowned, heavy-limbed bur oaks grew, park managers surmised that an oak savanna once stood. Initial burns eliminated some invading species and encouraged natives, but not all of the savanna's presettlement species reappeared. Grazing had been too intense.

In the 1980s, park staff enlisted schoolchildren and service groups to help collect native grass seeds from plants growing on Wild River's natural remnants. Other volunteers sowed the seeds the following spring. The park began to look like a savanna, but lacked many of the colorful, jewel-like native flowers that might number as many as two hundred species on a pristine savanna.

Enter park naturalist Dave Crawford and his Prairie Care Project. In 1993, starting with a handful of adult volunteers, he launched a program focusing on collecting seeds from easily identifiable flowering plants. Collectors each received an illustration of the plant's seed head and a map. Toting empty ice-cream buckets as collection pails, they went to small, undisturbed patches in the park and brought back seed—modest amounts at first, but still more than Crawford had seen from previous efforts.

Next, wondering if the program could be a teaching tool, Crawford asked two classes of elementary school children to collect blazing star seed. In twenty minutes—roughly a child's attention span—the kids had collected seed worth a thousand dollars.

Crawford knew he had a workable approach. In the ten years since its launch, the Prairie Care Project has blossomed and now engages more than fifty adult volunteers plus hundreds of schoolchildren. Many volunteers become species stewards and develop expertise on one or two species. We locate and observe "our" plants as they bloom, fade, and set seed. We scout out undiscovered populations in the park and collect as much seed as we can. Last fall, the total market value of the collected seed was twenty-five thousand dollars.

Actually, the seed is priceless. Since these populations grow on this patch of earth, their seeds are uniquely fitted to restore it. You can't buy such well-suited seeds in any store.

My charge is wild lupine, which produces seeds in midsummer. Late in June, Crawford hands me a small manila envelope weighted by several handfuls of last summer's seeds—about $250 worth. The seeds are white, like pebbles, about the size of split peas. "Just scatter the seeds in somewhat open areas where you think lupine might grow," he tells me. "Don't fuss too much—it should be fun."

Compulsive gardener that I am, I seek out the sandy earth of pocket-gopher mounds along the margins of woodland and grassy openings. I plant the seeds and carefully pat soil over them. My efforts are rewarded two weeks later when the smallest of seedlings, sporting tiny green whorls of leaves, poke through the soil. The lupine population increases.

The spread of wild lupine in the park could have consequences for a butterfly with a finicky appetite. The butterfly, the Karner blue, inhabits sandy pine or oak prairies and lakeshore dunes. Wild lupine is the sole host for its voracious caterpillars. Adult butterflies are small, with delicate cerulean wings marked with orange marginal spots. Karner blues are rare and listed as state endangered.

Karner blues do not inhabit Wild River State Park; but twenty miles north at Crex Meadows Wildlife Area in Wisconsin, the butterflies have a breeding population. The habitat is right for Karner blues at Wild River, though there is no indication they were ever present. Yet, when I sow my seeds, I walk north, consciously trying to bring the park's lupine population closer to Crex Meadows. I now watch for the flutter of blue wings, for a fleeting glimpse of azure at mud puddles or over meadows. We are waiting for a wandering Karner blue to discover this part of Minnesota.

Ah, the energy at Wild River State Park! Leaping flames tended by trained burn crews! Fifty volunteers with collection pails! More volunteers to pick and clean the collected seed over the winter! Still more volunteers to sow it in the spring!

With all the hand-collected seed gathered over a decade, Wild River State Park has gained about two hundred acres of replanted prairie—two hundred acres in ten years! It's a postage stamp on the broad face of the planet. That is just stage one of reestablishing a savanna.

In stage two, oaks will be reintroduced, probably by way of acorns sprouting into seedlings, then maturing into saplings, slowly, slowly becoming larger. After the oaks will come the plants that shun the full sun of a prairie but thrive in partial shade—woodland species that provide the mix that makes a savanna unique in diversity and plant structure. None of us involved in the restoration will live to see good savanna growing in the park. It will take longer than a human lifetime.

Dry-eyed critics of such meticulous restoration claim it is little more than a nostalgic attempt to bring back a lost Eden that vanished with the invasion of European settlers. "What value is it to choose a single moment in time as the aim of a restoration effort?" ask the authors of "Carving Up the Woods," a criticism of savanna restoration efforts in northeastern Illinois published in *Environmental Restoration.* "[It is] merely placing nature in a historical role and relegating its existence to that of an artifact, encased behind museum walls." In this case, a big museum—a state park.

Restoration ecologists counter by pointing out that their efforts are directed toward supplying an environmental force—such as frequent fire—and not a specific landscape. The heroic efforts of seed collectors have an end point—their function, to restore plant diversity, will someday be done. Then we will see if the savanna can maintain itself under its evolutionary conditions of disturbance by fire.

Still, are we sentimentalists, grooming a personal, though wild, garden? Wouldn't our efforts be better directed toward something really necessary for a healthy environment—such as persistently pestering our legislators to produce a sustainable energy policy, or addressing a consumer culture whose excesses cause a plethora of environmental woes?

I ponder these criticisms when I'm out in the field. Rather than picket signs, my thoughts turn to houses. The word *ecology* comes from the Greek word *oikos,* meaning "house," so I'm not completely off track.

Let's say I have a beautifully furnished house. One day, while I'm away, someone has a wild party in the house and trashes it—carpet stained, mirrors smashed, furniture broken. It is no longer fully functional or beautiful, but the roof is intact and still keeps out the rain. Is it sentimental to think that I ought to restore the house to its former condition?

The answer depends on the direction I am looking, forward or backward. If my aim in restoration is to re-create the house to the last detail in order to relive happy moments—birthdays, Christmases—of the past, then it might be a sentimental effort.

But what if my aim is to enrich my future life—to re-create beauty and functionality and to provide a worthy inheritance for my children? Is that sentimental?

What about the small furnishings? A china figurine—well, I really wouldn't need that. But a cell phone on the nightstand, to use in case of fire? That might save the house.

Like all analogies, mine has limitations. But the small items that might or might not be important are interesting, because ecologists will tell you that we don't understand any ecosystem well enough to determine whether we can get along without all the details. We know that ecosystems with a high level of biodiversity recover more quickly from disturbance, such as drought; but we don't know which species are essential to the ecosystem, and which ones won't be missed if they go extinct.

This lack of knowledge makes our efforts at Wild River seem less like paging through an heirloom photo album and more like sitting at a roulette table, trying to calculate how much we can afford to lose.

In my gloomy moments, I wonder if the charge of sentimentalism is, in truth, a refusal to come to terms with the loss of North America's wealth of life, and a rejection of any guilt in our collective abuse of the land. Yet, when I am at work on the nascent savanna, gloom and guilt do not exist. What I see is fresh and bountiful—big bluestem grass dripping with seed, dried lupine pods swollen with promise. The earth is incredibly lavish in its production of new life. Taking my cue from nature, I see that each new spring brings possibility. The hope it engenders ties us to the bountiful oaks adorned with May's flowers, to every savannah sparrow pioneering restored land.

GIVING THANKS ON THE PRAIRIE

Michael Furtman

 I PAUSED, PANTING ON THE PRAIRIE.

Despite cold fingers, numb where they gripped the old shot-gun, my steamed eyeglasses and a wet spot between my shoulder blades revealed the heat of my exertion.

I had caught up to my black lab, Wigeon, where she'd disappeared into cattails bunched along the edge of a frozen pothole, and marked her progress by the whipping tops of cattails scattering their downy seed pods. There was no hearing her over the sucking of my own breath. After the pause, I too stepped into the wall of cattails.

In that instant the prairie that had seemed so empty of all but the dog and me erupted into a confusion of life. A white-tailed deer burst from where it had been crouching to avoid the dog, so near to me that had I extended my shotgun I could have touched it. Snow, scattered from the cattails, hung momentarily in the air, each crystal glittering in the lowering sun. Had I time, I'd have paused to admire it. But the chase was still on.

The dog traded directions, and as she did, pheasants flew from the far end of the marsh. A great wave of birds launched into the sky, every one of them out of shotgun range, the roosters snubbing me with their cackling laugh. Wigeon surged into an opening before me, her tongue lolling and red with exertion, her face clouded by snow and cattail down. I called her to my side and calmed her before we scoured the rest of the marsh. Of the pheasants there was naught but their three-toed tracks and enough scent to drug the dog. Beaten, we walked wearily back toward the truck through the skiff of snow. On a rise, I turned to the slough and silently saluted the birds that had so handily eluded us.

From the knoll I scanned the horizon. The island of grass, so full of life, through which we had labored ended but a quarter mile away. Beyond, an ocean of black earth swept to the end of our sight, interrupted only by a few trees and some distant farm buildings. Roads diced the country into mile-sized squares—an immense checkerboard. This well-ordered world we saw—well ordered if you are a farmer—struck me then, as it always does, as a melancholy place, manipulated within an inch of its life.

Yet I love it here. Late in the year, when the sun never seems to rise much above half-mast, when thin gray clouds hinting of winter scud across the endless sky and cold winds hiss through the grass, I come to these grasslands to chase pheasants.

At least that's the excuse.

A creature of the north woods, I am nonetheless drawn to prairie Minnesota by its remnant wildness. Each autumn I long to walk where the horizon is unbounded, to feel the tug of tall grass at my boots, to listen to the geese and cranes pass overhead, and to watch the never-ceasing quartering of a fine dog as it is dragged along by the intoxicating scent of a pheasant. I drive past the ubiquitous No Trespassing signs—including a huge, hand-painted one (Don't Even Think of Hunting Here) that guards a barrens of dirt and stubble where, even if I had hunted, I would have had a hard time finding a field mouse. And when I pull up to a yellow Wildlife Management Area sign, or a green one proclaiming Waterfowl Production Area, I feel a huge sense of welcome and a debt of thanks to those who created these public lands.

But if the pheasants and the dog work are the public excuses for these visits, there are private reasons as well. I love to walk deep into these public oases, especially those that form a bowl, because from their centers, with the horizon formed by a grassy rim, I can almost believe that we are walking the untamed prairie, that part of Minnesota now more vanquished and vanished than any other. And when I sink to the ground to take a rest amid the Indian grass and side-oats grama, I can let my imagi-

nation run, and when it gallops, I believe I hear the pounding and groan-
ing of great seething herds of bison, hear the calliope-call of the prairie
elk. I imagine that when I top the next rise I will look down and see, not
my waiting pickup truck or a farmstead, but the smoking spires of the
Lakotas' tepees, hear their children laughing and the dogs barking, and
watch as the men leap to their ponies to chase buffalo across the plains.

Once, this land was as rich with wildlife as it is today lush with corn.
The Great Plains had been called the Serengeti of North America, and
Minnesota's portion was no less verdant. Grass unbroken from our western border east to where it met the oak savanna, it was dotted with un-
countable, glistening wetlands, which spawned huge autumn clouds of
waterfowl. And instead of pheasants lurking in the big bluestem and por-
cupine grass, prairie chickens chuckled as they flew, once so numerous
they were routinely found for sale in local markets.

Evidence of how many large animals once lived on the prairie was
the bone pickers, who, for years after the last bison and elk were killed,
labored to pick the prairie clean to sell the skeletons to fertilizer factories.
In 1878 St. Paul bone entrepreneur E. F. Warner found enough buffalo
bones, elk skeletons and antlers, and pronghorn antelope horns in Rock
County (around present-day Luverne) to gross seventy-eight thousand
dollars in a single year. So profitable was the business that a B. W. Hicks—
"Dealer of Buffalo Bones," according to his letterhead—set up shop on
busy Nicollet Avenue in Minneapolis to handle the incoming trade.

This testimony to change on a gargantuan scale is no indictment of
farmers, who perform a vital task. But as I drive the miles of roads, see
the fence-row-to-fence-row farms, tick off the seemingly endless miles
of drainage ditches, I cannot help but wish we had been as farsighted in
protecting prairie as we had been in reserving forests.

No greater champion of these prairies ever existed than Richard Dorer,
who, as state supervisor of game, dreamed of preserving prairie wetlands
and uplands at a time when their destruction was rampant. Part preacher,
part field general, Dorer talked in coffee shops and at meetings to all who
would listen of his Save the Wetlands plan for a surcharge on small-game

licenses to purchase some two hundred thousand acres of prairie lands and waters.

Despite his energy, the struggle must have been disheartening for this beefy man. With the post–World War II boom in full swing, he had to know he was working against an unrelenting headwind of contrary goals. Beginning in the late 1940s, as he wound his way across the state to preach, surely he saw yet more prairie plowed and watched draglines drain thousands of wetlands that vanished during the years it took for his dream to become law.

What sustains such dreams? Did he ever get angry as he drove the country roads trying to organize the state's then-unorganized hunters? If the prairie is a miracle of creation, so too is the will of a person so bent on its preservation that he can snatch thousands of acres away from the plow.

"Conservation is the militant defense of natural resources," Dorer wrote. The use of "militant" might today brand him as some kind of extremist. And in the 1950s, saving wetlands and grass might have labeled him as an oddball. But it took the organization of a military campaign to create his program, and though it then may have seemed odd, today it is clear that his plan to save prairie and wetlands was truly farsighted.

I could not help but think of Dorer as we trudged through the big bluestem toward the truck, weary but happy from hours of hiking. As we walked, Wigeon startled a prairie falcon from the grass. The handsome bird launched first downwind, flashing in the sun, then swung wide to our left, stroked into the breeze, and landed in a lone, bare-limbed cottonwood on the marsh's edge. It folded its wings delicately and watched us, waiting; and as we went forward, we saw why.

In the grass was a bowl of tossed feathers. In the bowl of feathers was the torn carcass of a pheasant. We had disrupted the falcon's meal, and I wondered if we hadn't even unknowingly helped provide it when we flushed the pheasants from the marsh.

Wigeon nosed it. I called the dog away and smiled.

At least one hunter in this little wild place had been successful. And at least there was this little wild place left in which it could be successful.

We hurried on so that the falcon might return to finish its meal. It knew nothing of the struggle to preserve such a place for it—and me—to hunt. But I knew.

As we closed in on the truck, we walked past the little sign that declared this to be public land. I paused, and thought of the giant of a man who made all this possible.

I turned to the grassland once more, and taking my hat from my head, said aloud something I felt needed saying.

"Thank you, Richard Dorer."

THE DROPPING DUCK

Tom Chapin

THE MODERN ERA OF DUCK HUNTING in America began in 1918, when centuries of uncontrolled commercial waterfowl harvest led to the enactment of the federal Migratory Bird Treaty Act, which banned the sale of wild waterfowl and imposed limits and other restrictions. Duck hunting was a top item on my agenda as a Minnesota game warden.

Since ducks migrate across borders, hunting is controlled by both state and federal regulations. The methods of taking waterfowl and daily limits differ to some extent between states; nonetheless, most migratory waterfowl hunting in this country is under similar restrictions. For example, it is illegal to chase and take ducks with a motorized vehicle, hunt in open water without vegetation cover, and use a shotgun that holds more than three shells. Most hunters comply with the rules, particularly when accompanied by children who need to learn the "right way" to conduct themselves in the blind.

Two weeks before season a few years ago, I was searching out a good spot to work on the morning of the upcoming opening day. I came upon a fresh campsite near a small lake just north of Lake Winnibigoshish. The remote, hourglass-shaped lake was situated a mile off the beaten path with only a walking trail leading to the access—a perfect spot for surveillance.

Prior to sunrise on opening morning, an officer from the Leech Lake

Indian Reservation and I approached the camp and hunkered down in a brushy area near the lake to await the noon start. Outfitted with binoculars and patience, we observed movement between tents and the water—seven men loading boats, organizing guns and decoys, and repairing blinds along the shore.

Because they were hunting in such an isolated area, it was unusual that we did not witness violations such as early decoy placing or shooting before noon. This crew appeared to be following the regulations as the first ducks were shot about 12:10 p.m.

We decided to hike a mile cross-country to an adjacent lake where we had heard shooting an hour before the season opened. We would return here later in the afternoon to check bags, guns, and licenses.

As we packed up, I took one last glance across the lake through my binoculars and caught a glimpse of a motorized boat with what appeared to be two occupants moving in the direction of most of the shooting. A short time later, I caught the glint of a gun barrel pointed out the side of the craft. Then, *boom* . . . *boom* . . . two reports from the shotgun out of the bow of the boat. They were motorboating ducks!

For the next hour, the boat skipped back and forth across the end of the lake, racing into the flocks of ringnecks while the hunter slayed ducks from the boat. We were hard-pressed to take action; we could only watch intently, scribble notes, and wait to confront them back at camp later in the day.

About 2 p.m. a second boat approached the narrows about a hundred feet away. I saw a man in a short-sleeved shirt with a shotgun lying across his lap operating his six-horse outboard at full throttle. I crawled to the edge of the water and crouched behind a clump of cattails. The boat ran directly down the middle of the lake and met up with the other two hunters on the water. At the same time, three other members of the hunting party had arrived back at camp and were moving behind me between blinds. I was only five feet from the trail they were using, so I was unable to move for fear of being spotted.

Ten minutes later, the single-occupant boat turned in my direction. At the same time, I heard the crunching steps of two other hunters passing within four feet of my ground-hugging body. Why they didn't see me, I'll never know. They must have been focused on the guy in the boat, who now started shooting.

Sneaking a quick look from my stomach position, I saw the operator hold his shotgun directly over his head and, at full speed, blast a duck out of the air. As the ball of feathers plummeted, I covered my head for fear it might hit me. The fat mallard landed with a big *thwop* twenty feet down the beach.

The two guys who had just passed me yelled, "Way to go, Weezer!" At least now I had a name. *Kerpow!* Weezer shot at another fowl but missed. "Go, Weezer, go!"—more encouragement from his buddies standing thirty feet to my left.

Weezer pursued his illegal antics for another fifteen minutes, busting another duck as he strafed the bulrushes along the opposite shore. Now everyone in the group was roaring encouragement to Weezer, lauding his exceptional ability to run down and dispatch ducks from a motorboat. By the time the whole team suspended their escapades and gathered back at the access, we had fingered five of the seven on various infractions.

Our intention was to make our presence known only when all the hunters were grouped in a cluster. We figured this would reduce the odds of escape if any had an inclination to leave the scene. We crawled toward the access, then stood up twenty feet away and just walked toward the whole bunch. Two of them noticed us immediately and turned to walk away.

"Hold on there a second. Game wardens! We'd like to talk to everybody at the same time. C'mon back here. C'mon back here!"

They turned in our direction and ambled back to the group.

I began. "How about everybody sit down and relax while I explain our intentions? We've been watching your hunting behavior since early this morning, and we'll be discussing our observations. First, why doesn't everybody pull out their IDs, hunting licenses, and duck stamps for inspection."

It soon became apparent that this was a good bunch of guys, cooperative and well educated on the finer points of legal duck hunting. We discovered this was the second generation of hunters who used this campsite on opening day every year, and they had never been checked by a warden in thirty years!

"We just got sloppy with the rules after all these years. It's probably a good thing you caught us. Otherwise, we would have gotten much worse," one of them said.

As I looked over the group, I gestured toward one of the more stout members and said, "Would you happen to be 'Weezer'?"

Sporting a shy, proud smile, he growled, "Yup. That's me!"

The other chimed in, "That's our Weez. That's the Weez-man!"

"That's what I thought. Maybe I'll talk to you first."

We all had a good laugh with the affable Weezer, now the center of attention.

Only a few had proper licenses. Four were charged with transporting loaded firearms in a motor vehicle. Three were issued tickets for taking migratory waterfowl from a motorboat and two for possession of lead shot. One shotgun was confiscated.

They eventually thanked us for a couple of warnings afforded them and declared, "I think we've learned our lesson. You won't have to worry about this place anymore."

I believed them. This case also reaffirmed an axiom for me that conservation officer visibility is one of the most important factors in deterring wildlife violations.

A HUNTER'S JOURNAL

Dave Schad

 WHENEVER I VISIT THE OLD DEER SHACK, I am inevitably drawn to the journal that rests high on a shelf. The typed entries, which start in 1946 and run until 1972, were compiled over the years by Eldon "Swede" Johnson, the unofficial leader and scribe for my father's deer-hunting gang.

The rustic cabin is nestled on a small ridge deep in the Nemadji State Forest, which lies along the Wisconsin border northeast of Hinckley. This cabin and the surrounding forests have been a central part of my life for as long as I can remember. And those journal entries, as much as anything, stimulated an interest in wildlife, hunting, and conservation, which eventually led to my career as a wildlife manager with the Department of Natural Resources.

While the journal tells of the camaraderie of a group of friends, it also chronicles our northern deer herd and efforts of my DNR predecessors to manage deer during the past fifty years.

My dad's hunting gang, most of them fresh out of high school and all from the Stillwater area, first ventured into the Nemadji in 1947.

Dave, Clayt, Ken Anderson & Eldon drove up in Model A and Chev Coupe. We camped north of fork in sled road, 2½ miles in from Daman's corner. Used dad's old tent, lots of snow. In trying to keep tent warm with oil heater, we almost gassed our selves. Ate outside under the birch & pine trees. Clayt shot 1 doe

& found another, Dave shot a doe & Ken shot a doe. Four doe for
4 fellows.

Similar camps had sprung up throughout the Nemadji and other
northern forests. The 1940s through the mid-1960s are often thought of
as the golden years of Minnesota deer hunting, when the rich tradition of
hunters going up north to deer camp began to flourish.

After the great pine forests were logged in the late 1800s and early
1900s, wildfires such as the Hinckley and Cloquet fires burned most
of what is now the Nemadji. A very young forest emerged. Mixed with
open meadows that had not yet reforested and farms established by early
homesteaders, it provided ideal deer habitat.

After World War II, thousands of war veterans returned home and
were eager to enjoy life in Minnesota. The number of licensed hunters in
the state jumped from 70,000 in the prewar years to more than 170,000
just after the war.

In those days, a $2.25 license allowed hunters to shoot deer of any age
or sex. In 1949 my dad (Ronny) shot his first deer.

Clayt, Ken, Paul, Dave, Babe, Mike, Ronny & Eldon were up this
year hunting. No snow to start with, but some came on Monday
morning. Last year we drove model A in, almost too much water
& mud, got stuck on the way out. Ken & Dave shot 1 doe each,
Paul a doe fawn, Ronny a buck fawn & Mike a big buck N.W. of
john deere shack. Two doe, 2 fawn & 1 buck for 8 fellows.

But the entry for 1950 indicated that the season was closed. Frequent
closed seasons through the 1930s had allowed deer populations to increase to high levels, leading to severe overbrowsing of much of the forest. The high deer numbers and depleted habitat led to large die-offs
of deer after severe winters, such as occurred in 1947–48 and 1949–50.
Because game managers did not have the authority to limit harvest or
even shorten seasons at that time, a closed season was their only option
to limit harvest.

Fortunately for the gang, deer populations rebounded quickly.
Starting in 1951, deer benefited from a series of mild winters, even though

the quality of habitat continued to decline as the forests aged. By 1955 hunting was better than ever for the gang.

> Dave, Al, Clayt, Paul, Prunes, Babe, Ronny and Eldon were up
> for hunting this year. . . . We had 10" of beautiful snow this year
> so we even had snowshoes with. Didn't use them though. . . .
> Four doe and Four bucks for 8 fellows.

New families, farming and business obligations, and the Korean War kept some members out of the woods almost every year, but the gang stuck with it.

> Sunday, November 12, 1961. Al, Neil, Paul, Clayt & Ronny left for
> home at 7:30, guess it's up to Eldon, Dave & Babe to fill out, what
> fun. Paul said, "I'm going to be better off next year, not so much
> corn and NO sows with little ones. Then I'll stay the full season I
> hope." Back to shack by 10:30. Rain this morning & cool tonight,
> someone said it was going to snow, that would be nice.

After struggling for years hunting from tents and makeshift cabins, the gang decided that they needed a new, permanent hunting cabin. They found a nice site on land leased from the state. It overlooked an alder and ash swamp, just off of one of the old logging trails that crisscrossed the forest. The shack they built there in 1963 still stands.

The single-room cabin includes six bunks, a wood stove, and a beautiful, handmade rectangular table with each hunter's name stenciled in black along the edge. The antlers from bucks taken during past hunts were hung on the walls, making it possible to match up the racks with deer mentioned in journal entries. No running water or electricity here— the cabin sits about three miles from the nearest maintained road, as close to wilderness as you can get this near the Twin Cities.

Shack construction brought my first visit to the Nemadji.

> Sunday, September 14, 1963. Up by 6:00 and building on the shack
> by 6:45. We had the wall panels, roof panels and felt roof paper
> down by noon. Dave, Carol, Jeanie, Sharon, Davy and Lynn K.
> came in about 9:00 or so. Lois, Elaine, David, Lori, Jimmy, Jean

Schad, David and Greg came about 11:30. The girls had chicken with for dinner and was it good.

That year everyone made an extra effort to hunt and spend more time than usual in their new accommodations, and the season was their best ever. It marked the first year that one of the gang's children was lucky enough to shoot a deer. They clearly enjoyed the 1963 season.

> Wednesday, November 13. Boy, did we see deer signs and deer. . . .
> We put Neil on a stand and made a drive to him. Neil shot his first deer, a nice buck fawn. He certainly was proud.

> Thursday, November 14. For supper we had tenderloins, mashed potatoes, green beans and apple pie with Reddi Whip on top. Man talk about live like kings!! This was Babe and Al's first meal of deer tenderloins.

Little did the gang know that these good times would be short lived. The forest was aging, and more than three decades of high deer populations had taken their toll on the forest. Severe winters in the 1960s began to deplete northern herds. High hunter numbers (now more than three hundred thousand) and no limits on the harvest of does and fawns allowed little opportunity for the herd to recover. Just two years after their banner season, the gang saw their first evidence of problems.

> Thurs., Nov. 18, 1965. Drew another blank today, in fact we didn't even see any fresh tracks. Dale, Eldon and Babe hunted east into Ash Swamp and old tumble-down shacks. Then north to John Deere Ridge. Deer had yarded up in this area last winter and you could really see it on the pine trees. Branches were eaten off 4 to 5 ft. from the ground.

In 1968 they failed to shoot a deer for the first time since they began hunting together. The next year's season was shortened to only five days as game managers struggled to reduce deer harvest. The gang hunted only two days, and saw four deer all weekend. They took two bucks, but were clearly discouraged. Prospects were even poorer in 1970.

Friday, Nov. 13. We thought last year was short, but this year it's only 2 day season. . . . Saturday, Nov. 14. Yes, you guessed it we drew a blank today. Rick & Bob hunted around John Deere country in morning and saw one. Paul & Eldon hunted west of camp, Eldon saw one, shot once with the 45-70 but didn't connect. Dave hunted on South Ridge then north to John Deere country & saw nothing. Chuck and Davie Carlson hunted east of Ash Swamp, but again they saw nothing.

Because even the short 1970 season resulted in a high harvest, the DNR was forced to close the statewide gun season in 1971, the first time since 1950. This crisis mobilized the hunting community, which began to work with the DNR and legislators to focus additional attention on the problems facing Minnesota deer. A large appropriation was provided to the DNR for habitat improvement, and was followed by a one-dollar surcharge on each deer license to provide permanent funding.

The 1971 season was to be my first spent hunting at the camp, and the closure was devastating to me. In 1972 the time for my first deer hunt finally arrived. Everyone seemed surprised that our first day in the woods produced success.

Friday, Nov. 24. Everyone hunted west & north of camp. Babe shot a nice 8 point buck north of camp by North Beaver ponds. Paul shot a nice spike west of camp by his old stand. No snow.

Another buck was shot the following day, and three more deer the next. To my young eyes, it seemed like a return to the good times, but the group's enthusiasm to hunt the Nemadji country had waned.

Sunday, Nov. 26. Everyone was back in camp by 12:00, we packed everything into Bergland's trailer & we were out to the white shack by 2:15. Home by 5:30 after registering our deer in Bruno. . . . Looks now like we might look into some other country to hunt deer in, possibly north of Flood Wood.

Even though they remained friends, the gang quit hunting the Nemadji after that year and eventually turned the cabin over to their children, who have maintained it since then. Most of the other deer hunting camps that used to dot the tote roads were also gone by this time, and the woods surrounding the shack became quiet in November.

In 1975 the DNR developed the antlerless permit system, which placed annual limits on the harvest of does and fawns, but not adult bucks. Though a few permits first became available in the Nemadji area in 1977, the gang had long since given up.

The antlerless permit system slowly brought populations back. Deer also benefited from mild winters statewide through most of the 1980s, habitat improvement funded by the continued deer license surcharge, and more logging of the aging forest.

In 1995, after an absence of twenty-three years, the gang held a reunion of sorts at the Nemadji. While the shack was still sturdy, deer hunting had changed in the time they had been away. Licenses now cost twenty-two dollars, and hunters had to apply for antlerless permits. The number of hunters in the state had increased to more than four hundred thousand, and deer were now abundant statewide. Certainly, the gang could have found places to hunt closer to home. Instead, they chose to return to their old cabin.

That first morning, as the hunters moved out to their favorite stands, they found that the woods had also changed. Much of the area had been recently logged, the first harvest of timber since near the turn of the century. The cutting had drawn in both deer and new groups of hunters. However, the old stands were still productive, and though the gang no longer hunted as hard as they once did, deer once again hung on the meat pole outside the shack.

Since then, members of the gang have continued to get together at the shack for deer hunting. The recent severe winters have dealt another blow to deer in the area. But with continued management of the deer herd and improved habitat, the deer will return to the Nemadji, just as the old hunting gang has.

THIS OLD FARMLAND

Blane Klemek

I ONCE ASKED ELDOR OMDAHL if there were many deer around when he was a boy, and he answered simply, "None."

Eldor Oliver Omdahl, ninety-seven, was born January 6, 1910, in Polk County in far northwestern Minnesota. He and his wife, Stella, eighty-eight, live on the land where Eldor grew up and later farmed. Throughout their thirty-seven-year marriage, they have been stewards of the land. They turned their eight-hundred-acre farm into a wildlife refuge by planting trees and creating ponds, waterways, and nature trails. In 1981 their place became the Wetlands, Pines, and Prairie Audubon Sanctuary.

Eldor is amazed at the plentiful deer now on the land. He never would have imagined seeing deer in the days before the Depression. By the 1950s he was noticing deer. Year after year, he saw more and more deer. One day he decided he must begin hunting them because there were more than the land could sustain.

Today, a November deer hunt is a leisurely pursuit for Eldor. He rises early and chooses one of several hunting spots. For many years, he chose an old chair atop a hill he built. From such vantages, Eldor has taken deer on numerous occasions.

I first met Eldor Omdahl more than seven years ago at the sanctuary near Warren. I was interested in becoming the sanctuary's new manager, and

I wanted to meet the man who donated his farm to the local chapter of the Audubon Society.

Parking my truck next to the visitor center, I noticed an elderly gentleman in a nearby woodlot, cutting up a large branch with a chainsaw. Seeing me, he shut down the saw and approached. I introduced myself, and we shook hands.

His firm handshake, cloudy blue eyes, square jaw, and tall, slim physique impressed me. He wore glasses, a long-sleeved button-up shirt, denim pants, and running shoes with Velcro closures. A mesh baseball cap, flecked with sawdust and cocked slightly on his head, covered what appeared to be ample gray hair. He spoke clearly, smiled often, and listened to me intently. I had no idea he was, at the time, ninety years old.

Eldor's grandfather emigrated from Norway in 1893 and homesteaded the 160 acres surrounding today's visitor center. In 1949 Eldor purchased the farm. Over the years, he acquired adjacent properties to expand his farming operation.

Eldor credits his parents for his conservation ethic: "Yes, my dad was a tree planter, and I helped him. We put up birdhouses as a young boy too." Eldor learned from his parents that planting trees helped reduce soil erosion from wind and rain. He saw that trees attracted wild birds, some of which used the birdhouses mounted there. Realizing the conservation value of trees and shrubs, Eldor began to plant them.

The story of the sanctuary unfolds as marvelously as blooming prairie forbs. With lush, grassy fields; shaded hiking trails; and woodlots, wetlands, and waterways teeming with wildlife, the acreage is an oasis of life surrounded by flat Red River valley farmland.

The Omdahls' home, which Eldor designed, stands kitty-corner through the woods from the sanctuary manager's house, which had once been their farmhouse. Black willows, cottonwoods, and other trees planted by Eldor shade their home beside a pond dug by Eldor.

Nearly every morning when I began my workday at the visitor center office, Eldor—sitting atop his four-wheeler—would stop for coffee before departing on his rounds to feed birds and squirrels along the Bluebird

Trail, a meandering two-mile loop lined with bluebird houses. During our chats, we often discussed wildlife habitat projects, which usually involved planting trees.

Eldor loves trees, and I often joked with him that he should be living in the forest instead of the prairie. Trees historically were not abundant on the prairie. As settlers replaced sod-forming grassland plants with crop fields and farmsteads, and tried to suppress fires, trees invaded the open landscape. Still, Eldor planted trees and shrubs as well as native grasses and forbs to control erosion, beautify the homestead, and provide food and shelter for wildlife. Eldor's trees and grasslands are living testament to the man's vision, conservation values, and longevity.

Sometimes, as we stood together admiring his mature cottonwoods, I'd find myself gazing at him in wonderment as he devoutly discussed the lofty giants like an adoring father talking about the lives of his grown-up children.

By all accounts, trees *are* Eldor's children. My old friend never had children of his own. The care he gave each seedling was genuine and rooted in a lifetime of farming knowledge.

A stroll with Eldor on mowed and winding trails beneath the limbs of his beloved trees is a walk from the past into the present. He recalls digging the pond and adjoining canals with a dragline many decades ago. Conversations weave from when the property's productivity was measured by bushels to the acre of wheat to today's grassy fields with nesting bobolinks, meadowlarks, and mallards.

Enormous hills of earth—carefully placed, shaped, and seeded with native grasses by Eldor as he excavated ponds with his tractor and loader—feature benches on each summit. Sitting there, I've often wondered if sanctuary visitors realize just how gifted and generous a man Eldor is: he who returns to nature the land from which he once hauled truckloads of grain.

Eldor retreats to these summits on crisp November mornings to hunt deer. In earlier years of hunting, he was out the door well before sunrise. These days, after a light breakfast of eggs, toast, and coffee, he departs for the woods around 8 a.m. or so. Carrying his .30-caliber rifle and packing sandwiches, Stella's home-baked cookies, and a thermos of coffee, the seasoned deer hunter ambles slowly to his stand.

After Eldor harvests a deer, he and Stella work together to process the venison. Eldor does the butchering; Stella does the wrapping and canning. Yet I suspect that Eldor's reasons for hunting deer have less to do with securing venison and more to do with seeking solitude and being outdoors to watch wildlife. And, like the late Aldo Leopold, he understands that too many deer on the landscape are harmful to the environment.

I once asked Eldor if he could give a bit of advice to others about how to live a good life. He answered thoughtfully, "Be active in world events and conditions around you." I then asked him what has changed the most during his lifetime. "This was old farmland," he said. "Now it's trees, shrubbery, prairie grass, and ponds."

Finding Home

THE GRACE OF THE WILD

Paul Gruchow

AT THE NARROWS OF THE LAKE, I cross over a little arch of land and put in at the river, which, in this shadowy morning light, looks like a dark artery, or vein, running deep in the dense body of a forest so tropically profuse that it seems impervious, foreign, organismic, a place where the trees cannot be seen for the forest. I stifle my breath, so raucous it seems in the surrounding stillness, and paddle my way dreamily upriver, turning the blade at the end of each stroke and pulling it forward underwater so as not to violate the reverential air.

Around one bend I pass a huge beaver lodge; around the next, a reedy marsh in which a bull moose, magnificently racked, feeds without interruption, as if I were merely a bit of flotsam; and around the next, a pileated woodpecker, which takes precipitously to the air, its scarlet crest glowing in a shaft of sunlight, crying what sounds a curse. The cry echoes back, and the forest falls silent again.

Faintly at first, like a whisper of wind, I hear the sound of running water. As I approach it, its language becomes more distinct, the babble of many voices in an unfamiliar language. And then I am upon the rapids, the water slipping over stones like liquid silk, its voice now a low murmur, the sound of an astonished crowd.

I portage around the falls, a distance of a few rods, and when I arrive at its upper end and am about to take to the river again, I see a flash of yellow in the shallows beside the canoe. A clump of irises blooms there. I know from their goldenness, the indigenous irises being blue, that they, like me, have traveled far to reach this place. They are fleurs-de-lis, specimens of which were carried by traders on the Silk Road from Asia to Europe, becoming there the ensign of the kings of France, and from Europe to North America by French fur traders, who thought them a touch of home—the sort of confusion that perhaps all vagabond humans share. Once when I was a newspaper editor, I sent a young journalist to interview the poet John Berryman on the occasion of some new prize, and when she asked him about his roots, a phrase then in currency, he exploded. "Roots!" he bellowed. "What do you think I am, some goddamn plant?"

Thoreau, reading Gray's *Manual of Botany*, was inspired to think how nearly like plants we in fact are, if we are healthy, especially in the matter of roots. "The mind is not well balanced and firmly planted, like the oak," Thoreau wrote in his journal, "which has not as much root as branch, whose roots like those of the white pine are slight and near the surface. One half of the mind's development must still be root, —in the embryonic state, in the womb of nature, more unborn than at first. For each successive new idea or bud, a new rootlet in the earth. The growing man penetrates yet deeper by his roots into the womb of things. The infant is comparatively near the surface, just covered from the light; but the man sends down a taproot to the centre of things."

This is not, by and large, the country of oaks. Here the shallow-rooted white pines reign, or used to before the days of the lumbermen, and in any case, given the shallowness of the soil and the impenetrability of the bedrock that lies just beneath it, deep taproots are not generally an option. I see, however, how firmly the balsam that lies uprooted just up-river has embraced that rock, raising a massive chunk of it as it fell, even though it had not been grounded in the darkest regions of the earth.

And I see how successfully, how gracefully these Asiatic irises have taken hold here at an ancient crossroads of the global village, not one of the highways traveled by the birds or the winds, but a lane opened by the wanderlust of enterprising humans. If the fleurs-de-lis are not by now indigenous here, if they will always be, as the botanists say, alien, still they look securely at home.

They remind me that although we think of this place now as wilderness, as a refuge where nature might make a last defense against the ravages of culture, and although it is a forbidding place in which to make a living, nevertheless it has been occupied by humans for at least eight thousand or nine thousand years. It is likely that the portage I have just crossed was already in more or less continuous use before the first artifact of my own civilization was struck. The ancient crossings may sometimes now be obscured, Sigurd Olson, the bard laureate of this country, has written in *The Singing Wilderness,* but "they are always there, and when you pack your outfit across them you are part of a great company that has passed before. . . . The way of a canoe is the way of the wilderness and of a freedom almost forgotten. It is an antidote to insecurity, the open doorway to waterways of ages past and a way of life with profound and abiding satisfactions. When a man is part of his canoe, he is part of all that canoes have ever known."

I paddle again upriver until I round another bend and come upon the widening of it that I have sought. Along one bank, an ice-polished face of granite rises, perhaps three hundred yards long and fifty feet high. When I draw near to it, I see that it slopes toward me and find myself enshrouded in its perpetual shadow. The rock is dark, stained, and rifled with cracks, but unsullied by lichens, and when I draw very close, I can see a long line of markings, just above the level of my eyes, the color of old blood, but faded, some beyond recognition.

I paddle to the head of the cliff and drift past the paintings, turn and do it again, and again. A few of the markings are immediately recognizable: a canoe, a moose, a human figure, a thunderbird. Others, including the most prominent figure here, which looks to me like the backside of a mission-style rocking chair, are utterly mysterious. The markings were, it is thought, applied with pigments made from animal grease, or the eggs of gulls, or the roe of fish, and tinctures of iron-bearing oxides, probably, judging from their durability, by people who lived here within the past two thousand years. One or two of them, in a rudimentary way, are even readable. The thunderbird, for example, was a supernatural creature living high in the heavens. It bellowed and flashed its presence by flapping its wings to make thunder and by blinking its eyes to produce lightning.

Beyond these few facts little is known. It is not clear why they were made; or why they were made *where* they were made; or what, in general, they signify; or to whom they were addressed. This much seems clear: that they were messages; and this much more can be conjectured: that not all of the messages were addressed to humans, that some of them, at least, were meant to be—perhaps still are—communications with the gods, who were once thought to dwell in this land, and perhaps still do.

These people, whoever they were, were not indigenous. They also came from somewhere else—they may even have come from the home place of the fleur-de-lis—and followed the glaciers of the last Ice Age northward as they melted, and settled here, and came to know the place spiritually as much as physically. When the Europeans arrived, these forecomers were the natives, and so they remain. It may be that this is what it means to be native to a place: to know it intimately enough so that one can say where lives its spirit, or spirits.

"Whatever their interpretation," Sigurd Olson writes of the painted rocks in *Listening Point*, "they marked the period during which Stone Age man emerged from the dark abyss of his past into the world of mind and soul." Olson was not indigenous to this place either, but he stayed long enough, once he had arrived, to notice, to take account of—to discover—and so at last to learn to sing its poetry. Let us also agree that this was sufficient to have made him native.

BATTLE FOR THE COTTONWOOD

Evelyn Wood Moyle

IN MY YARD, DOWN BY THE LAKE, stood a big, dead cotton-wood. The tree was branchless except for a few stubs, barkless, and leaning slightly toward the water. To my undiscerning eye, it appeared to be good for nothing but firewood—and not very good for that. But the cottonwood was vitally important to others. That much was brought to my attention dramatically by the desperate avian battles fought every spring for nine years over possession of the tree. Slowly I came to see that to certain birds it was prime housing material, potentially as valuable as life itself. I also came to see that for the birds, as for people, time and labor are required to add value to raw material and, furthermore, that even among the birds it is not always the laborer who benefits from his toil.

The first of the workers whose activities were in time to convert a dead tree into prime housing was a handsome redheaded woodpecker whose early arrival and aggressiveness made me assume it was a male. Perhaps originally he was attracted to the tree by the carpenter ants, who were busily engaged inside in survival projects of their own and whose fat, helpless offspring probably made the bird many a nutritious meal. Then, finding the pecking easy, the wood dry and well seasoned, the woodpecker set to work to make a home high up on the trunk. Before long a mate joined him, and the two birds worked in shifts every fine day for a month.

It was an arduous task to excavate a hole with one tool, a beak, which had to serve as hammer, chisel, and tongs. Since by woodpecker custom and necessity the nest cavity had to be at least ten inches deep and four inches or more in diameter, the birds had to convert a considerable volume of wood to small chips and sawdust. Moreover, once they had gotten the shaft well started downward, they had to lift all the debris beakful by beakful and drop it out over the entrance. As the weather warmed, whichever bird was working frequently poked its head out of the hole and panted from heat and exertion. But they continued to work steadily. By the first week in June, the job was done, and the woodpecker pair could proceed with their part in perpetuating the species.

The pair went about this task with such quiet efficiency that they were scarcely noticed until their two young poked their heads out of the hole to complain loudly about the food service. For a while there was much noise and activity around the tree, but it ceased suddenly when the woodpecker family flew off to seek more abundant hunting grounds. So for the rest of the summer, the cottonwood was just a dead tree, useful only as a perch for passing birds.

Thus it was not until the following spring that I became aware of the increased value of the old tree. For now the tree had a fine, unguarded nest hole for the taking—and there were takers.

The first claimants were a flicker and a small group of starlings. The flicker apparently had the advantage of size and aggressiveness, and he confidently went to work cleaning out the hole. However, on their side the starlings had numbers and a certain rudimentary social organization. That is, as long as the flicker stayed in or close to the hole, the starlings would retreat when threatened with voice or beak. But let the flicker leave, as eventually it would, and there was always a watching starling to take immediate possession. When in turn this starling left, another, its mate perhaps, would take its place. Once settled inside, beak facing out through the hole, the starling was ready and willing to take on the returning flicker. Usually the threatening beak, loud voice, and puffed-out feathers of the entrenched bird were enough to make the flicker retreat for a short time. But becoming desperate, or catching the starling outside the entrance, it would attack, and a heart-stopping battle would ensue. Sometimes a well-directed blow from the beak would send the starling squawking. At other times the birds would lock together and fall twenty feet or so to the ground, breaking apart just as they landed. They never seemed to be seriously hurt by these falls, only dazed and rumpled, and after a time the fights would resume.

I was not to see the eventual outcome of these battles, for the situation was complicated by the reappearance of the redheaded woodpecker (or perhaps its offspring). The woodpecker immediately attacked the flicker as it perched on the cottonwood (apparently the winner of the last starling-flicker battle) and drove it off with a loud and rattling cry. The flicker, not easily discouraged, returned again and again, but each time with less conviction until it finally stopped coming altogether.

The redheaded woodpecker, even though joined by its mate, still did not have clear title to its old home. The starlings stayed nearby, ever alert to claim ownership by right of possession. The woodpeckers never learned to leave a guard or to act as a team. When one was trying to drive off the starlings, the other never tried to help either physically or vocally. Inevitably the starlings gained possession. This did not end the battling. The woodpeckers simply drilled a new hole above the old one and continued the war with the starlings below. It was not clear that they still wanted to use the old hole, but they surely did not want the starlings there, and with good reason. For no sooner did the woodpeckers complete the second hole than another pair of starlings tried to move in. The second pair of starlings used the same tactics as the first: never leaving the hole unguarded by at least one of the pair and giving at least vocal support when the other was fighting with a woodpecker. Moreover, other resident starlings gathered around with loud cries—surely a psychological advantage for the starling. And so, although the woodpeckers won most of the beak-to-beak battles, the starlings eventually won that hole too.

The indefatigable woodpeckers now moved to the other side of the tree and excavated still a third hole, this one out of the direct line of vision of their opponents. Perhaps the location helped, but more likely, the starlings were now too occupied brooding and then feeding their offspring to make more than token gestures of attack when one of the redheads flew by. So after an expenditure of time and energy made greater by the starlings, the woodpeckers also nested successfully. By the time their nestlings emerged, the starlings were long gone.

One of the redheaded woodpeckers, however, stayed on (again I assumed it was the male), continuing to defend the cottonwood as vigorously as before. No bird or squirrel venturing near was safe from attack. Even a pileated woodpecker, several times his size, backed off from the onslaughts of its belligerent cousin.

Though the human observer might hope the redheaded woodpecker was finally thinking ahead to secure nesting rights for the following season, it was soon evident he was defending his current feeding and sleeping grounds. As fall came, the bird excavated one more hole. So he now had clean sleeping quarters for shelter during the long winter. As it happened, little snow fell that winter, and the bird was able to supplement his food stores with the abundant acorns that lay on the wind-bared ground. He obtained drinking water from icicles on nearby roofs. So he came through the winter in fine shape to resume his arduous spring duties when his mate returned.

As the days lengthened and warmed, the starlings returned to the old cottonwood, and the battles for nesting space began again. The redheaded woodpeckers again showed no evidence of having learned from experience, while the starlings seemed bolder than ever: One even ventured into the hole where a redhead was at work. It was impossible, of course, for someone below to see what went on inside, but the remaining starlings gathered on the tree in great excitement, pecking at the entrance and chattering shrilly. In a few seconds, a badly disheveled starling tumbled out and flew off in an erratic, dazed manner. The woodpecker soon followed, looking ruffled. Immediately, its partner entered the hole and began carrying out bits of wood and straw. One would guess that the interior had been messed by the struggle and the proprietor was cleaning up. Despite this apparent defeat, the starlings did not give up, and the battles continued. In the end the woodpeckers once more gave up their hole and moved around the tree to excavate another.

. . .

And so it went, with minor variations every spring: dramatic battles, sometimes between woodpeckers and starlings, sometimes between woodpeckers and woodpeckers of the same or different species. Twice flickers raised their young there, once even throwing out the starlings. And once purple martins, eyeing the growing number of holes, tried to move in. They had no luck at all and soon went back to their annual contest with the house sparrows for human-made apartments. The house sparrows themselves did better: They took over a weathered open hole that interested neither the woodpeckers nor the starlings, stuffed it with grass, and raised a family without interference from the battling birds below. But always the starlings secured for themselves at least one hole, usually two, while the woodpeckers built anew until finally the top half of the cottonwood had more than twenty-five holes. Oddly, the numbers of woodpeckers and starlings contending for the holes remained about the same year after year—two pairs of starlings to one of woodpeckers. Perhaps it could be said that both won their local battle for survival even though the woodpeckers were forced to provide the housing.

But in the ninth year of the cottonwood's role as high-rise housing, a new dimension was added. A pair of pileated woodpeckers, arriving on the scene before any of their smaller cousins, hammered out a hole much bigger than any previously on the site. It was a fine, large oval that would in time lead to an equally capacious inner chamber. To accomplish this, the pileateds, like their relatives, worked in shifts from dawn to dusk on fine days, staying away only on rainy or cold ones. As the days became longer and warmer, the pair worked longer hours. When both birds were on hand, though there was room at the hole for only one, the second would tap impatiently on a nearby branch and call loudly. The worker would reply with loud calls of its own and after a few minutes would fly off. Whereupon the partner would quickly take its place and send the chips flying. The birds would repeat this scene in reverse a short time later and many times over.

Perhaps the noisy tappings inadvertently advertised newer and larger housing. Whatever the reason, new sets of hopeful home seekers arrived. A gray squirrel and then a pair of wood ducks were easily driven off. The starlings returned and quickly settled in their old holes. But then came a new, more menacing pair that brought trouble for the big woodpeckers. The newcomers were kestrels—handsome, sleek, and patient. A small species of falcon, scarcely bigger than redheaded woodpeckers, they appeared to be harmless: they spent their time reconnoitering, looking over the collection of holes one by one or sitting on the bare treetop for hours, just gazing out over the countryside. The little male soon found himself a hunting territory over the nearby marsh and railroad tracks, while the female frequently ranged up the lakeshore to some vacant lots planted to alfalfa. Seemingly satisfied that they could live here, they laid siege to the pileated's hole.

At first the pileateds had the advantage, with their greater size, long chisel-like bills, and powerful neck muscles. From inside the hole, they were invulnerable. Each time one of the kestrels looked in, it quickly withdrew and retired to a perch above. In time the woodpecker would fly off, announcing its departure with loud, rattling cries. Immediately, one or both of the falcons would give chase, usually with no visible results.

As a drama for spectators, the contest was poorly staged. Sometimes the big hole stood empty for hours, especially during cold, cloudy weather. Sometimes one woodpecker worked inside while the other hunted dinner nearby with no interference from the falcons. Sometimes the falcons seemed to possess the hole, going in and out as if they had already settled the issue of ownership. But then, suddenly, a pileated would appear at the entrance, and immediately the female kestrel would attack from behind with deadly intent. Once, twice, she landed on the back of the bigger bird and dug in with claws and beak, pecking savagely at the head. Each time the birds fell together to the ground with a shocking crash and piercing screams. Each time it seemed as if the falcon might get in a fatal blow, but each time the woodpecker shook her off and flew into the nearby woods.

After several such attacks, the pileateds visited their hole less often. Indeed, they could be seen looking with care at other old trees in the neighborhood. Nevertheless, they did not readily relinquish the hole on which they had already spent so much energy. They continued to watch for times when the kestrels were away, and then they flew back to the cottonwood to resume their labor.

The advantage seemed to be with whichever bird could get inside the hole first in the morning, since both sets of birds roosted elsewhere. Either understanding this or, more likely, finding the compartment now to be of comfortable size, the female kestrel changed her tactics. She began spending the night inside the tree and so she was there to confront the woodpeckers when they arrived in early morning.

All this time other home seekers also kept trying to take over the bigger hole. Here too the kestrels prevented them. A pair of wood ducks got as far as the entrance, but both falcons chased them far down the lake. A redheaded woodpecker made a tentative survey of its former home, but left quickly at the urging of the kestrels. Only a pair of starlings dared remain on the cottonwood to brood eggs in one of the old holes. However, they seemed unusually quiet, slipping in and out as unobtrusively as possible. The starlings held no more social gatherings around the tree. But they could not escape the kestrels' attentions. Occasionally, one would approach the starlings' hole, spread its wings wide over the trunk, and peer in. The starling would respond with thrusts of its sharp beak. The kestrel would retreat with startled and indignant screams to the nearest branch, where it preened its ruffled feathers back into shape. For the starlings this must have aroused a conflict of instincts: the instinct to defend their nest and eggs versus the instinct to stay away from falcons, however small.

But the birdwatcher was not to see the outcome of the contests between the kestrels and their competitors. Over the years the forgotten galleries of carpenter ants had been taken over by organisms too small to excite the appetites or territorial instincts of the birds above. Unnoticed, bacteria and fungi slowly consumed and weakened the old cottonwood from within. Thus one fateful night in early May, a burst of wind from a tornado snapped the upper half of the tree and sent it into the water. Propelled by the wind, the broken trunk sailed out across the lake into dark oblivion. Within, settled for the night in their respective compartments, were the starling and female kestrel. They had little chance to escape and so probably died of shock or drowning.

In the morning the male kestrel circled the spot where his mate and home had been, then flew swiftly off and never returned.

Perhaps from the human standpoint, justice was served: the villains received their desserts, and the industrious woodpeckers lived on to continue their capital improvements on other, sturdier trees. Still, it would have been fascinating to watch the kestrels raise a brood there and to see whether or not the starling young could have survived such neighbors.

IRON RED HOME

Margaret A. Haapoja

 THE MINE PERMEATED EVERY PART of my childhood in the village of Calumet on Minnesota's Mesabi Iron Range. Ore dust colored my world as it sifted through the cracks and turned everything the same rusty shade of red. China rattled in the cupboards as blasts shook every house in town. School days were punctuated by the rattle of rocks being dumped, the squeal of electric shovel cables, the rhythmic thumping of the churn drill, and the clash of colliding oar cars. The sounds emanated from the Hill Annex Mine, a gaping pit just a block from the edge of our playground. Neighbors were knit together by their connection to the mine.

At times, seven sharp whistles blew and sent chills up my spine, for that signal meant there had been an accident. Mining was a dangerous occupation, and casualties were not uncommon. Veteran miners remember a train running over a man, cutting him in half. They recall one time when railroad cars dumped the wrong way, knocking over the brakeman and burying him alive under the load of ore. The father of one of our school friends lost his life in a truck accident at the Hill Annex. One of our neighbors was killed in the mine.

Our house, which once had ore-stained white siding that Mother insisted on painting dark brown, stood within fifty feet of the railroad tracks. Mallets—large steam locomotives pulling nearly two hundred ore cars—thundered through town three or four times every twenty-four hours.

When the large engine had to wait for the track to clear, it would stand behind our garage, panting like some prehistoric dragon snorting smoke and fire. Visiting relatives marveled that we could sleep through the night, but we had grown accustomed to the slam-banging of cars as the engineer dynamited the brakes and to the mournful whistling as he signaled for the crossing a block away. Predating the modern diesel engine, these monstrous black machines weighed well over a million pounds. No wonder the ground shook as they rumbled by.

When we were very young, we used to wave at the mallet engineers as they steamed past our backyard. My sister and I often walked down the tracks with our neighbor, a retired depot clerk. One day, as we sauntered along, searching the railroad bed for agates, a sudden whooshing sound startled us. We whirled around to see a mallet bearing down on us. Its massive black face and eight pairs of driving rods working in unison posed a menacing presence that sleek diesel successors would never match.

My dad, a railroad man at heart, worked in the Hill Annex for more than forty years. He began in 1921 at the age of sixteen as a mule skinner for Guthrie Brothers, contractors who worked the mine before the Interstate Company took over. From that job he moved up to locomotives, first as brakeman and then as engineer. When the company abandoned locomotives, he switched to driving haulage trucks. He remembered the days when a laborer earned $3.50 for a ten-hour day, a locomotive engineer earned $6.20, and a shovel runner made $10.

My father worked different shifts all the time I was growing up, and he wasn't always easy to live with when he was on nights or "swing shift." Probably the most difficult to survive, swing shift consisted of two day shifts, two afternoon shifts, and two night shifts consecutively. It's no wonder miners working such a topsy-turvy schedule got a little cranky. My sister and I learned to tiptoe around the house and to wait until Dad was awake before we practiced piano.

Lazy summer days I often spent on Grandma Will's front porch swing, watching the comings and goings next door. Grandma and Grandpa lived next to Findlay's, a boardinghouse on the corner of our block. Miners rented rooms there and ate at Findlay's small café.

Findlay's was one of the few boardinghouses left in my lifetime, but back in the 1920s and '30s, several miners boarded at my grandparents' home. The men slept in a bunkhouse out back, along with my dad and his younger brother. Paneled with beaverboard and heated with an oil stove, the uninsulated building got frosty on winter nights, but card games that lasted well past midnight helped raise the room temperature. The dollar a day Grandma received from each man for bed, board, and laundry eased the Depression years for her and her family. Town women vied with each other to see who could cook the best meals and pack the best dinner pails.

Calumet was a microcosm of the Iron Range's melting pot. Men moved to town from many countries, and nationalities learned to live together, sharing their dependence on the Hill Annex Mine.

Perhaps to avoid spelling or pronouncing unfamiliar names like Orazio Dipangrazio, men came to be called Curly Smith, Mud Lake Joe, Black Sam, Pickles, Prunes, Big Roddy, and Little Roddy. Whatever the reason for their nicknames, we were accustomed to the sight of several of these old bachelors sitting on a Main Street bench any time of day or night. We kids never knew these men personally, but they were part of the local landscape. Most had immigrated here in search of good jobs, leaving wife and family behind in Europe. They worked at the Hill Annex the rest of their lives and died alone in this, their adopted country.

Guthrie Brothers built a pair of two-story fifty-room bunkhouses near the pit. Many of the single men roomed there and grew accustomed to sleeping amid the cacophony. Nearby stood a dining hall with long wooden tables set with twenty-four tin plates turned upside down. My dad tells me the men weren't allowed to touch anything until the cook gave the signal; then there was a deafening din as the men turned over the plates. Women called "hashers" waited tables, while others worked as dishwashers, cooks, and helpers called "cookees." These women slept in separate quarters referred to as "the doll house," and two policemen patrolled the camp around the clock to preserve order.

My dad was a shy young boy whose job it was to pick up the lunch box for his three-man train crew from the kitchen each day. The girls teased him unmercifully, he recalls. "Holy gosh," he says. "There was enough food there to feed six men." Often the girls would slip my dad a whole pie, which he hid in the bib of his overalls until he got outside.

During my teen years, I assumed the chore of packing dinner pails for Daddy when my mother resumed her nursing career. His heavy tin pail had a drawer that slid out. I'd line it with wax paper and slip in a meat sandwich along with his favorite peanut butter and jelly sandwich, cookies or cake, and an apple, orange, or banana. Sometimes he ate with fellow workers in a changing room he referred to as "the dry." In later years, Daddy drove a forty-ton Euclid haulage truck and ate his lunch "on the fly." That often meant grabbing a bite of sandwich as he waited to dump at the "pocket," where a conveyor belt carried the ore up to the washing plant. Or he might eat his apple while he was waiting at the shovel to be loaded.

One Johnny Doughboy Day, an annual celebration we eagerly anticipated, my father drove his Euclid in the parade, and my sister and I sat in the spacious cab with him and waved to our friends below. The pavement shuddered beneath the giant tires. The truck dwarfed all the other floats, yet next to today's two-hundred-ton monsters, that Euclid would look like a toy.

Another of my weekly chores was helping with the wash. I can still picture those white sheets hanging on the clothesline behind the house. The wind covered the wash with ore dust from the mine dumps that circled town. When Mother heard a train coming in the distance, she'd holler and we'd run to help her take in the sheets before they were sprinkled with cinders from the steam engine.

Because he had so much seniority—more than thirty years at the mine—my father was seldom laid off in the days when unions were all-powerful on the Range. Mining natural ore was seasonal work, however, and some winters many men were laid off. It wasn't a bad life, and the leisure time allowed the men to see more of their families. Sometimes my dad would go skating or sliding with us during slack winter days. In those years before television, we town kids whiled away most evenings at the skating rink. There, beneath a sky sparkling with constellations, we played pompom pull away and practiced twirls and spins without ever having watched the Olympics.

Strikes were infrequent but catastrophic. The strike of 1959 was memorable. Even my dad was out of work for a long time. Many men sought jobs away from home. My uncle worked as a carpenter in Duluth that year. Union members took turns walking the picket line and made do with strike pay. Everyone endured months without a regular paycheck.

Tourists today sometimes mistake our "dumps" for mountains, but they are the remains of soil stripped from the surface to uncover the iron ore. Nothing grew on the dumps in those days when we children scrabbled up the sides, slipping and sliding, until our clothes and shoes were stained ore-car red.

From the top of the dump nearest town, we had an impressive view of our homes. A neighbor boy spent even more time on the dumps than we did, and he had amassed quite a collection of shark's teeth to show for it. Tansy grew on the flat fields atop the dumps. Even today, the smell of tansy takes me back to those sultry summer days.

Since I was a child, trees have sprung up on the dumps surrounding Calumet, making them look more like mountains than ever. Green grass creeps over the edges of the pit, as if seeking to heal that open wound in the earth's red surface. An azure lake conceals the depth of the pit.

My hometown, once a vibrant community, is sleepy now. The school was demolished years ago. Gone too are the movie theater, grocery store, café, drugstore, and lumberyard. The years have erased the ore-colored tire tread marks leading to and from the mine. Calumet's lifeblood has ebbed away.

Yet Hill Annex Mine State Park preserves pictures of my past. Tourists now climb the worn, wooden staircase of a museum, a building once known as "the clubhouse," where townspeople held parties and dances. Among the displays and artifacts are my dad's dinner pail and photos enlarged from Grandma and Grandpa Will's family album. From the museum's front steps, I can see what was our school playground. Park picnic tables surround the spot where the merry-go-round once whirled. Standing there, I can still hear the voices of my schoolmates and echoes of the Hill Annex Mine.

HOME IS WHERE THE HEARTH IS

Mary Hoff

BOUNDARY WATERS CANOE AREA WILDERNESS, dusk. Hunched like an old woman against the chill floating in from across the lake, I sprinkle twigs over the little mound I've made from crumpled paper and bits of bark. I circle the tinder with sticks, leaning them inward like stiff soldiers sleeping on a hill. I light a match, hold it hopefully to the base of the heap. Tendrils of smoke and flame lick the edges, explore the twigs, stretch out to the dusk, beg for more. My numb fingers comply, feeding the flickers with ever-bigger offerings.

After fits and starts, the fire finally settles itself into a comfortable complacency. Warmed inside and out by its glow, I am suddenly and surprisingly at home in this place I have never been before.

Fire as home is an ancient equation, far older than written records, perhaps older than consciousness itself. In ritual and legend, through all time, fire has meant: You Are Here.

Moses found God in a burning bush. Sam McGee found eternal warmth in a derelict ship's flaming furnace. Somewhere in our history, we humans traded an instinctive fear of deadly fire for a deep longing for its life-giving presence. And so we yield, over and over again, to the perverse and pervasive urge to invite it into whatever space we happen to occupy. Hence we have campfires, cookouts, birthday candles. Hence we have hearths and gas fireplaces.

Last winter my husband, our son, The Dog Who Eats Sofas, and I spent the good part of a Saturday morning together in the woods in a place that was not a place, turning an old, downed granddaddy of a dead willow into fodder for our hearth back home. By noon we had a tall stack of fat logs to show for our work. Wet and weary, with sawdust and brush cuttings strewn around us and lunchtime approaching, we figured it was time to either leave or find a good excuse to stay. So we decided to build a fire.

But where? Looking around, we searched for some self-evident center to this place in the woods, but found none. Undaunted, we gathered a few slabs of thick wet bark and laid them side by side on a randomly chosen patch of snow in the middle of the trail. On top of them, we crumpled a pocketful of paper, perched tiny twigs from a nearby pine, and stacked bigger sticks from our logging leftovers.

My pyro-apprentice begged to light the match. I let him, and I let him again, and eventually spark and paper met and became a flicker, and the flicker grew into a healthy orange spire. We watched first in pride and then in dismay as flames grabbed the edges of the old news, ate the pine bits, leapt at the dry sticks propped about them, then faltered and faded.

Like anxious parents, we scurried from one brush heap to another in search of something to feed this hungry infant. It ate and grew, until eventually it turned into a teenager of a fire, and we were content to leave it at least partly to its own business, intervening only occasionally to feed it, prod it, keep it from straying too far outside our limits.

Finally, we felt at home. We knew where we belonged: We Were Here. This random act of fire gave us a focal point. It gave us something to hang around, something to look at, something to come back to after we went somewhere else.

We warmed our fingers, chewed an apple, admired the morning's work of fuel for future fires.

"Should we cook a potato?" I asked. Pyro Boy thought that sounded like a good idea, and went to fetch one from the house. When he got back, we poked holes into it with a stick to keep it from exploding and wrapped it in tinfoil. Reaching down into the pit the fire had carved out for itself in the snow, we buried the potato in the white-coated coals.

Pyro Boy and Sofa Dog wandered off to do whatever it is that boys and dogs do in the woods. When they were sufficiently cold and snow-covered and hungry, they wandered back.

"Is it time yet?"

"Not yet." Wandered off again, shook a tree, followed a trail, wandered back again.

"Yet, Mom?"

Over and over the fire and the potato drew him, a yo-yo of a kid tied by an invisible string to the fingers of flame that held, for the moment, our place in the universe.

Finally it was time, and we dug the smoking, black-shrouded lump from the coals. Together we peeled back the foil to expose the fire-charred skin. When we broke it open, fragrant steam burst from the innards. With sooty fingers we shared the sacramental potato—half-cooked, ash-covered, and still so very good.

We finished the potato, crumpled the foil, licked our fingers, then watched the fire burn down to nothing, and with it, our ad hoc home in the woods. We admired the crater it left, decided we'd tell anybody who asked that a spaceship had landed there. Loading the sled one last time, we headed toward the house and the fires we would make there.

I hiked out to our makeshift hearth last week. The ashes remained, rimmed with a tangle of gooseberry and woodbine. But the place no longer beckoned.

Still, I know that the next time I touch match to tinder, whether on a wind-blustered rock on the edge of nowhere, or under a government-issue grate with Pyro Boy and Sofa Dog and the whine of mosquitoes and tent-trailer occupants all around, I'll be mindful of that hearth in the woods. And I'll be mindful, in some small way, of all the fires that have burned and burn and will burn, in lantern, stove, and imagination—fires that reassure us, wherever we may be: You Are Here.

CALL ME ISLAND

Bill Holm

I'M NOT SURE I WAS LOOKING FOR WISDOM when I invented islands on the prairie as a boy. Like most children, I longed for a private world with boundaries unassailable by adults, or even by other children. Maybe only children like me discover the essential isolate quality inside human beings before others, but I'd guess that all humans discover it in the course of an average life; pain, disease, failure, betrayal, death, all have proved themselves adequate instructors.

My father's island was his hilltop farm from which he could survey the roof peaks of his neighbors' barns and the twenty-mile-distant line of glacial hills that rose southwest of his house. My island was not his island, despite the fact that we shared a name. The farm seemed to me a bottomless pit with its practical labor, animal smells, grain dust, whirling eternal winds, barbed-wire boundaries. I discovered the imagination early, then fed it with books, music, and daydreaming till it grew to the usual monstrous human size. I lived in a private mental world, sure that no other human being on the face of the earth had any remote notion of the strange goings-on inside my head, or what singular oddities gave me pleasure. I found my comrades among the dead: Poe, Hawthorne, Shakespeare, Icelandic sagas in literature; the fiercer and stranger books of the Bible: Job, Ecclesiastes, the Song of Solomon; the romance of the Arctic: Fridtjof Nansen, Vilhjalmur Stefansson, Robert Peary, and Frederick Cook, the search for the lost Franklin expedition. I savored the gothic and the horrible: Frankenstein, Dracula, stories of zombies, of corpses risen from their coffins for revenge, mischief, self-assertion.

Though I think I was a friendly enough boy in my functions on the surface of life, I was always convinced at bottom of my utter disconnection from humanity. Who else longed for violin music, dog sleds mushing over frozen ice floes, old heavy leather-bound books, eerie scratchings on night windows from inhabitants of the next world? I would look in the mirror at my pink, soft, fleshy head, crowned with a mop of bright red hair, adorned with thick black plastic glasses and think: There is someone else trapped inside this body—another life, another possibility. The universe has made some mistake here.

So in the brief subarctic Minnesota summer after the box elders and cottonwoods leafed out and the legions of insects hatched, I would journey out with my equipage to furnish and fortify my private island. It was not a long trip. Trees were scarce on the prairie and aside from farm groves and river courses grew one or two at a time in odd places, along fence lines or in the middle of fields, where the birds had shat out or the wind had scattered as if by random chance, a seed that actually amounted to something and grew up to be a real tree. A fine old cottonwood sat on a little island of grass in the middle of the field just west of the house. You passed through a grove of Chinese elms and box elders to arrive at the field's edge and there it stood, as if out to sea—either corn, wheat, alfalfa, oats, or flax. An ambitious farmer might have cut down the tree to reap another bushel or two and to avoid plowing around this impediment to agricultural progress, but my father was willing to circle it and leave nature well enough alone. I furnished my island always with food (I was and remain a happy eater), bottles of water, books, paper, and pens. I used fallen branches and pulled up weeds and farm scrap to make the island invisible to prying eyes, though my father could always follow my progress from his tractor seat. Such are the illusions of youth in its pursuit of a private world.

The illusion of island life always looked best in years when my father planted the hilltop with flax. Flax is the loveliest of all crops on the northern prairie. When it flowers, the field turns into a sea of bright blue blossoms, pitching and rolling in that omnipresent prairie wind. Now my island of green grass with its single tree had the look of a real tropical island. I don't think I ever pretended to canoe through the flax to arrive there, but I might have with some justice. My imagination wasn't as big as I thought. Corn provided the best cover. When it arrived at its stately mature height, the island turned invisible even to my father. Had I been able to invent secret and terrible rites, I could have practiced them undisturbed, at least until my mother summoned me for a meal. Even the imagination doesn't like missing dinner. It must be fed too—sometimes with pork chops and rhubarb pie.

What did I do on my namesake island? I practiced geography, naming and mapping it, charting its chief natural features, its cities, industries, resources. I did what young liars do: I made it up. I imagined invaders and the means I might use to repel them. I populated the island with large, plump, nerdy boys who, astonishingly, shared my odd tastes. I had scintillating and witty conversations with them. Puberty hadn't arrived in my island days, so I probably didn't imagine colonies of beautiful black-haired women, but I confess to having done so since. Thoreau had his flute at Walden, but I had my black plastic Tonette on Holm's Holm, so I composed and wrote down whole symphonies—one tune—and labeled them, like my hero Beethoven, with opus numbers: Grand Symphony for Tonette in D Minor by William J. Holm, Opus 12, 1953. I began to assemble my collected poems, though I think I was a little premature in that. I folded, then bound them either with Scotch tape or string. I don't remember assembling festschrifts in honor of my upcoming Nobel Prize, but I might have. Isolation breeds grandiosity in human character. If no one can see what you're at, you may as well be extraordinary. It doesn't cost any more than Lutheran modesty.

I drove by Holm's Holm last summer, but found it gone. The tree must by now have died, or the new farmer cut it down when he sensibly reshaped the hilltop field in terraces to prevent the downward slide of topsoil, a conservation practice my father never discovered. But, of course, the island goes on existing where it always existed: in my mind's eye, the same ocean that holds Crusoe's island, Dr. Moreau's, Lilliput, Laputa, Brobdingnag, and Treasure. Like Thoreau, I wanted to drive life into a corner, to see what it was made of. The big world seemed too strange, too hostile, too unsuited to my nature, but we all discover, as we age, that in at least one sense, our interior islands grow even larger. We find that we are, in fact, connected, that John Donne may have been no fool when he said we are not islands—entirely. Those connections may not always please us, and we may sometimes long to return to the private and forti-fied island surrounded by flax. We may even conspire to remove the other islands that we imagine get in the way of our vision. Islands are necessary for us to be able to think about what is true at the bottom of our own char-acter; we need to reduce the world for a while to count it and understand it. But finally no island is without fine threads traveling mostly invisibly under the ocean floor to every other island; we are, like it or not, part of the gang, and the gang, like it or not, had better get used to that fact. You can safely take all this sound advice from me: call me island and I will answer, though probably to other names as well. Walt Whitman thought we were all continents, even planets, each and every one of us, and that might be true too.

MARKING TIME

Tom Baumann

THE NAME NEATLY PORTRAYS THE IRONY of such a place: Sunrise Cemetery.

Curious name for a cemetery? Not for one perched high on a sandy knoll above the Sunrise River, just up the hill from a smudge of a town called Sunrise.

But like the name, this pioneer cemetery can conjure up an odd mix of emotions for a visitor who might wander through its century-old white pines, which mark life, and the etched, weathered stones, which mark those who have left life behind.

Many years ago, when working as a Department of Natural Resources forester in Chisago County, I would sometimes travel the gravel road that runs from the town of Sunrise north to forestland. On occasion I would stop by the cemetery for a short while and wander the grounds. There was no real reason for me to do so; none of the names held personal meaning for me. But this place had an eerie allure, which I find hard to understand and harder to explain.

Sunrise Cemetery was officially chartered the year Abraham Lincoln was assassinated, the year the Civil War ended. The nearest settlement then, as now, was Sunrise. However, most of the once-bustling logging town disappeared shortly after the timber ran out. What's left clings periously to each side of the riverbank.

The white pines, now the sentinels of the cemetery, were probably too young and small to bother with during the heavy logging in the mid-1800s. Now their trunks are thick and squat, the bark coarse and dark. Their crowns range from full and sweeping, to thin and tattered from growing so many years on so exposed a site. In places, massive roots erupt from the ground, pushing and tipping some of the gravestones.

On cloudless days, sunlight streams through the branches; some places in torrents, others in mere trickles. Where the life-giving light finds the ground easily, young white pines are popping up, taking advantage of the opening in the overstory.

Thrown loosely across the undulating ground beneath the huge pines are the monument stones. Like the trees, the stones occur in random patterns—clustered here, open and sparse there. Most are small and plain. There are none of the massive monoliths or crypts found in some cemeteries.

Etched on the stones are names and dates, and sometimes a bit more. The inscriptions give a glimpse of the past—like reading a history book with many pages missing. Yet the reality of this place tells a more intriguing and heartrending story than any book could create.

A small stone near the front of the grounds carries a name and epitaph: "Died June 24, 1859, Age 1 month 8 days." This was one of the first stones to find a resting place under the thick blanket of pine needles.

Among another cluster of stones, a family marker tells a bit of history. Mother and Father married in 1875. Ten years later Mother died at thirty-two years of age. Nearby lies a line of three stones, each no bigger than a sheet of typing paper, engraved with the names "Bessie 1878," "David 1881," "Baby 1884." A feeling of sadness still hangs in the air. Did Mother's heart just break after losing three children in six years? And what about Father?

In another part of the cemetery, beneath another family marker, a stone simply states: "Baby 1885–1885."

Both local history and military history are recounted on a memorial board near the back of the cemetery. Listed there are the names of American war veterans: twenty-one from the Civil War, thirteen doughboys from "the war to end all wars," twenty-nine from World War II, and three Korean War veterans—three of the handful of more recent markers added to this place.

Many years have passed since I worked in the Sunrise area, and even more have gone by since I wandered through the cemetery. Recently, I was drawn back to Sunrise Cemetery. Which again raises the question, Why?

Is it the lure of the majestic white pines, which gained their spot on earth a century ago and might cling to it for another hundred years? Is it the history of the people, carved on the stones and memorial board, of the babies, the heroes, and the plain folks of another era, when life was more tenuous and a lifetime much shorter?

Now, as I wander less and wonder more, the irony of the name begins to part, like a morning fog being pushed away by a stiff breeze.

No sun can rise unless it has set. Here in the Sunrise Cemetery, young white pines germinate and survive in openings created by the decline and passage of the large white pines. And while the Sunrise Cemetery surely suggests the pain and sadness of death, it just as surely highlights the possibilities of life.

Perhaps it is the expectation and hope, jointly fashioned by nature and humans in this place, that draw me back.

ACKNOWLEDGMENTS

I am grateful to the following individuals for their assistance in bringing this book to publication. At the Department of Natural Resources, Kathleen Weflen, editor in chief of *Minnesota Conservation Volunteer;* Gustave Axelson, managing editor of *Minnesota Conservation Volunteer;* David Lent, management analyst; and Laurie Martinson, deputy commissioner. At the University of Minnesota Press, Todd Orjala, senior editor; Andrea Patch, editorial assistant; Laura Westlund, managing editor; Rachel Moeller, production coordinator; and Douglas Armato, director. Thanks also to the authors and publishers who generously donated their work, and special thanks to my wife, Nancy, and to our daughter, Grace, to whom this book is dedicated.

PUBLICATION HISTORY

All essays in this volume previously appeared in *Minnesota Conservation Volunteer*, a donor-supported magazine encouraging conservation and careful use of Minnesota's natural resources. (St. Paul, Minn.: Minnesota Department of Natural Resources).

"Trapper's Cabin" was originally published in Sigurd F. Olson, *The Singing Wilderness* (New York: Alfred A. Knopf, 1956). Copyright 1956 by Sigurd F. Olson. Copyright renewed 1984 by Elizabeth D. Olson and Alfred A. Knopf, Inc. Reprinted by permission of Alfred A. Knopf, a division of Random House, Inc.

"Heart of the Hunt" was first published in *City Pages* (Minneapolis), December 9, 1998. Copyright 1998 by Terri Sutton. Reprinted by permission of the author.

"The Bog" was originally published in John Henricksson, *Gunflint: The Trail, the People, the Stories* (Cambridge, Minn.: Adventure Publications, 2003). Copyright 2003 by John Henricksson. Reprinted by permission of the author.

"Fishless Waters" was originally published in Jan Zita Grover, *Northern Waters* (St. Paul: Graywolf Press, 1999). Copyright 1999 by Jan Zita Grover. Reprinted by permission of the author.

"Kayaking the Wild Shore" is adapted from Greg Breining, *Wild Shore: Exploring Lake Superior by Kayak* (Minneapolis: University of Minnesota Press, 2000). Copyright 2000 by Greg Breining. Reprinted by permission of the author.

GEOGRAPHICAL INDEX

Essays set in multiple biomes are listed more than once.

Coniferous Forest (North Woods)

"Trapper's Cabin," by Sigurd F. Olson (Ely)   3

"My First Trip Up North," by John S. Sonnen (Park Rapids)   7

"Deer Camp," by Phil Aarrestad (outside Brainerd)   12

"The Path Between," by Holly Atkinson (Lake Beltrami)   16

"Sugar Bush Journal," by Anne M. Dunn   21
(Leech Lake Indian Reservation)

"Drawing Life from Nature," by Vera Ming Wong   31
(Boundary Waters Canoe Area Wilderness)

"Heart of the Hunt," by Terri Sutton (Ely)   44

"A Perfect Start," by Dan Brown (Chippewa National Forest)   57

"The Road to Wild Places," by Don J. Dinndorf (Baudette)   63

"The Bog," by John Henricksson (Boundary Waters Canoe Area Wilderness)   66

"The Wagon Wheel," by Joel M. Vance (between Duluth and Minneapolis)   70

"The Strike Tree," by Peter M. Leschak (Beatrice Lake)   74

"A Search for Whitewater," by Hal Crimmel   115
(rivers of northeastern Minnesota)

"River Passage," by Janet Blixt (St. Louis River)   120

"Kayaking the Wild Shore," by Greg Breining (Lake Superior)   124

"Down at Miller Creek," by Shawn Perich (Duluth)   132

"Boundary Waters Wilderness: January," by Laurie Allmann   137
     (Boundary Waters Canoe Area Wilderness)

"Brittle Beauty," by Rick Naymark (Boundary Waters   141
     Canoe Area Wilderness)

"Lake Superior, Winter Dawn," by Gustave Axelson (Lake Superior)   146

"Rivering on the Onion," by Stephen Regenold (Onion River)   150

"Me and Joe," by C. B. Bylander (Mille Lacs)   154

"A Thousand Chandeliers," by Will Weaver (Lake Bemidji)   165

"Elusive Orchids," by Erika Rowe (Clearwater and Becker counties)   174

"A Great Small Universe," by David Czarnecki (Itasca State Park)   178

"My Night Life with the Boreal Owl," by Bill Lane (Lake and Cook counties)   188

"The Dropping Duck," by Tom Chapin (near Lake Winnibigoshish)   218

"A Hunter's Journal," by Dave Schad (Nemadji State Forest)   222

"The Grace of the Wild," by Paul Gruchow (Boundary Waters   235
     Canoe Area Wilderness)

"Iron Red Home," by Margaret A. Haapoja (Calumet)   247

"Home Is Where the Hearth Is," by Mary Hoff (Boundary Waters   253
     Canoe Area Wilderness)

"Marking Time," by Tom Baumann (Sunrise)   260

Deciduous Forest (Big Woods)

"Mother's Day in Rattlesnake Country," by Susan Maas   26
     (Whitewater State Park)

"Lessons from a Young Explorer," by Steve Dibb (Moonan State   33
     Wildlife Management Area)

"Birding in the Fast-Food Lane," by D. Scott Shultz (St. Paul)   39

"Heart of the Hunt," by Terri Sutton (south of West Concord)   44

"The Apple Tree Stand," by Marsha L. Kessler (southeastern Minnesota)   55

"The Road to Wild Places," by Don J. Dinndorf   63
     (Upsala, southeastern blufflands)

"Adventure Underground," by Cary Griffith   79
    (Forestville/Mystery Cave State Park)

"I Flew with Eagles," by John K. Grobel (Lake Pepin)   82

"The Lurker," by Tony Capecchi (St. Croix River)   84

"Around the Next Bend," by Tim Holschlag (upper Mississippi River)   92

"Fishless Waters," by Jan Zita Grover (Minneapolis)   98

"The River," by Sheila Deyo (St. Paul)   104

"Fishing the Ice," by John Brandon (Buffalo)   158

"A Flash of Summer," by Jason Abraham (Plainview)   162

"Memories of the Landscape," by Nancy Sather (Island Lake, Poplar Lake) 171

"A Ribbiting Adventure," by Philip C. Whitford (southeastern Minnesota) 182

"Count Your Loons," by Eric Hanson (Battle Lake)   192

"Solo Sojourn," by Joan Galli (Carlos Avery Wildlife Management Area)   196

"Land Use: A Bird's-Eye View," by Kim Alan Chapman (Twin Cities)   200

"One Seed at a Time," by Sue Leaf (Wild River State Park)   207

"Battle for the Cottonwood," by Evelyn Wood Moyle (Lake Minnetonka)   239

Prairie Grassland

"Birding with Ben," by Mary Kroll (southern Minnesota)   36

"Why I'm a Bowhunter," by Tom Conroy (New Ulm)   52

"Heron Lake Legacy," by Lacey Rose Horkey (Heron Lake)   89

"Going with the Flow," by Jim dale Huot-Vickery (Red River of the North) 109

"Giving Thanks on the Prairie," by Michael Furtman (prairie)   213

"This Old Farmland," by Blane Klemek (Warren)   228

"Call Me Island," by Bill Holm (Minneota)   256

CONTRIBUTORS

PHIL AARRESTAD is a commercial and advertising photographer. His work appears in regional, national, and international publications. He lives with his family in Waconia.

JASON ABRAHAM grew up fishing for trout in southeastern Minnesota. He works in the wildlife management section of Minnesota's Department of Natural Resources and writes frequently for *Minnesota Conservation Volunteer*.

LAURIE ALLMANN is an environmental writer whose work finds expression in a variety of media. She received a Minnesota Book Award for *Far from Tame: Reflections from the Heart of a Continent;* was a member of the writing team for the public television documentary series *Minnesota: A History of the Land;* and has been an essayist and a commentator for Minnesota Public Radio's *Voices from the Heartland* series.

HOLLY ATKINSON is a nature writer whose essays have been published in numerous national magazines. She is the author of *Drinking Shadows,* a collection of stories, and *Snow Is Coming,* a children's book. She lives on a farm in the Ozarks near Rolla, Missouri.

GUSTAVE AXELSON is managing editor of *Minnesota Conservation Volunteer* magazine. He moved from Chicago to Minnesota in the 1990s and wrote "Lake Superior, Winter Dawn" shortly after his first winter visit to the North Shore.

TOM BAUMANN worked for many years at the Minnesota Department of Natural Resources as a field forester and in the Bureau of Information and Education in St. Paul. He lives in Isanti.

JANET BLIXT lives in Duluth and works in marketing communications at Lake Superior College.

JOHN BRANDON is a freelance writer. His articles have been published in *Coastal Living, Wired, PC* magazine, and the *StarTribune* (Minneapolis–St. Paul). He lives in Fergus Falls with his wife and four children.

GREG BREINING, former managing editor of *Minnesota Conservation Volunteer,* is the author of *Wild Shore: Exploring Lake Superior by Kayak* (Minnesota, 2000); *Super Volcano: The Ticking Time Bomb beneath Yellowstone National Park;* and *A Hard-Water World: Ice Fishing and Why We Do It* (with photographer Layne Kennedy). He lives in St. Paul.

DAN BROWN is a human services director who lives in Taylors Falls with his wife and sons. He writes a weekly column for the *Chisago County Press* called "Discover the Outdoors" and is a member of the Outdoor Writers Association of America. He is also a fly-casting instructor and trout guide.

C. B. BYLANDER is the outreach chief for the fish and wildlife division of Minnesota's Department of Natural Resources. He finds comfort in sitting on a slab of ice in winter.

TONY CAPECCHI lives in Inver Grove Heights and works as a web editor for *North American Fisherman* and *North American Hunter.* He has written freelance articles for the *StarTribune* (Minneapolis–St. Paul), *In-Fisherman,* and *Walleye In-Sider.*

TOM CHAPIN spent most of his twenty-nine-year career as a game warden in the district of Grand Rapids, Minnesota. Now retired, he teaches and promotes ethical hunting and fishing in Grand Rapids.

KIM ALAN CHAPMAN is a principal ecologist with the consulting firm Applied Ecological Services. He works with people and organizations to find new ways to design, build, and live sustainably.

CONTRIBUTORS

TOM CONROY is an information officer for the Department of Natural Resources, an outdoors enthusiast, and a widely published writer. He lives in New Ulm.

HAL CRIMMEL is associate professor of English at Weber State University in Ogden, Utah. He is the author of *Dinosaur: Four Seasons on the Green and Yampa Rivers;* the editor of *Teaching in the Field: Working with Students in the Outdoor Classroom;* and coeditor with Laird Christensen of *Teaching about Place: Learning from the Land.*

DAVID CZARNECKI (1947–2006) was a professor of biology and curator of the Freshwater Diatom Culture Collection at Loras College in Dubuque, Iowa. He was a visiting professor for twenty-two summers at the University of Minnesota's Itasca Biological Station and Laboratories in Itasca State Park.

SHEILA DEYO is communications project manager at the Minnesota Department of Natural Resources.

STEVE DIBB has been a teacher and school administrator for thirty-one years. He lives in Farmington with his family.

DON J. DINNDORF lives near St. Augusta in central Minnesota.

ANNE M. DUNN, an Ojibwe author and storyteller, lives in Deer River.

MICHAEL FURTMAN, author of more than a dozen books, has been a full-time freelance writer and photographer for twenty years.

JOAN GALLI was the nongame wildlife specialist in the Twin Cities metropolitan area for the Minnesota Department of Natural Resources for twenty-two years. She and her husband reside on a farm of two hundred acres in northwestern Pennsylvania, where they raise "a few beef cattle and lots of wildlife."

CARY GRIFFITH is the author of *Lost in the Wild: Danger and Survival in the North Woods* and *Opening Goliath: An Exploration of Caves.* He lives in Rosemount.

CONTRIBUTORS

JOHN K. GROBEL is a writer and lives in Falcon Heights.

JAN ZITA GROVER is author of *North Enough: AIDS and Other Clear-Cuts* and *Northern Waters*.

PAUL GRUCHOW (1947–2004) was the author of seven essay collections about the Minnesota landscape, including *The Necessity of Empty Places*, *Grass Roots: The Universe of Home*, and *Boundary Waters: The Grace of the Wild*.

MARGARET A. HAAPOJA is a freelance writer who lives on Little Sand Lake, five miles south of where she grew up in her "Iron Red Home." Her work has been published in a variety of magazines, including *Audubon*, *National Wildlife*, and *Wild Bird*.

ERIC HANSON has coordinated the Vermont Loon Recovery Project for the Vermont Center for Ecostudies since 1998. He edits and writes the annual newsletter *Loon Caller*, which is available at www.vtecostudies.org. The Minnesota Loon Monitoring Program is now in the middle of its second decade of volunteer monitoring.

JOHN HENRICKSSON is the author of three books about the Gunflint region (*A Wild Neighborhood, Gunflint,* and *The Gunflint Cabin*) and the editor of two *North Writers* anthologies for the University of Minnesota Press. He and his wife divide their time between their Gunflint Lake cabin and their home in Mahtomedi on White Bear Lake.

MARY HOFF is a freelance science writer from Stillwater.

BILL HOLM (1943–2009), a native of Minneota, Minnesota, was a poet and essayist whose books include *The Heart Can Be Filled Anywhere on Earth, Eccentric Islands: Travels Real and Imaginary,* and *The Windows of Brimnes: An American in Iceland*. He taught for twenty-seven years at Southwest Minnesota State University in Marshall.

TIM HOLSCHLAG, a fishing writer and guide, is the owner of the Web site smallmouthangler.com.

CONTRIBUTORS

LACEY ROSE HORKEY resides in Sioux Falls, South Dakota, but often returns to rural Minnesota to enjoy hunting and fishing with her father, as well as other adventures that inspire essays about growing up Minnesotan.

JIM DALE HUOT-VICKERY is the author of *Wilderness Visionaries, Open Spaces* (winner of the first Sigurd F. Olson Nature Writing Award), and *Winter Sign* (Minnesota, 1998). He is a native of northwestern Minnesota's Red River Valley and during the past twenty-five years has lived in a cabin near Ely, on the edge of northeastern Minnesota's Boundary Waters Canoe Area Wilderness.

MARSHA L. KESSLER writes, raises quail, and trains her horses and bird dogs on a bluff-top farm in southeastern Minnesota.

BLANE KLEMEK is assistant area wildlife manager for the Minnesota Department of Natural Resources in Bemidji and a freelance writer.

MARY KROLL writes about the natural world from her home in rural central Minnesota.

BILL LANE migrated to Minnesota's North Shore and now calls Cook County his home. He continues to monitor breeding owl populations each spring, twenty-two years after his first night in Minnesota's boreal forest.

SUE LEAF is the author of *Potato City: Nature, History, and Community in the Age of Sprawl* and *The Bullhead Queen: A Year on Pioneer Lake* (Minnesota, 2009). She is president of the Wild River chapter of the Audubon Society and lives in Center City.

PETER M. LESCHAK is the author of ten books, including *Letters from Side Lake: A Chronicle of Life in the North Woods* (Minnesota, 1992). A native of Minnesota, he makes his living as a firefighter.

SUSAN MAAS is a writer, editor, nature lover, and budding herpetologist. She lives with her family in Minneapolis.

EVELYN WOOD MOYLE is coauthor, with her husband John B. Moyle (1909–1977), of *Northland Wildflowers: The Comprehensive Guide to the Minnesota Region* (Minnesota, 2001). She lives on Lake Minnetonka.

RICK NAYMARK was born in Duluth and lives in Minneapolis. He owns a marketing company and writes about Minnesota and Minnesotans.

SIGURD F. OLSON (1899–1982) was an award-winning conservation activist and best-selling author. He lived in Ely most of his life.

SHAWN PERICH is a writer and publisher in the North Shore community of Hovland. He is the author of several books, including *Fly-fishing the North Country*. He writes a column in *Minnesota Outdoor News* and is a co-owner of Northern Wilds Media, Inc., which publishes *Northern Wilds*, the outdoor newspaper of the north.

DANIEL J. PHILIPPON is associate professor of English at the University of Minnesota–Twin Cities. He is the author of *Conserving Words: How American Nature Writers Shaped the Environmental Movement*. He lives in St. Paul.

STEPHEN REGENOLD is a Minneapolis writer. His syndicated column "The Gear Junkie" runs in a dozen publications nationally and on www.gearjunkie.com.

ERIKA ROWE is a plant ecologist with the Minnesota County Biological Survey of the Department of Natural Resources. She grew up in St. Paul and now lives in Minneapolis.

NANCY SATHER has spent more than two decades as a botanist and ecologist with the Minnesota Department of Natural Resources. A freelance environmental educator and writer, she has taught at Metropolitan State University, Hamline University, and Southwest Minnesota State University, and her writing has been published in *Isotope, Orion,* and the book series Stories from Where We Live.

DAVE SCHAD is director of the fish and wildlife division of Minnesota's Department of Natural Resources. A lifelong Minnesotan, he still tries to make it back to the old shack each fall.

D. SCOTT SHULTZ, husband, father, and licensed falconer (on hiatus), enjoys watching all birds—predatory and prey.

JOHN S. SONNEN (1913–2008) was a real estate appraiser and freelance writer in St. Paul.

TERRI SUTTON is a freelance writer from Minneapolis.

JOEL M. VANCE is the author of *Grandma and the Buck Deer; Bobs, Brush, and Brittanies; Down Home Missouri;* and *Autumn Shadows.*

WILL WEAVER lives on the Mississippi River east of Bemidji. His Web site is www.willweaverbooks.com.

KATHLEEN WEFLEN joined *Minnesota Conservation Volunteer* as associate editor in 1986 and became editor in chief and publisher in 1989.

PHILIP C. WHITFORD is a biology professor at Capital University in Columbus, Ohio. His work has appeared in *Bird Watcher's Digest,* the *Passenger Pigeon,* and the *Michigan Botanist.* The research on which his essay "A Ribbiting Adventure" was based was supported by funds provided by the Minnesota Department of Natural Resources and Winona State University.

VERA MING WONG is an artist and natural science illustrator who works in a variety of media for publication in books and magazines. She cofounded and teaches in the Botanical and Zoological Arts and Illustration Program in St. Paul; founded and leads Project Art for Nature (www.projectartfornature. org); and is a member of the Guild of Natural Science Illustrators. She lives in River Falls, Wisconsin.